ECHOES OF TIME

Senior Authors
Carl B. Smith
Virginia A. Arnold

Linguistics Consultant
Ronald Wardhaugh

Macmillan Publishing Co., Inc.
New York

Collier Macmillan Publishers
London

ACKNOWLEDGMENTS

The publisher gratefully acknowledges permission to reprint the following copyrighted material:

"Alexander and Bucephalus," from the book *Each in His Way* by Alice Gall and Fleming Crew. Copyright 1937 by Oxford University Press. Copyright renewed 1965 by Louise Crew Bell. Reprinted by permission of Mrs. Louise C. Bell.

"The Altamira Cave," adapted from *All About Prehistoric Cave Men* by Sam and Beryl Epstein. Copyright © 1959 by Sam and Beryl Epstein. By permission of Random House, Inc.

"The Animal's Point of View," from *The Language of Animals* by Millicent E. Selsam. Copyright © 1962 by Millicent E. Selsam. By permission of William Morrow & Company.

"Antonio Stradivari" by Irene Bennett Needham, from *Highlights For Children,* November 1972. Copyright © 1972 Highlights for Children, Inc., Columbus, Ohio. All rights reserved.

"Babe at the Circus," adapted from *Tall Timber Tales, More Paul Bunyan Stories* by Dell J. McCormick. By permission of the Caxton Printers, Ltd.

"Bush Prairie," adapted from *Black Courage* by A. E. Schraff. Copyright © 1969. By permission of Macrae Smith Company.

"La cancion del camino" by Francisco Icaza, from *Some Spanish-American Poets,* translated by Alice S. Blackwell. Copyright 1929 by University of Pennsylvania Press. By permission of University of Pennsylvania Press.

"Carmen and Miranda," adapted from *Zoo Year* by Alice Schick and Sara Ann Friedman. Text copyright © 1978 by Pongid Productions and Sara Ann Friedman. By permission of J. B. Lippincott, Publishers: New York and Writers House, Inc.

"Change," from *River Winding: Poems by Charlotte Zolotow.* Copyright © 1970 by Charlotte Zolotow. By permission of Thomas Y. Crowell.

"Commercials and You" by Dawn Kurth is reprinted with her permission.

"Connie's New Eyes" is an adapted text excerpt with selected photos from *Connie's New Eyes,* written and photographed by Bernard Wolf. Copyright © 1976 by Bernard Wolf. By permission of J. B. Lippincott, Publishers.

"Coyote Cry," from *Coyote Cry* by Byrd Baylor. Copyright © 1972 by Byrd Baylor. By permission of Lothrop, Lee & Shepard Co. (a Division of William Morrow & Company), and World's Work Ltd.

"Daniel Craig," adapted from *Heroes of Journalism* by Elizabeth D. Squire. Copyright © 1974 Fleet Press Corporation, New York. By permission of the publisher.

"Dr. Schumacher's Discovery," adapted from *From Anna* by Jean Little. Copyright © 1972 by Jean Little. By permission of Harper & Row, Publishers, Inc.

This work is also published in individual volumes under the titles: *Moments, Partners, Signals, Wonders, Outlets,* and *Explorations,* copyright © 1983 Macmillan Publishing Co., Inc. Parts of this work were published in earlier editions of SERIES r.

Macmillan Publishing Co., Inc.
866 Third Avenue, New York, New York 10022
Collier Macmillan Canada, Inc.

Printed in the United States of America
ISBN 0-02-131850-6
9 8

Contents

Introduction to **MOMENTS** **17**

Emma Lazarus
A biographical sketch by Virginia O. Shumaker **18**

The New Colossus
A poem by Emma Lazarus **23**

Coyote Cry
A story by Byrd Baylor **24**

SKILLS: **A Place for Everything**
(Classification) **38**

Exploring the Mind
An article by Arthur Alexander **40**

One Must Rise Above It
From a biography by Adele deLeeuw **44**

Dream Variation
A poem by Langston Hughes **51**

Practice
A story by E. L. Konigsburg **52**

What Do They Mean?
Language activities **65**

SKILLS: **Who's Who?**
(Characterization) **66**

The Lost Dog
A story by Lois Lenski **68**

The World's Work, The Artist, *and* The Clockmaker and the Timekeeper
  Chinese fables told by Isabelle C. Chang **82**

Phrases from Fables
  Language activities **85**

Dr. Schumacher's Discovery
  A story by Jean Little **86**

My Inside-Self
  A poem by Rachel Field **100**

Prefixes That Make Antonyms
  Language activities **101**

Bush Prairie
  A story by A. E. Schraff **102**

Change
  A poem by Charlotte Zolotow **109**

SKILLS: **Word Detectives**
  (Context Clues) **110**

Conclusion for MOMENTS **112**

Introduction to **PARTNERS** 113

The Altamira Cave
A fictional account by Sam and Beryl Epstein 114

Nal and the Wolf
A story by Laurence Swinburne 120

SKILLS: Turning the Tables
(Tables and Graphs) 132

Monster in the Ice
A fictional account by Laurence Swinburne 134

A World of Languages
Language activities 143

People Domesticate Animals
An article 144

Alexander and Bucephalus
A historical story by Alice Gall and Fleming Crew 148

Galloping
A poem by Cordelia Chitty 159

How Animals Helped the North American Indians
A chart compiled by Hermann Dembeck 160

Kemi
A story by Mary and Conrad Buff 162

American-Indian Names
Language activities 169

SKILLS: Don't Jump to Conclusions
(Unsupported Generalizations) 170

Red River Crossing
A biographical story by Marjorie Filley Stover **172**

Wilderness Rivers
A poem by Elizabeth Coatsworth **180**

People and Places
Language activities **181**

Connie's New Eyes
A biographical sketch by Bernard Wolf **182**

On Safari in Kenya
A photo-essay by Robert Bell **190**

Carmen and Miranda
A story by Alice Schick and Sara Ann Friedman **198**

Where in the World Are the Animals From?
A poem by Mary Ann Hoberman **205**

 SKILLS: **Word Magic** *(Prefixes)* **206**

Conclusion for PARTNERS **208**

Introduction to SIGNALS 209

The Animal's Point of View
An article by Millicent E. Selsam 210

Hope at Last
A story by Alma Whitney 216

Write It Down!
An article by Sam and Beryl Epstein 220

Say It with Symbols
Language activities 226

What Do You Know About Newspapers?
An introduction to newspapers 227

The Daily Banner
A newspaper facsimile 228

Daniel Craig
A biographical sketch by Elizabeth D. Squire 234

SKILLS: **What's New?**
(Newspaper Usage) 240

Radio
An introductory essay 242

King Midas and the Golden Touch
A radio play by Nila Mack 245

Zooming In on Zoom
A photo-essay by A. Whitney 264

SKILLS: **Prove It!**
(Evaluation of Ideas) 272

Commercials and You
An autobiographical essay by Dawn Kurth **274**

The Language of Advertising
Language activities **289**

At Home in the Future
An essay by Alma Whitney **290**

We Could Be Friends
A poem by Myra Cohn Livingston **300**

 SKILLS: **What Do You Mean by That?**
(Multiple-Meaning Words) **302**

Conclusion for SIGNALS **304**

Introduction to WONDERS 305

Earth, Moon, and Sun
A poem by Claudia Lewis 306

Galileo Galilei
From a biography by Arthur S. Gregor 308

Five Degrees from Polaris
A biographical sketch by Nina Link and Alma Whitney 315

Thoughts from Many Lands
Quotations compiled by Natalia Belting 328

Using Metaphors
Language activities 331

SKILLS: Fact Finding
(Sources of Information) 332

Just One Moon
A poem by Alma Whitney 334

From the Diary of Yeddo Ski-Kredo
A science-fiction story by Caroline D. Henry 336

Looking to the Stars
An introductory essay 344

Freedom Star
A historical play by Wade Hudson **345**

Sky Words
Language activities **361**

The Moon
An article by Isaac Asimov **362**

SKILLS: **All Things Considered**
(Drawing Conclusions) **368**

A Trip to Mars
A photo-essay by Alma Whitney **370**

The Escape
A fantasy by Robert Heinlein **380**

Language of the Future
Language activities **396**

Night
A poem by Sara Teasdale **397**

SKILLS: **Words Under the Microscope**
(Content-Area Vocabulary) **398**

Conclusion for WONDERS **400**

Introduction to OUTLETS **401**

Music
A poem by Eleanor Farjeon **402**

Mariko Plays the Koto
A music essay by Merrill O'Brien **404**

A Little Culture
A story by Dina Anastasio **408**

Peanuts
A comic strip by Charles Schulz **415**

Drawing Funny Pictures
A "Do-It-Yourself" article by Jack Markow **416**

Vinnie Ream: Sculptor of Lincoln
A biographical sketch by Elisabeth P. Myers **420**

SKILLS: **At a Glance**
(Skimming) **430**

The Yellow Bowl
A story by Carolyn Sherwin Bailey **432**

Katchina Dolls
An art essay **444**

13

Spanish in English
Language activities **445**

Journey into Jazz
A story by Nat Hentoff **446**

SKILLS: What's the Idea?
(Main Idea) **456**

Listen to the Angels Laughing
A story by Thomaline Aguallo **458**

When I Learned to Whistle
A poem by Gordon Lea **466**

Antonio Stradivari
A music essay by Irene Bennett Needham **467**

Sam Clemens of Hannibal
A biographical play by Margery C. Rutherford **472**

New Year Journal
A humorous essay by Mark Twain **491**

Which Trunk Is the Right Trunk?
Language activities **492**

Sometimes
A poem by Eleanor Schick **493**

SKILLS: For Many Reasons
(Character Behavior) **494**

Conclusion for OUTLETS **496**

14

Introduction to EXPLORATIONS 497

Wheels
A poem by Claudia Lewis 498

Prairie Schooners
An essay by Glen Rounds 500

Westward Ho!
A map of the western frontier 512

A Pioneer Family
An autobiographical story by Laura Ingalls Wilder
Going West 514
Crossing the Creek 527

SKILLS: **Follow the Trail**
(Map Reading) 536

Sweet Betsy from Pike
An American folk song 538

Babe at the Circus
A tall tale by Dell J. McCormick 540

SKILLS: **Different Voices**
(Literary Genre) 550

Alfred Jacob Miller, Painter of the Old West
A biographical sketch by Judith Lechner 552

La canción del camino
A poem in Spanish and English by Francisco Icaza 566

My Dear Cousin
A letter by Virginia Reed **568**

Wheel Ruts
A poem by James Daugherty **579**

Tabitha Brown
From a fictional biography by Evelyn Sibley Lampman **580**

 SKILLS: **What and Why?**
(Cause and Effect) **590**

Conclusion for EXPLORATIONS **592**

Glossary **593**

MOMENTS

Moments—a lot can happen in the space of a few short moments. A brief experience can leave you with a lasting impression. Everything you see, hear, and do affects you in some way. Your experiences can change the way you think and feel. Each experience, every moment, is part of a learning process that takes a lifetime.

In "Moments," you will meet real people and fictional characters. Each changes in some way because of his or her experiences. In just a short time, a boy's enemy becomes his friend. A girl puts on glasses for the first time and discovers a whole new world. A young woman encounters some newcomers to America and is inspired to write a poem.

Some of the experiences you will read about may be similar to moments in your own life. As you read, try to figure out why each character feels or acts a certain way. Then think of a time when you or someone you know has felt the same way.

EMMA LAZARUS

Virginia O. Shumaker

The young woman put down her pen and leaned back in her chair to stretch. The calendar on her tidy desk read: November, 1883. Outside the draped windows, the city streets were quiet. As usual, she had been writing far too late into the night.

She listened for a few minutes to the night sounds around her—the ticking of the hall clock, the brittle tapping of the stiff branches against the cold, polished windows. Everyone else in the house was asleep, she knew. Good! No one would ask why she was not yet in bed.

Emma Lazarus glanced down at what she had written and frowned. "Is it clear?" she wondered. "Will others who read the poem understand what I'm trying to say?"

Her mind turned back to the day it all began, a few years ago. Someone—she couldn't remember who—had asked her to join a committee visiting Ward's Island in the New York harbor. Emma had known that Ward's Island was the place where people, or immigrants, from other countries entered America for the first time.

Most of these people were poor and in need of help, so Emma had agreed to go with the committee. Wealthy young women were expected to do such things—visit the poor, the sick, or the needy, to see what could be done to help them. Sometimes, the committee's families and friends would donate food or clothing, or the committee would plan a social event to raise funds to help.

Emma had also agreed to join the committee because she was curious. She had heard of the unfortunate people who had been driven from their homes and lands. She knew many had been forced to flee for their lives. How would these people look? How would they feel about their new homeland? How could she really be of help to them?

The visit took place several days later. When Emma arrived at Ward's Island, hundreds of Russian immigrants were crowded into the vast building. Sounds of a foreign language filled the air. Long lines of people, waiting to be examined by doctors, snaked around the room.

The American immigration officers sat behind wooden tables, asking questions and filling in forms. Opposite the tables sat men, many with long, black beards, struggling to understand the strange language of the officers. Nearby, frightened families clutched their few shabby belongings—everything they owned and had been able to bring with them. Children cried from exhaustion.

Emma Lazarus looked at the scene before her in shocked silence. Every pair of eyes that met hers was filled with the recent memory of having fled from a homeland. One question could be read on all the troubled faces: Are we safe now in this strange place called America?

That visit happened years ago, but Emma never forgot it. She recalled it now, as she got up from her desk, walked to the windows, and pulled back the draperies. Looking down at the empty sidewalk, Emma thought of the poem she had just written and of the statue that was its subject—the statue being sent to America as a gift from France.

She hadn't seen the statue yet, but she had heard about it. She knew that the sculptor, Auguste Bartholdi, had created the huge statue of a woman representing *Liberty*. In one hand, the woman held a giant torch; in the other hand, a tablet with the date, July 4, 1776, the day America became a free country. The statue was to stand in

New York harbor, not far from Ward's Island where Emma first began to understand what the word *freedom* meant.

Emma Lazarus was just one of many people who were asked to write something in honor of this gift from France—this statue of Liberty. She had worked on her contribution for several days, and now it was finished. She smiled as she thought again of the title: "The New Colossus." She hoped people would remember their Greek history and recall the "old" Colossus.

According to ancient Greek history, a giant statue was once erected on the island of Rhodes in the Mediterranean Sea. Legend said that the statue was so large that one foot rested on one side of the harbor while the other foot rested on the other side. The statue had been built as a symbol of thanks for victory in an important battle. It was called the Colossus of Rhodes and was one of the Seven Wonders of the World.

The new American statue would also be large—over 150 feet high from the foot of the statue to the top of the torch. But Emma did not write her poem about the size of the statue. She wrote about the immigrants she had seen many years earlier when she visited Ward's Island. She wrote her poem for and about all the people who had ever come to America seeking freedom and searching for a better life.

Emma walked back across the room and picked up her poem once more. She reread it slowly. Then she put it back on her desk, turned down the lamp, and slipped into bed. Little did she know that a part of her poem would one day be engraved on the base of the Statue of Liberty, where millions of visitors—from America as well as other lands—would read it every year.

THE NEW COLOSSUS

Not like the brazen giant of Greek fame,
With conquering limbs astride from land to land;
Here at our sea-washed, sunset gates shall stand
A mighty woman with a torch, whose flame
Is the imprisoned lightning, and her name
Mother of Exiles. From her beacon-hand
Glows world-wide welcome; her mild eyes command
The air-bridged harbor that twin cities frame.
"Keep, ancient lands, your storied pomp!" cries she
With silent lips. *"Give me your tired, your poor,*
Your huddled masses yearning to breathe free,
The wretched refuse of your teeming shore.
Send these, the homeless, tempest-tost to me!
I lift my lamp beside the golden door!"

—*Emma Lazarus*

COYOTE CRY

Byrd Baylor

It is night.

A boy and an old man sit beside their campfire, listening, listening . . . waiting.

Finally, from somewhere across the hills, from some rocky ledge, from some steep ravine, comes the high, windy cry of a coyote.

At first they hear only one. But from other hills and other ledges and other ravines, coyotes answer. Ay-eee. Ay-eee.

In the darkness, far back from the small flickering campfire, coyotes sing and yap and howl and whine.

The boy, Antonio, stiffens.

He does not like that sound, that wailing, that yapping. And anyway, Coyote is his enemy. Antonio never forgets that, even at the end of a day, when he is almost ready for sleep.

"Coyote is my enemy," he says. "And I am his."

But the old man, the grandfather, has no enemies. Sometimes he even makes excuses for Coyote.

He says, "It is hard to enjoy a supper of rocks and sand, and so Coyote does what he must to stay alive."

"Even so, he is my enemy."

"He is our neighbor, our compañero," the grandfather says. "We share the same rocky land."

"Even so, he is my enemy."

The grandfather and the boy have nothing else to do now that the sheep are quiet in their night pen, now that the beans and green chiles and tortillas and wild honey have been eaten, now that the stars are out.

So they listen to coyotes. The old man has seen coyotes gathered together for company. He is sure of that.

"And they play games—those coyotes—chasing each other until they have to lie down, panting. I have looked at tracks that ran around and around. I almost think that on those nights Coyote dances."

But Antonio does not wish to think of Coyote dancing on some sandy ledge. Coyote is his enemy. He only thinks of him *that* way.

"He won't be dancing after

he meets me. Then he'll be running. *Cuidado,* Coyote. *Cuidado.* Watch out for me."

It is like this every night.

They sleep—they even dream—still half-listening for the sheep they must take care of day and night.

If a wildcat prowls, if a night bird screeches, if a coyote comes close, the sheep will run in fear. If the sheep move, the old man always wakes first, faster than Antonio, and he runs to the pen. He runs, calling out to calm his sheep. And his eyes peer into the shadows to find what it is they fear.

Too often it is Coyote he finds there. And Coyote must be kept away from the summer lambs, which still run, playing and jumping in the pen long after their mothers are quiet.

Usually the long-haired yellow collie Blanca sleeps where she too can guard the sheep.

Like the old man, this dog's whole life, as far back as Antonio can remember, has been caring for that flock of sheep . . . herding them across the valley to graze, bringing them back in the evening, keeping them safe all through the night.

27

But now Blanca does not run beside the old man when they go down the trail in the morning. Neither does she stay beside the sheep at night, because she has four new pups hidden under a manzanita bush not far from the glow of the campfire. There, the small branches twist down and touch the earth, and the pups lie curled together among the shadows, pale and soft.

But now in the first gray half-light of dawn, the pups stir. One of them stretches and yawns and rolls away from the others until he lies beyond the shelter of the manzanita branches.

The old man, too, moves restlessly in his sleep. Even in sleep, he seems to know that something is not as it should be. Without opening his eyes, he lifts his head to listen.

There is nothing but silence—silence and crickets. He drifts back into sleep. . . .

It is the wild barking of the dog Blanca that wakes Antonio and the grandfather at sunrise. They leave their blankets and go running toward the manzanita, where Blanca is sniffing the ground, circling back and forth, growling.

Antonio kneels beside the pups, stroking them, whispering to them. "But you are all right. Nothing is wrong here. . . ."

And then he sees that one of the pups is gone.

"Coyote!" he screams out. "Coyote was here."

And he is right. Already the grandfather is bending over coyote tracks in the sand.

The tracks circle the manzanita bush. They tell of one coyote, alone, quiet as a shadow.

Antonio is angry, and his anger is loud. He fills the dawn with his shouts, with his threats. He wants every coyote in the hills to hear him.

"I'll get you, Coyote. *Cuidado,* Coyote. Watch out, Thief."

Even though it is still too dark to see far beyond the light of their lantern, they both search for the pup. Perhaps, after all, he has just crawled away. Perhaps the coyote tracks mean nothing.

But the grandfather says, "The pup made no tracks. No tracks at all."

He looks off toward the hills, shaking his head, wondering. . . .

There is only one hope—to find where these coyote tracks lead. This will be Antonio's job.

While the old man takes the sheep to pasture, the boy follows the tracks from the small twisting tree, past the sheep pen, along the damp, sandy creek and up toward the first hills. But now the earth becomes rocky. Time after time, Antonio sits down on the ground and studies the faint footprints, trying to decide which way to turn.

Often the ground is too hard to hold a footprint. Or grass may hide it. Or there may be only rocks.

Antonio stops to listen. Even the slightest voice could tell him something. But the wind carries no coyote sounds today, no pup sounds. Only jack rabbits watch him from the far hills.

And when he calls out, "I'll get you, Coyote!" there is only an echo of his own small voice in the ravine: "I'll get you, Coyote."

But he does not get Coyote. All that afternoon, he does not even see Coyote.

Days go by. Now it is morning—another morning.

Antonio and his grandfather have taken the sheep a different way this time, along the other side of the creek. They have just walked across a little hill, and they stop to rest near the bottom of the slope.

There has been rain, and the air is cool and the far blue mountains seem closer. The grandfather bends down to look at a cactus flower blossoming pink and white from a crack in a rock.

Just below them at the foot of the hill, the rock juts out and forms a shelter, a small overhang not large enough to call a cave. The boy and the old man stand for a minute here on the slope of the hill, looking down. They are not in a hurry.

Something moves. They see a flash of yellow fur among the tall weeds. Antonio hardly breathes. The grandfather is as still as a rock or a tree. They wait.

Below them the small furry thing moves back into the rock shelter and then again comes bounding into the sunlight.

Now they are sure. It is the pup . . . Blanca's pup.

Antonio wants to run to the pup. But the old man puts out his hand to stop him. They stay there, watching.

31

Now something else comes into sight. A coyote—a mother coyote—puts her paw against the pup and plays with him the way any mother dog plays with her own babies. The pup rolls and nips and jumps. The coyote watches him.

Antonio's hands are tight. His eyes blink. He cannot believe what he is seeing. It is as if the hills he has walked all his life had turned suddenly into a strange and unknown land.

"Coyote," Antonio whispers. "Coyote. . . ."

Antonio does not wait to see what the grandfather wants to do. He goes leaping across the rocks to the bottom of the hill.

At the first sound, the coyote and the collie pup both run toward the rock shelter. There, the pup has been carefully taught, is safety. But Antonio is beside him in an instant. He grabs the pup up into his arms.

The coyote looks at the pup, but there is nothing she can do to hide him now. She turns and runs, and Antonio, holding the pup tightly against him, sees the coyote look back before she disappears in the low brush. The pup whines and tries to twist loose, but

Antonio says, "No, stay with us. You're no coyote."

Antonio runs and takes the pup to Blanca. Blanca sniffs the pup and walks around him, looking at him carefully. She smells the touch of coyote on her pup, and it puzzles her. Like Antonio, Blanca has been at war with coyotes for a long time. Yes, finally she decides to take the pup back, and she pushes him toward his brothers.

The pups no longer stay under the manzanita branches. Now they are old enough, strong enough, to come out into the world, to explore, to taste, to blink in the sunlight, to jump at Antonio.

Antonio watches the pup he has just carried home from the coyote's den. He is a dog again, not a coyote. Yet Antonio wonders. . . . When the pup grows up, will he remember those days? Will the sound of a coyote cry mean anything to him? Will he remember a den hidden among the rocks?

The old man and the boy listen carefully at night. Who knows whether the coyote will come back? Perhaps she is waiting in the shadows. Perhaps she will try to take the pup again. . . .

But that night passes. And another. And another.

And they put it out of their minds.

Then one cool dawn—still dark but with the first streaks of orange in the night sky—the old man lifts his head from his blanket. He sees two eyes shining. It is Coyote. He reaches over and touches Antonio and puts his finger to his lips. "Shhh."

They make no sound.

Now they see the pup moving toward the spot where Coyote stands. Coyote comes no closer. She waits. Then pup peers into the darkness to make sure. Then he goes to the coyote, and they touch noses. That is all. Just that. The pup goes back to his sleeping brothers.

When they look again, Coyote is gone.

She does not come back.

They know her tracks now, and every day they search for them around the camp. But she does not come back.

Yet even now that summer is past, the old man and the boy remember her.

They still lie under the stars, listening, listening as they always have for the night's first faraway coyote song.

Ay-eee.

And then they wait for other voices to come from the moonlit hills, from the deep ravines.

Ay-eee. Ay-eee.

Could one of the voices be *that* one?

"When she comes back again, that coyote . . . I'll give her something for supper. A melon, if we have it," Antonio says. "You saw how skinny she was."

"A melon for your enemy?" the grandfather asks, surprised.

"Maybe Coyote is not my enemy now," Antonio says very softly.

And then after awhile, it seems to him that the coyote voices have changed. He hears in them now a sound he must never have noticed before.

It is a song that coyotes sing only to the moon. You hear it only when the moon is yellow and low.

The boy knows suddenly what that song is about. He *knows*.

It is about being alive. It is about this rocky land, these windy hills where Coyote runs.

So Antonio says, "Someday I will be one of those people who can tell you what things Coyote is saying."

And the coyote song rises to the moon.

Ay-eee. Ay-eee.

37

A Place for Everything

Imagine that you have opened a sports shop. You sell equipment for twelve different sports. The equipment is scattered around the shelves. Soon, customers stop coming in because they can never find what they need.

How might you improve your store? You could arrange the pieces of equipment according to the sport for which each is used. For example, you might put all baseball equipment in one section, all tennis equipment in another, and so on.

Grouping items according to type is called *classification*. Each group is a *category*. In your sports shop, one category would be baseball equipment. *Items* are the things in a category. The items in your baseball-equipment category would include bats, balls, and gloves. Here is another example:

Category: ski equipment
Items: skis, ski boots, poles

ACTIVITY A Read each group of items below. Then choose the category that names the group. Write the answer on your paper.

1. **Items:** penny, dime, nickel, quarter, half dollar
   Category: bills, coins, stamps

2. **Items:** jacket, coat, shirt, sweater, hat
   Category: toys, furniture, clothing

3. **Items:** Bob, Nancy, Joe, Betty, Fred
   Category: names of people, names of boys, names of cities

ACTIVITY B Read each group of words. One word in each group names the category. The other words name items in the category. Write the word that names the category.

1. buzzes, honks, hums, sounds, clicks, taps, clangs
2. bears, horses, cows, pigs, dogs, animals, lions
3. rivers, bodies of water, lakes, streams, oceans
4. canoes, rowboats, sailing vessels, steamships, tugs
5. daisies, tulips, flowers, roses, daffodils

ACTIVITY C Read each group of items. Think of a category name for each group. Write the category name.

1. branch, twig, bark, leaf, root, trunk
2. nouns, verbs, adjectives, adverbs, pronouns
3. car, train, boat, bicycle, airplane, bus
4. kitchen, dining room, porch, living room, attic
5. second, minute, hour, day, month, year

ACTIVITY D Read each group of items. On your paper, write the item that doesn't belong in the group. Then write a sentence explaining the reason for your choice.

1. eye, nose, toe, finger, touch, ankle, ear
2. January, March, Monday, April, July, October
3. orange, pear, lemon, apricot, spinach, lime
4. liter, kilometer, centimeter, milligram, mile

ACTIVITY E Read the name of each category. Think of four items that belong in the category. Write the items on your paper.

1. Category: colors
2. Category; sports
3. Category: holidays
4. Category: vegetables

EXPLORING THE MIND

Arthur Alexander

In very important ways, each of us is different from everyone else in the world. Not even twins are exactly alike. They may look the same. But their hidden selves may have many differences.

Think of how each of us behaves when we don't get our way about something.

Suppose a class has been looking forward to an outing. Each boy and girl has been counting on it. No classes! Something new and exciting!

But on the day of the outing, the teacher tells the class that they will not be able to go. Something has happened to make it impossible.

Everyone is disappointed. But not everyone shows his or her disappointment in the same way.

Mark, for instance, finds tears in his eyes. "Something always happens to spoil our fun," he blurts out between sobs.

Ellen is disappointed, too. But she takes it out on Mark. "Cry-baby! Cry-baby!" she shouts. "Mark's a cry-baby!"

Michael blames the teacher. "This always happens," he whispers. "If we

could only have a different teacher, we'd have more fun. All she ever wants to do is work."

Susan answers Michael with: "Well, I didn't want to go, anyway. I'd much rather stay in school. I like school. It's much more fun than going on any old outing."

Caroline doesn't say anything. She feels like crying. But she "puts it out of her mind."

Johnny doesn't say anything, either. But he begins to imagine that he is on the outing. In his mind he is doing all that he looked forward to doing. All that day Johnny's mind is not on his work. He is daydreaming.

If we could look inside the mind of each girl and boy in the class, we would see that each one of them is taking the disappointment in his or her own way.

GALILEO

H. Einstein

ANTON VAN LEEUWENHOEK

M. Montessori

42

It is not easy to say why we act in so many different ways. It is just as hard to tell why we often act alike.

Like other scientists, the psychologist, who is a mind-scientist, is an explorer. He or she wants to know why we are alike in so many ways and why we are different in others.

"How do we learn?" this scientist asks. "Why do we remember the things we do?"

Psychologists explore our feelings, too. They want to find out what causes emotions like anger, jealousy, love, happiness, and fear.

Why do some of us seem to get along better with certain people than with others?

Why do some boys and girls get better marks in school than others?

All of these questions are difficult to answer.

Mind-scientists are not magicians. They cannot "read" minds. They must study and experiment and think—just as all scientists, no matter what their science, must.

The physicist tries to answer questions about light, heat, sound, and motion.

The biologist looks for the secrets of life.

The psychologist examines the part of people that cannot be seen or felt: the mind.

All scientists seek to answer questions. Many people say that psychology is the most difficult of all the sciences.

Certainly today we know more about the outside world than we know about the inside world—the mind.

The thing that makes psychology so interesting is that it is about us—you and me. The discoveries of the mind-scientists help us to see our own "invisible selves."

One Must Rise Above It

Adele deLeeuw

This story is about Betty Marie Tallchief, daughter of a full-blooded Osage Indian. When Betty Marie was eight years old, her family moved from an Indian reservation in Fairfax, Oklahoma to Beverly Hills so that she and her sister could have the best possible dance and music training. Today the whole world knows Maria Tallchief, one of the finest ballerinas that America has ever produced.

A classmate stopped Betty Marie Tallchief in a hall of the Beverly Hills High School. "Telephone your mother after class," she said, hurriedly, "and ask if you can come home with me. We could have a game of tennis, and then you could stay to supper."

Betty Marie said, "Oh, I would like that! But I have piano practice—"

"Well, when you've finished, come on over."

"I wish I could," Betty Marie said, "but I go to ballet class at five, and it lasts for two hours." She tried to make her voice sound a little regretful, but really she was not sorry. Ballet was the highlight of her day.

"Good heavens!" the other girl cried. "What a life!

Maria - 21 months old

Brother Jerry, Maria
and Mother

Maria's
first toe-
dance at
home, Fairfax

45

You must enjoy it to work so hard."

"I love it!" Betty Marie said, and now her voice was full and excited. "The ballet class is with Madame Nijinska, you know."

"Who's she?"

"Oh—oh, you must have heard of her! She's the sister of the famous Russian dancer, Nijinsky. He's dead, but he was as famous as Anna Pavlova. Madame is a marvelous teacher and a well-known choreographer—"

"What's a choreographer?"

"Someone who designs dances. She's done that for the Ballet Russe de Monte Carlo—"

"There's the bell," her friend said quickly. "See you!"

Betty Marie walked on slowly. Her friend wasn't really interested, it was obvious. But it didn't matter.

The world Betty Marie lived in, which was something strange to her friends, was real and exciting to her.

When Nijinska came to Hollywood to open a studio, it had been an event. Mr. Belcher, Betty Marie's former teacher, had said to Mrs. Tallchief, "I've had your daughters for four years. I feel I shouldn't keep them any longer when someone like Nijinska is available."

Nijinska had watched Betty Marie and her younger sister, Marjorie, perform.

"Umm," she said. "I can do something for you, both of you." Her gaze focused on Betty Marie. "You especially, little one, if you are willing to work."

Betty Marie had found no words, but her eyes answered for her.

Madame Nijinska kindled a kind of awe in Betty Marie. She wanted to please Madame,

Top Left – Maria, Mother and Marjorie at entrance to home in Fairfax.

Top Right – First dance learned at home in Fairfax – Highland Flin

Alex Tallchief – Maria's Father

47

to be a credit to her. When Madame praised something she had done, she was in seventh heaven. If she fumbled or was awkward and Madame frowned, a cloud covered the sky for the rest of the day.

Mrs. Tallchief was quietly proud that her daughters were doing so well in the studio. But she did not want Betty Marie to consider ballet more important than the piano. So Betty Marie worked twice as hard as she might ordinarily have done. Aside from practicing the piano twice a day, she got up early every morning to do her first dance exercises.

One day Betty Marie practically flew home from ballet class. She was fifteen, a sophomore in high school. "Mother, I'm to do a solo!" she cried breathlessly. "Madame has given me a soloist part in her *Chopin Concerto!* She's done the choreography for Chopin's E Minor Piano Concerto No. 1. Oh, I forgot to tell you— Madame's been asked to put on the ballet in the Hollywood Bowl. Isn't that thrilling?"

Betty Marie practiced as she had never practiced before. She dreamed of the coming event. The music was in her heart; now she could express it in her toes. She would dance in the Hollywood Bowl, the huge open-air auditorium where so many famous artists had performed.

The night of the performance was clear and cool, a beautiful starlit night. Row after row of people waited in the huge Hollywood Bowl. Betty Marie knew that she would make Madame proud.

And then, while dancing, Betty Marie fell onstage! It was a horrible moment, lying flat on the hard floor, with the other dancers swirling around her. She rose swiftly and re-

Maria – 4 years old

Tallchief and Bruhn in the Nutcracker Suite

49

sumed her place, but the awfulness of the moment stayed with her. She wanted to cry, but pride kept her dry-eyed.

When it was over she rushed into the wings, into Madame's arms. "I ruined it!" she wailed. "It was so lovely, and I ruined it!"

"You did well," Madame said calmly. "Every dancer experiences moments of that sort."

"But my first real solo! Oh, Madame—"

"Ssh," said Madame. "The world is not yet lost. Did you ever hear of Irina Baronova? She was dancing at a command performance, before royalty. She leaped—and landed on her head!"

Betty Marie smiled faintly.

"And then there was another dancer—I forget her name for the moment. She was dancing the bird-woman in

The Firebird. Her shoulder straps broke onstage, and her costume began to come off. What to do? Fortunately her partner had his wits about him. He snatched some feathers from her skirt and held them over her until she could exit."

Betty Marie's smile broke into a giggle.

"So you see, little one, it happens everywhere. One must rise above it. You did the right thing. It may never happen again. But the risk is always there." She shrugged. "That is part of dancing."

Next day the newspaper critics spoke of Miss Tallchief's dancing with kind words. It helped soothe her wounded spirits. Just the same, it had been a bad moment that Betty Marie would not forget, even after she had become Maria Tallchief, one of America's finest ballerinas.

Dream Variation

To fling my arms wide
In some place of the sun,
To whirl and to dance
Till the white day is done.
Then rest at cool evening
Beneath a tall tree
While night comes on gently,
   Dark like me—
That is my dream!

To fling my arms wide
In the face of the sun,
Dance! Whirl! Whirl!
Till the quick day is done.
Rest at pale evening....
A tall, slim tree....
Night coming tenderly
   Black like me.

— **Langston Hughes**

PRACTICE

E. L. Konigsburg

Mark Setzer doesn't know what to think when his mother becomes manager of his Little League team. But things look good when Mrs. Setzer convinces Spencer, Mark's older brother, to be team coach. Mark expects Spencer and his mother to give him extra pointers at home and special attention on the field. But Mark soon learns that on his mother's baseball team, all players are treated equally.

The orthodontist tightened my braces late on the Saturday before our first practice. On Sunday I was in pain. But pain.

Aunt Thelma and Uncle Ben came to dinner on Sunday. Although Mother didn't like to have both cooking and baseball on her mind at the same time, she put out a nice meal. Pot roast and cheesecake. Mother is great with cheesecake. She tops it with strawberries.

Aunt Thelma was dieting; dieting is part of Aunt Thelma's character. Dieters annoy Mother. When she was pot roasting and cheesecaking, she expected everyone to eat a lot. Because of the braces I let her down, too.

Mother commented as she was clearing up, "I'm putting away more than I put out." She always said that when we had company.

Aunt Thelma and I made an effort to help Mother clean up. But when Mother is annoyed, she is very difficult to help. Like when I asked, "Where should I put the leftover roast?" Mother didn't answer. Looking straight at me, she wrapped it in aluminum foil and then with movements like a ballet dancer, put it in the refrigerator.

As she closed the refrig, she said, "I started keeping leftover roast in a refrigerator five minutes after it got invented."

By the time we arrived at the practice field, Mother was very tired, and Spencer was annoyed. Dad had decided to stay home and read. Uncle Ben stayed with him. As soon as we got there, Aunt Thelma ran out onto the field full of enthusiasm. But after getting her shoes stuck in the mud, she sat on the bench and watched. The trouble with the way

Aunt Thelma looked was that when she walked, nothing moved but her legs. When Mother walks, it's like she carries a private breeze with her. And that's much nicer.

The team arrived in dribs and drabs after we did. Mother herded all the kids into the dugout and began by introducing herself and Spencer. "My name is Mrs. Setzer. Here is Spencer, who is your coach." There was dead silence. Mother smiled and cleared her throat, "I'm your manager."

There followed one loud snort from the left end of the dugout. Mother ignored it and continued, "I think we can be a winning team if you listen to me and to Spencer and work hard and train hard." The snort was louder and longer this time. Mother ignored it again. "After this we'll practice every Tuesday afternoon and Friday before sundown unless there is rain." Again the snort. Everyone began to laugh. "Does someone here have trouble with adenoids?" she asked. Spencer was getting nervous. He began picking imaginary dust off his pants, a sure sign that he was nervous.

Hal Burser pointed to Botts and said, "Botts wants to know why we have to have a woman manager. Like why can't we have a man?"

"If Botts wants to know, let Botts ask," Mother said.

Botts asked. "Why do we have to have a woman manager?" His voice kind of trailed off.

Mother said, "The question has been asked and seconded, 'Why do we have to have a woman manager?' There is only one possible explanation." She paused, took a deep breath, and with her hands straight down at her sides, said, "The reason why you have a woman manager is because the earth revolves around the sun."

Long, long pause. No snorts. Nothing. We all waited, but Mother said nothing more.

Finally Hersch said, "But, Mrs. Setzer, that about the earth is just a fact of life."

Mother didn't give his sentence a chance to cool off before she pressed in hers, "And so is your having a woman manager! It's just a fact of life, and you have to face it. You have to face facts." She shrugged her shoulders and smiled at the boys. "Now that we have that over with, can we play ball?"

Spencer laughed first. I was second. We gave everyone the cue that it was all right to laugh, and they did.

Sidney Polsky raised his hand and said, "Mrs. Setzer, would you mind repeating that so that I can tell my mother?"

Mother responded, "All right, you guys. Now repeat after me: The reason why you have a woman manager is because the earth revolves around the sun."

And we all repeated after Mother; that was our first lesson in baseball that season. As the kids left the dugout for the playing field, they chanted it to themselves.

After those introductions, we began exercising. Every time I leaned down to touch my toes, I felt rivers of pain leap up in my head. And when we ran around the bases to loosen up, the vibrations set my whole head to quaking each time I put my foot down. After doing awful two times at bat, I retired. Spencer was pitching batting practice, and he could have fed them to me a bit softer. He being my brother and all. Besides, he knew about the braces. As I walked to the bench, I said to myself, "If only I had a more dramatic ailment than just crooked teeth. Great pains make great heroes, but toothaches just make lousy batting averages." So I sat out and watched.

Our best players, the twins, were terrific. They were like two pros among us. Simon and Sylvester looked as if they were looking in a mirror when they faced each other. Completely identical except that one was right-handed and the other was a lefty.

They were both great at pitching as well as batting. But if you're looking at narrow differences, the lefty was a little bit better. A tiny bit. Not enough to hurt the other's feelings. Both of them were good-natured and kind to the other kids.

Barry Jacobs was also good at batting, but he wasn't so kind to other kids. I guess it's easier to be kind when you're as superior as Simon and Sylvester than when you're just working-at-it good like Barry. Simon and Sylvester giving out smiles and helpful hints to the others was like a gift from the Ford Foundation; there was still lots there, and they didn't do it for profit.

Aunt Thelma helped measure the boys for uniforms, and I helped give them out. Sidney cried when he found out that he wouldn't have his baseball pants right away. His mother mentioned to Aunt Thelma that he was a little overweight. Actually Sidney was rather fat. His pants would have to be ordered. Sidney was wiping the tears from his eyes with his fists the way infants do, when his mother came swooping down onto the field looking like a jagged streak of yellow lightning in her yellow stretch pants.

Mother was standing behind Hersch telling him to choke up a bit more on the bat.

"Mrs. Setzer," Mrs. Polsky began.

Mother waved a hand impatiently. She wanted to finish with Hersch.

"Mrs. Setzer," Mrs. Polsky repeated.

Mother finished with Hersch and then said, "Yes, Mrs. Polsky?"

"Isn't there some way Sidney can get into a pair of pants?"

Mother glanced from Mrs. Pol-

sky to Sidney and then back again. "Sure," she said, "tell him to lose about ten pounds." She looked over at Sidney again and added, "Around the hips would be best."

Spencer came over and added that he had a new training rule: All the boys were to walk to practice and to the games. They all needed the leg work.

Mrs. Polsky sputtered, "But my Sidney doesn't get home until 3:15. By the time he gets a little snack and changes his clothes, how can he have time to walk to practice?"

Spencer thought a minute and answered, "He can skip his snack and ride his bike."

Mother looked at Spencer and said, "That's a great idea."

Aunt Thelma chimed in, "I think, Mrs. Polsky, that it would be a very good experience for Sidney to ride his bike to the games."

Mother said, "What's this about a good experience? It's a training rule; Spencer said so."

Sidney asked, "Can I? Can I?" and Mrs. Polsky said, "We'll see. We'll see." She glared at Mother quite a lot.

After exercising and measuring for uniforms, we had a practice game. It was hardly that, though. For example, Barry hit a low grounder on which he easily made it to second. That was because the ball kept rolling out of the first baseman's hand. I happened to be the first baseman. When I finally got enough hand on the ball, Barry had just rounded second. I threw it to Louis LaRosa on third. He caught it, surprisingly enough—the first firm catch of the afternoon. But when he caught it, he was so pleased with himself that he stepped off base to look around and see if his mother was watching (she was), and he neglected to tag Barry out. Barry made it to home even before the throw.

Spencer continued not giving me any special breaks. He kept referring to himself as *let's* and to me as *kid.* "Let's beef up that swing, kid." "Let's run as if it counts, kid."

When practice was over, Spencer threw the equipment into the back seat next to me and Aunt Thelma. He sat in front.

I leaned over the front seat and asked my brother, my coach, "How did I do?"

He said, "You act as if you're afraid of the ball, kid."

We had all of six players out of fifteen who didn't act afraid of the ball. Maybe I was afraid because I was conscious of the fact that if the ball hit anywhere near my mouth, I'd be swallowing about $950.00 worth of braces and fillings. I don't know what reasons the others had.

I decided not to mention my reasons. Instead I asked, "How do you become unafraid?"

"Mostly by becoming more sure of yourself," he answered.

That's like telling a poor man he would stop being poor if he had more money! I figured that I didn't even have to answer Spencer, my brother, my coach, if that was the way he was going to be big-hearted about giving me advice.

As we came back into the house, I realized that my mouth had stopped hurting. "What's to eat?" I yelled.

We had leftover pot roast. I shouldn't have asked.

What Do They Mean?

In the story "Practice," Mark's mother told one player to "choke up a bit more on the bat." In the same story, another player "rounded third." If you play baseball or if you are a baseball fan, you probably know that *to choke up on the bat* means "to grip the bat farther up on its handle." *To round third* means "to touch third base and run on toward home plate."

To choke up on the bat and *to round third* are expressions which are special to the game of baseball. Words or expressions that are used by people in a particular occupation or profession are called *jargon*.

Do you think you can understand the jargon of people who work on newspapers? Both sets of sentences below say the same thing. But the sentences on the left contain jargon. Read these sentences. Then read the sentences on the right to find out how well you understand newspaper jargon.

The reporter called, "A big story is breaking. Be ready to check something out in the morgue."

The reporter called, "An important story is developing. Be ready to check some facts in our library of reference books and files of previous newspapers."

The editor shouted, "Cut that headline! Kill this paragraph! This paper must be put to bed in five minutes!"

The editor shouted, "Shorten that headline! Get rid of this paragraph! This paper must be ready for the printing presses in five minutes!"

Who's Who?

Suppose you found a picture of a stranger. You could describe the stranger's looks. However, you could not describe the stranger's personality. You would need to meet the person first. You might also need to get descriptions from the stranger's friends.

The people in a story are called *characters*. They are strangers to you at first. You learn about each one in several ways. Often you learn from a character's own words and actions. Sometimes, you learn from the author's descriptions of the character. Other times, you learn from what other characters in the story say.

Think of what you learned about Betty Marie Tallchief in "One Must Rise Above It." For example, you learned that Betty Marie enjoyed ballet. The author told you directly, "Ballet was the highlight of her day." Betty Marie herself admitted that she enjoyed ballet when she said, "I love it!" Then, one of her friends said to her, "You must enjoy it to work so hard."

Betty Marie was also proud of her ability as a dancer. When she fell onstage, her actions showed this pride: she recovered immediately. The author also said of her: "She wanted to cry, but pride kept her dry-eyed."

Remember: You learn about a character from three sources:

1. the character's words and actions
2. the author's descriptions of the character
3. what other characters say about the character

Read the story below. Pay close attention to the character named Joey.

Joey watched the basketball game from the bench. He was happy because his team was in the championship game. But he was also sad because he wasn't playing.

"Joey's not a good player," the other players had whispered. They thought Joey hadn't heard them, but he had. Joey turned to the coach standing nearby.

"Coach, I know I'm not the greatest," he admitted. "But can't I play in the game—just for a few minutes?"

The team led by only three points. "Maybe a little later," the coach answered.

With only a minute left in the game, Tom Allen hurt his ankle. Joey had to replace him. Happily, Joey ran onto the court. He bounced nearly as high as the ball.

Then, the team fell behind by a point. With only five seconds left, Joey caught the ball. He tossed it with all his might. Everyone watched as the ball hit the backboard, fell, and circled the rim of the basket. For a moment, the gym was silent. Then, the ball dropped into the net. Joey had scored *two* points!

The gym exploded with sound. The players and the crowd cheered. They carried Joey off the court on their shoulders. He was thrilled that he helped win.

On your paper, write a sentence from the story that tells the following:

1. The author describes Joey as being sad.
2. Other characters say that Joey is a poor player.
3. Joey admits he is not a very good player.
4. Joey's actions show he's happy to be in the game.
5. The author describes Joey as being thrilled.
6. Other characters show they are proud of Joey.

THE LOST DOG

Lois Lenski

Felix and his family had recently moved from the small California town of Alameda into bustling San Francisco. Felix had trouble adjusting to the new home and to the city. Several of the boys in the neighborhood were mean to him, probably simply because he was new. The only boy who was slightly friendly was Roger, who shared a paper route with Felix.

Felix stood by the high brick wall on the roof of the apartment house. He could see boats coming and going in San Francisco Bay. His eye could follow the Bay Bridge over to Yerba Buena Island and beyond, where the shore line melted in a blue haze. If only he had a telescope, he could see all the way to Alameda.

It was warm up on the apartment house roof in spite of the wind. The roof was the next best thing to a real yard, and the children liked to play there. The boys could run and jump around, except when the Yicks in Apartment No. 7 below complained. There were chimneys and skylights and water tanks on the roof. There were clotheslines where Mother hung her clothes to dry. There were radio and television antennas.

In one corner of a small fenced-in yard, Father had several salted fish hanging on a line to dry. Baskets of shrimp and other seafood were spread out in the sun. Behind the chimney, Felix's sister, Mei Gwen, had a dollhouse made from a cardboard carton. Father had told her to give her dolls to Susie, and Grandmother said she was too old to play with them. So she kept them hidden up on the roof. Now she got them out and began to play.

Mother called the twins, Frankie and Freddie, and they helped her bring up a basket of wet clothes, ready to hang on the line. Seeing Felix standing alone, looking so sadly across the water, Mother went over to him. She spoke softly so the others could not hear.

"You must not grieve so much, my son," she said. "Only time will ease the pain of homesickness. All of us who were born in the old country have felt it, too."

Felix made no sign that he heard her words.

Aloud, Mother said, "Go to the grocery store, my son, and get me a box of soap powder." She handed him some money. "I still have all the blue jeans and shirts of Father and my three boys to wash. They will make another washer full."

Felix turned and went slowly down the steps.

Did Mother really want soap powder, or did she just want him to go for a walk? Felix was not sure. There were grocery stores in almost every block, but he just kept on walking. He would take a walk anyhow, and pick up the soap powder on his way back.

Just then a cable car came clanging along Mason Street from Fisherman's Wharf. How about a ride? Felix had money of his own in his pocket, so he got on at Jackson Street. At Washington, the cable car turned south to Powell. When it stopped at Sacramento, Felix jumped off.

He walked down Sacramento Street. The hill was so steep that traffic was one-way, and cars were parked going up only. People could go both ways on the sidewalk, but it was hard to walk up the hill on windy days.

Hearing shouts, Felix looked behind him. Two boys were coming down on a new kind of scooter. Each boy had placed a book on a single roller skate, and was sitting on it, with knees bent up in front of him. Felix stepped out of the way, laughing. What fun to do that! He knew the boys, too. They were in his class at school—Ronnie Chow and Ralph Hom. They rolled on past him, gathering speed as they went.

Then all at once, another boy came zooming from behind on a soap-box scooter. Felix heard him coming and jumped out of his way. It was Sammy Hong and he whistled like a diesel engine to let people know he was coming. At Stockton Street, the three boys waited for a green light and crossed over. Felix followed them to the playground.

When he came in, Ronnie and Ralph and Sammy were throwing a baseball. Sammy tossed it to Felix, shouting, "There, see if you can catch it!" It was unexpected and Felix was not ready for the ball, so it landed on the back of his neck and bounced off. Ralph Hom caught it and threw it back to Sammy. The boys began to call Felix names. It was no use—Felix walked away and sat down on a bench.

It was then that he saw the dog come running into the playground. It was a small dog with long light brown hair and floppy ears and a short tail. The boys teased the dog with sticks. They chased it, saying, "Get out of here. We want to play our game." The dog ran into the street, and Felix ran after it. It came to him when he called. He sat on the curb-stone and patted it.

"What's your name, doggie?" he asked. "Where is your home? Are you lost in the big city?"

The dog wagged his tail and looked at Felix with his big brown eyes. "Oh, if I could only keep him," thought Felix, "how happy I would be. I would not mind living in the city, if I had a dog of my own." He held the dog in his arms, and it seemed contented there.

"That's not *your* dog," someone said.

Felix looked up. Sammy Hong was standing near, leaning on his scooter.

"He's got a collar with a tag on it," said Sammy. "That means he belongs to somebody."

"If I can find the owner," said Felix, "I'll give the dog back. But if I can't, I'll keep him myself."

Felix went into the playground and sat on a bench. The boys saw the dog and began teasing him again. They threw balls at the dog to see if he could catch them. They threw sticks and tried to get the dog to bring the sticks back. They kept the dog running in circles and barking loudly.

The dog was yelping so, Felix knew he was unhappy. He picked him up and went out the gate, starting for home. He carried him all the way to the apartment.

Would Mother let him keep a dog in the apartment?

What would Father say? Would he approve of having a pet in the city?

The dog ran all the way up the three flights of stairs. He followed Felix and came when he called. At the top, the door stood open and there was Mei Gwen.

"Did you bring the soap powder?" she asked. "Mother has been waiting hours for it."

"No, I forgot about it," said Felix. "I found a dog. Look what a nice little dog I found."

"A dog!" she cried. "What do you want a dog for?"

"Of course it's not my dog," said Felix. "I suppose it belongs to somebody."

Hearing voices, Mother and little Susie came to the front room. Mother asked for the soap powder. Maybe she really needed it after all. Felix had to explain all over again. Little Susie put her arms around the dog's neck. The dog stood very still while she patted him on the head.

"He likes Susie," said Felix.

"Have you looked at his dog tag?" asked Mother.

Felix looked at the tag dangling from the dog's collar. "It's got his license number," he said. He turned the tag over. "It says, 'If this dog is lost or injured, please phone 621-1701 for name and address of owner.'"

"That must be the dog pound, the place where they keep lost dogs," said Mother. "You should telephone that number."

"I don't want to," said Felix. Deep in his heart, he did not care to find the owner, because he wanted to keep the dog.

"You must find the owner quickly," said Mother. "When a dog gets homesick, it will not eat or drink. It will die."

"I will feed him," said Felix. "What does a dog eat?"

"Dog food," said Mei Gwen promptly. "I have seen it at the grocery."

"I have my own money," said Felix, looking at his mother. "I will buy him dog food. I will buy you the soap powder, too."

"Let me go with you," said Mei Gwen.

Mother said nothing, so the children started out. The dog followed them to the store and back again. Mei Gwen gave the soap powder to Mother. Felix opened the can of dog food with a can opener and smelled it.

"My dog will like this," he said. "It smells something like pressed ham."

Felix put some of the food on a dish. He set the dish on a cloth on the floor. Mei Gwen brought a pan of water. The dog ate and drank.

Mother came down from the roof, bringing some of the clothes that were dry. She asked, "Have you telephoned the dog pound?"

"No, Mother," said Felix. "The dog likes it here. He is not going to die of homesickness. See how he eats! I will spend all my paper-route money to buy him good food."

Mother spoke crossly, "Mei Gwen, what was that number on the dog's tag? Go to the telephone and call it. Find out who owns this dog, so he may be restored to his owner." She turned to Felix. "When a dog is lost, it is a kindness to restore it to the owner. If you try to keep a lost dog, it is the same as stealing it."

Felix's heart sank. Now he knew—there was only one thing to do. It was a hard thing to do because already he loved the little dog so much. "I would like to keep him if the owner does not want him," he thought. "Maybe the owner will say that he does not want him—then he will be mine." But Felix knew this was a foolish hope.

"I will take him for a little walk on the street, Mei Gwen," said Felix, "while you do the telephoning."

Mei Gwen called 621-1701, and a woman said, "This is the S.P.C.A."

"What's that?" asked Mei Gwen.

The woman explained that it was the Society for the Prevention of Cruelty to Animals. Mei Gwen gave the dog's license number, and the woman told her the owner's name and address. Mei Gwen looked up the owner's number in the telephone book. She called the number and a man answered. She asked him if he had lost his dog and he said that he had.

Meanwhile, Felix sat in the downstairs doorway and held the dog on his knees. At first he thought of saving the dog by running away with him. But where could he go to keep the dog safe? Then he remembered his mother's words. He patted the dog and talked to him.

"I am trying to bring you back to your master as fast as I can," he said. He told the dog this, so the dog would understand. He wanted the dog to know he was trying to help.

Just then Mei Gwen came to the front door and called. Felix went over to her. "He's coming," she said.

"Who?" asked Felix.

"The owner," said Mei Gwen.

"Did you tell him where we live?" asked Felix.

"Yes," said Mei Gwen.

"Oh, why did you do that?" groaned Felix.

"So he can come and get his dog," said Mei Gwen. "The dog's name is Rusty," he said.

"Rusty—I like that name," said Felix. "Did he sound like a nice man—like a kind man?"

"He was okay," said Mei Gwen.

"Where does he live?" asked Felix, unhappily.

"Up on Nob Hill," said Mei Gwen. "The man said that when he took his car out of the garage this morning, he forgot to close the door, so the dog ran away."

"The dog was happy," said Felix, "because he was free. Maybe he felt like Frankie and Freddie when they run away. They don't like to be cooped up in a little crowded apartment. The dog did not like to be locked in a garage. That is why he ran away. To run away does not always mean that one is bad. Maybe it just means a person is unhappy. A dog could be unhappy, too. Maybe the man does not treat him well."

Mei Gwen and Felix sat in the doorway and talked. The dog lay contentedly in Felix's arms.

It seemed no time at all before a taxi pulled up and a man stepped out. He called, "Here, Rusty!" The dog heard it and jumped up and down, he was so glad to see his master. He barked a little, too—happy barks, not angry barks. The man wanted the dog back. It was useless for Felix to ask if he could keep him. The man talked to the children, but Felix did not hear a word he said.

The man put a leash on the dog's collar. The dog stood still and let him snap it on. That settled the matter. The dog was willing to go back to his master.

Felix and Mei Gwen said goodbye to the dog. Felix's voice was shaking. He hated to see the dog go away. The man got into the taxi, and the dog jumped in after him. The taxi drove off down the street and turned the corner. The dog was gone.

Standing there, Felix looked down and saw that he held a dollar bill in his hand.

"Where did I get this?" he asked, astonished.

"The man gave it to you." said Mei Gwen. "He said it was your reward."

"Did he?" asked Felix.

What was it—the motto? *Better to keep a friend than to have a dollar.* In his mind, Felix changed it: *Better to keep a dog than to have a dollar.* No amount of money could make up for the loss of the dog.

Everyone has felt like Felix at one time or another—sad and friendless. Often, animals seem to be especially comforting at unhappy times like these. Why is this so?

Felix's unhappiness in San Francisco slowly dissolved as he learned more about his new home and found new friends. You can read the rest of Felix's story in *San Francisco Boy*, the book from which this excerpt was taken.

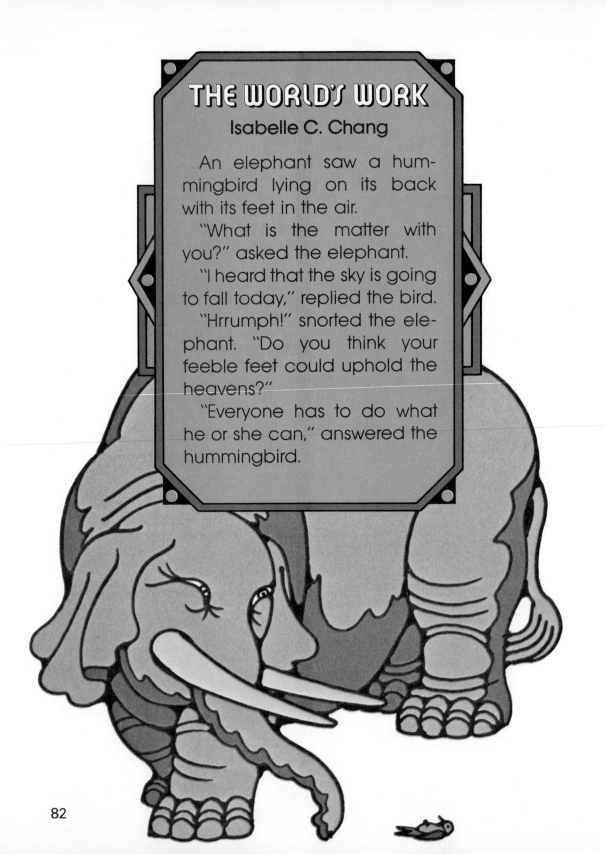

THE WORLD'S WORK

Isabelle C. Chang

An elephant saw a hummingbird lying on its back with its feet in the air.

"What is the matter with you?" asked the elephant.

"I heard that the sky is going to fall today," replied the bird.

"Hrrumph!" snorted the elephant. "Do you think your feeble feet could uphold the heavens?"

"Everyone has to do what he or she can," answered the hummingbird.

The Artist

Isabelle C. Chang

There once was a king who loved the graceful curves of the rooster. He asked the court artist to paint a picture of a rooster for him. For one year he waited and still this order was not fulfilled. In a rage, he marched into the studio and demanded to see the artist.

Quickly the artist brought out paper, paint, and brush. In five minutes a perfect picture of a rooster emerged from his skillful brush. The king turned purple with anger, saying, "If you can paint a perfect picture of a rooster in five minutes, why did you keep me waiting for over a year?"

"Come with me," begged the artist. He led the king to his storage room. Paper was piled from the floor to the ceiling. On every sheet was a painting of a rooster.

"Your Majesty," explained the artist, "it took me more than one year to learn how to paint a perfect rooster in five minutes."

The Clockmaker and the Timekeeper

Isabelle C. Chang

There was once a clockmaker who had a shop in the center of the village. Every day a man stopped by and looked in the window, before hurrying on his way. After a year, the clockmaker hailed the man one day and asked him why he always hesitated by the window but never entered the shop.

The man replied, "I am the timekeeper for the town, and I have to ring the church bells at exactly twelve o'clock noon. To be accurate, I always check with your clock first."

"Ah," said the clockmaker, "but I always set my clock after I hear the chimes of the church bells."

PHRASES FROM FABLES

An old fable has it that crocodiles cry bitterly after eating a victim. Their tears are to show how sorry they feel for the innocent person. So the expression *crocodile tears* has come to mean "make-believe sorrow or sadness."

One of Aesop's fables tells of a fox who wanted some beautiful, sweet-smelling grapes. The fox tried and tried to get the grapes, but they were just a bit higher than he could reach. When the fox realized that he couldn't reach the grapes, he walked away. As he left, he told himself that the grapes were probably sour and that he really didn't want them. Now, when someone says something bad about something they want and can't have, we sometimes say that they are experiencing *sour grapes.*

Another of Aesop's fables is about a dog who guarded a manger full of hay. Even though the dog couldn't use all the hay, she wouldn't share it with anyone. So a selfish person is now sometimes called *a dog in the manger.*

Unlike her four older brothers and sisters, nine-year-old Anna Solden seemed clumsy, slow, and stupid. She couldn't even learn to read. She hated school, and she hated reading. Anna's brothers and sisters were always teasing her. But Anna learned to pretend she didn't care what they said. She got used to keeping her thoughts and feelings hidden. And she got used to being alone.

Anna's father inherited his brother's store, and the Soldens moved from Germany to Canada to run it. The children had to have medical examinations before they could start school in Canada. That is when Dr. Schumacher made an astonishing discovery. And that is when Anna met an optometrist.

DR. SCHUMACHER'S DISCOVERY

Jean Little

Dr. Schumacher's waiting room was shabby and crowded. When the Solden family arrived, the two boys had to stand up against one wall with their father because there were not enough chairs.

"All right," Dr. Schumacher smiled, "who's first?"

Rudi stepped forward. Mama got up to go with him. He scowled at her.

"I'm not a baby," he muttered.

"Let him go in by himself, Klara," Papa said. "Go ahead, Rudi." He came over and, taking Anna on his knee to make room, sat on the bench beside his wife.

"It will be fine," he told her.

Mama was not convinced. She was used to taking her children to the doctor only when they were sick. They all had injections before they came to Canada, but that had been so hurried that she had not had time to think about it. Suppose this doctor she did not know found one of her children had some terrible disease?

"One healthy one!" Dr. Schumacher said. "You're next—Gretchen, is it?"

This time Mama sat still, although her eyes followed Gretchen every step of the way until the door closed behind her.

"Do you think she looked pale?" she asked Papa.

Ernst Solden laughed, a big laugh that filled the room. "Gretchen—pale! She has cheeks like roses, and you know it."

Anna snuggled closer to him and laughed, too. It was funny thinking of Gretchen as pale.

"She was green on the ship," Anna offered.

"Now, Anna, that is not tactful," her father said. "Just because you were the only sensible one..."

Mama shushed them both sternly.

Papa chuckled again and gave Anna an extra squeeze.

Gretchen came back, her cheeks as rosy as ever. Frieda went and returned. Fritz was a couple of minutes longer.

"Maybe something is wrong with Fritz..." Mama began, her eyes growing wide.

"He let me listen to my own heart," Fritz bragged, bouncing out into the waiting room.

"A fine family, you Soldens," Dr. Schumacher boomed, stretching out a broad hand to Anna. She slid off her father's knee at once and put her hand in the doctor's. Papa smiled. So someone else had discovered a way to reach his Anna!

As they disappeared, Mama gave a deep sigh of relief.

"Didn't I tell you?" her husband teased.

She had to nod. Only Anna was left—and Anna had not been seriously ill in her entire life.

"Let me hear you read the letters on this card," Dr. Schumacher was saying to the youngest of the Soldens.

Anna froze. Reading! She couldn't....

She looked where he was pointing. Why, there was only one letter there. That was easy!

"E," she told him.

"And the next line down?" Dr. Schumacher asked.

Anna wrinkled up her forehead. Yes, there were other letters. She could see them now, when she squinted. They looked like little gray bugs, wiggling.

"They're too small to read," she said.

Ten minutes later, when he had made very sure, the doctor came out to the waiting room with the little girl.

"Did you know that this child can't see?" he asked sternly.

Ernst and Klara Solden's blank faces told him the answer. Feeling sorry then, he tried to soften his voice, although he was still angry on Anna's behalf.

"At least she can't see much," he corrected himself.

Mama reached for Anna. Had Anna known it, at that moment she was the only one who mattered. But Anna did not guess. She pulled away from her mother and stood out of reach.

"Of course she can see!" Klara Solden gasped, turning away from the child to this foreign doctor whom she had not trusted from the beginning. "What do you mean? Don't be silly!"

The doctor looked from one of Anna's parents to the other.

"She sees very poorly, very poorly indeed," he said. "She should be wearing glasses. She probably should have had them two or three years ago. But before we go any further, I want to have her examined by an eye doctor."

This time Mama would not be left behind. The others stayed in Dr. Schumacher's waiting room while Anna was taken upstairs to see Dr. Milton.

It was all like a nightmare to Anna. Once more, she had to read letters off a faraway card. Once again, she could only see the big E. The new doctor peered into her eyes with a small, bright light. He made her look through a collection of lenses. All at once, other letters appeared.

"F...P," Anna read in a low voice. "T...O, I think...Z."

"Now these," Dr. Milton said, pointing to the next row of letters. But they were too small.

Dr. Milton clucked his tongue. He began to talk to Mama in rapid English. Mama threw up her hands and rattled German back at him. Dr. Milton took them back down to Dr. Schumacher's office, and the two doctors talked. The Soldens waited anxiously. Anna looked sullen, her usual touchy, difficult self. She was trying, inside, to pretend that she was not there. It was not helping.

Dr. Schumacher took her to yet another room, where she sat on a chair and was fitted for frames.

"What a nice little girl," the optician said heartily.

Anna glowered.

"Even with the glasses, she will not have normal vision," Franz Schumacher explained when they were back in his office. The grown-ups took the chairs. Anna stood near Papa, but she did not look at him. Instead she scuffed the toe of her shoe back and forth on the worn carpet. Maybe she could make a hole in it. That would teach Dr. Schumacher.

"She'll have to go to a special

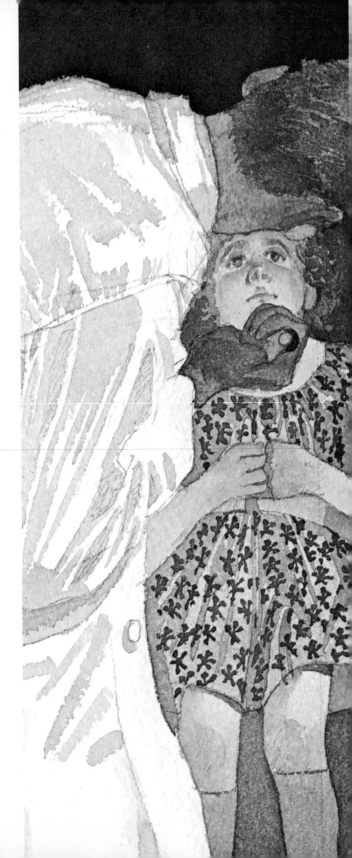

class, a sight-saving class," he went on. "Lessons are made easier there for children with poor eyesight."

"Not go to school with the others!" Mama asked hoping she was not understanding.

Dr. Schumacher switched back to German. He spoke gently, soothingly.

"It is a nice place. She'll like it there. You will, Anna. You'll like it very much," he finished.

From the beginning, he had been drawn to this little girl. Now, guessing at how hard life must have been for her since she started school, he wanted more than ever to be her friend.

All of this was in his voice as he spoke straight to her. He not only tried to reassure her about the special class; he also said, without actually putting it into words, that he, Franz Schumacher, liked her, Anna Solden.

Anna went on scratching her shoe back and forth on the bare place in his carpet. She did not look up or answer. He had become part of the bad dream in which she was caught.

She hardly heard what he said. What she did hear, she did not believe. How could she like school?

In the days that followed, the Soldens were busy settling into their new home. Papa went over everything in the store, finding out what he had, trying to decide what he needed to order. Since Karl Solden's death the store had been kept running by hired help, but now Papa planned to look after it by himself.

"I think he's worried about it," Rudi told the others.

Anna thought so, too. Her father seemed to have no minutes to spare, no special smiles to give. She tagged after him, trying to help. Both of them were surprised when she really was a help. She counted cans of peaches, boxes of arrowroot biscuits. She was good at counting. When Papa checked, she was always right. Frieda came, too, one day; she made mistakes.

"You hurry too much, daughter," Papa said to Frieda.

Anna listened wide-eyed. Could it be that being slow was sometimes a good thing?

Then, three days before school was to begin, Anna's new glasses arrived. Perched on her nub of a nose, they looked like two round moons. She longed to snatch them off and hurl them into a far cor-ner. Instead, she peered through them suspiciously.

For one startled moment, an utterly new expression came over her small plain face, a look of intense surprise and wonder. She was seeing a world she had never guessed existed.

"Oh, Anna, you look just like an owl," Frieda laughed, not meaning any harm.

The wonder left Anna's face instantly. She turned away from her family and stumped off up the stairs to her room where none of them could follow without permission. Papa, though, came up alone a minute or two later.

"Do you like them, Anna?" he asked quietly.

She almost told him then. She nearly said, "I never knew you had wrinkles around your eyes, Papa. I knew your eyes were blue, but I didn't know they were so bright."

But she remembered Frieda's laughing words. How she hated being laughed at!

"Do I have to keep wearing them, Papa?" she blurted.

Papa looked sorry for her, but he nodded.

"You must wear them all the time and no nonsense," he said.

Anna reddened slightly. It was not right, fooling Papa like this. But she was not ready to share what had happened to her. Even her father might not understand. She could hardly take it in herself.

"All right, Papa," she said, letting the words drag.

Wanting to comfort her, her father put his hand gently on top of her bent head. She squirmed. He let her go.

"Would you like to come back to the store with me?" he asked.

Anna nodded. Then she said in a muffled voice, "I'll be there in a minute. You go on down."

Ernst Solden started to leave. Then he turned back, stooped suddenly, and kissed her.

"Soon you'll get used to them, *Liebling*," he consoled her. "Wait and see."

Anna felt her blush grow hotter. She was glad that the light in her room was dim.

When he was gone, she lifted her right hand and held it up in front of her. She moved her fingers and counted them. Even though the light was poor, she could see all five. She examined her fingernails. They shone faintly, and they had little half-moons at the bottom. Then she leaned forward and stared at her red wool blanket. It was all hairy. She could see the hairs, hundreds of them.

Everything, everywhere she turned, looked new, looked different, looked miraculous.

At last, knowing she was safe, Anna smiled.

adapted from: *From Anna*

MY INSIDE-SELF

My Inside-Self and my Outside-Self
Are different as can be.
My Outside-Self wears gingham smocks
And very round is she,
With freckles sprinkled on her nose,
And smoothly parted hair,
And clumsy feet that cannot dance
In heavy shoes and square.

But, oh, my little Inside-Self—
In gown of misty rose
She dances lighter than a leaf
On blithe and twinkling toes;
Her hair is blowing gold, and if
You chanced her face to see,
You would not think she could belong
To staid and sober me!

—**Rachel Field**

PREFIXES THAT MAKE ANTONYMS

Find the words with prefixes in the speech balloons below.

Help me untie these water wings, please.

I'm going to disappear. Watch me go!

I can swim four laps nonstop.

Did you find three words? What is the base word in each word? What is the prefix in each word?

The prefixes *un-*, *dis-*, and *non-* all mean the same thing: "not." Adding one of these prefixes to a base word gives the base word its opposite meaning.

$$un + tie \Rightarrow untie$$
$$dis + appear \Rightarrow disappear$$
$$non + stop \Rightarrow nonstop$$

The prefixes *im-*, *in-*, and *de-* may also mean "not." Add one of the prefixes in the box to each base word below the box. Write the new words with their opposite meanings. Use your dictionary to check your new words.

im-	dis-	un-	in-	de-	non-

possible	considerate	sense	direct
comfortable	approve	frost	safe
dependent	afraid	polite	obey

BUSH PRAIRIE

A. E. Schraff

"I hear water rushing," Owen Bush said. He stood up in the wagon. He was eight years old, and this was just about the most exciting thing that had ever happened to him. This was Oregon Country in 1845. Owen and his parents had come all the way from Pennsylvania across mountains and deserts.

"Yeah, I hear the water, too," George Washington Bush, Owen's father, said. "That's what the American Indians call Tumwater."

Owen and his father had black skin. They had lived in Pennsylvania and in Missouri. Owen did not really know why they had moved from those places, but sometimes the small boy heard his mother and father talking. Owen thought it had something to do with the neighbors' not liking black people.

"This land looks good," George Bush said to another man, Mike Simmons. Mike was a white man from Kentucky. He was a good friend of Mr. Bush's. They had come together to Oregon to start new lives.

"Looks great, George," Mike said.

And so they settled down right there. They called the place Newmarket.

Mike wanted to build a flour mill. George lent him the money to start out. Then the black pioneer found some good land, and he started farming.

"We'll make this a good farm," Bush told his son.

"I'll help you, Dad," Owen promised.

"Sure you will," Bush smiled. He was proud of his son. Owen was a very good boy. He could be trusted to do all kinds of jobs.

Bush's first crop was very good. He had enough food for his family and even some to give away to his friends.

One day, a new family moved into Newmarket. They had a small boy named Jim. He was also eight years old, and Jim and Owen quickly became friends.

Jim's family was very poor. During the first few months that they lived in Newmarket, they had very bad luck. George Bush helped them out by giving

them supplies and lending them money. When Jim's father was finally on his feet, he said to Bush, "George, you're the best friend I ever had. But now that I have some money, I want to pay you back."

"You can't pay me with money," Bush smiled. "You can pay me back by doing a favor for somebody else in need."

"Well, at least I can say thank you, George."

Bush smiled. "Yes. And I can say you're welcome."

Rain was expected in the next few weeks, but the rain did not come. Newmarket had a drought. The days were hot and dry. People kept looking into the sky and hoping for a cloud, but there never was one.

The dry weeks turned into dry months. All the crops died because there was no water. However, thanks to George Bush, the people of Newmarket got along fairly well. Bush had a lot of food stored in his barns. He shared it with all his neighbors, and everybody made out all right until the rains finally came.

Then, one day, a stranger came to Bush's house. "Is this Bush Prairie?" he asked Owen.

"Yes. That's what they call my father's farm," Owen said. Owen did not like the stranger. He had a cold look on his face.

"I want to see your father," he said.

"Yes, sir." Owen ran to the house and got his father.

"Mr. Bush," the stranger said, "I'm afraid I have bad news for you."

Owen listened, but he was very quiet.

"What is the news?" Bush asked.

"You do not own this land you call Bush Prairie," the man said.

"You mean I don't own my own land? The land I've been farming?"

"That's the way it is," the stranger said, "because there is a law in Oregon that says a black man cannot own land. And you are a black man."

Owen looked up at his father. Owen could not understand this. When the stranger left, Owen asked his father, "Do we have to move?"

"I don't know," George Bush said sadly. But he knew he had had to move before because he was black.

"Dad, why don't people like us?" Owen asked.

"Most people like us," George Bush said. "Mike Simmons likes us, and Jim's parents, and all the people at Newmarket. They are all our friends, Owen."

Owen went to see his friend Jim. "Jim, we have to leave Newmarket. A man came and said we have to leave because we're black. So I guess I will be moving away, and we can't play together anymore."

Jim looked very angry. "I'm going to tell my dad! He'll do something so you won't have to leave."

Jim told his father about the trouble, and all the people of Newmarket got together for a meeting. They decided to write a letter to the United States Govern-

ment in Washington. They said that George Washington Bush was the best friend anybody in Newmarket had. They also said that if there was some silly law against black people owning land in Oregon, then the law should be changed. Everybody in Newmarket signed the letter, and they sent it to Washington.

The United States Congress read the letter from Newmarket. And then Congress passed a law saying that George Washington Bush could stay on his farm. The silly law about black people was changed so that Bush Prairie still belonged to George and his family.

So George Bush of Bush Prairie continued to live at Newmarket with his friends. Owen grew up to be a fine, tall man and won all kinds of prizes for being a good farmer. His father was very proud of him. Nobody ever forgot George Bush and what he had done for them all. He was one of the finest pioneers in the American West.

CHANGE

The summer
still hangs
heavy and sweet
with sunlight
as it did last year.

The autumn
still comes
showering gold and crimson
as it did last year.

The winter
still stings
clean and cold and white
as it did last year.

The spring
still comes
like a whisper in the dark night.

It is only I
who have changed.

—Charlotte Zolotow

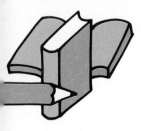

Word Detectives

Have you ever watched detectives on television at work? They search carefully for clues. The clues will help them solve the puzzle.

Sometimes, an unfamiliar word is like a puzzle. You find the word in your reading. You don't know the word's meaning, but there are clues to help you figure out the meaning. The clues are the other words and sentences near the unfamiliar word. Read the following paragraph from "Bush Prairie":

> Rain was expected in the next few weeks, but the rain did not come. Newmarket had a drought. The days were hot and dry.

You know that Newmarket is a town, but you may not know the meaning of *drought*. There are clues to help you figure out its meaning. The first sentence says that rain did not come for weeks. The third sentence says that the days were hot and dry. From these clues, you should be able to figure out that a *drought* is a long period of dry weather. The clues that helped you figure out the meaning of drought are called *context clues*.

ACTIVITY A   Use context clues to help you choose the correct meaning of each underlined word. Write that meaning on your paper.

1. It was a perilous journey across the icy mountains. Three people slipped and broke their legs.

    a. enjoyable   b. dangerous   c. short

2. Pat forgot to turn off the faucet. Soon, the bathroom was <u>inundated</u> with water.

   a. melted   **b.** baked   **c.** flooded

3. I like the country because it is <u>placid</u>. There are no constantly loud noises to disturb me.

   a. peaceful   **b.** expensive   **c.** nearby

4. The scientist <u>lured</u> the bees with honey. They followed her into the laboratory.

   a. painted   **b.** watched   **c.** attracted

5. The mail carrier delivered the <u>parcel</u>. We quickly unwrapped it.

   a. mailbox   **b.** package   **c.** string

ACTIVITY B On your paper, write what you think is the meaning of each underlined word. Then check your answer in a dictionary or in the glossary of this book.

1. With one leap, he was <u>astride</u> the horse. He took up the reins and galloped away.

2. The annual garden party was a very <u>staid</u> affair. Everyone was very solemn and talked quietly.

3. The large boulder tumbled down the mountainside, bounced on the deserted road, and hurtled into the deep <u>ravine</u>.

4. The tug pulled the ship into the harbor. There, the sailors tied the ship to a <u>wharf</u>.

5. The building was a blur when she viewed it through her camera. Then she <u>focused</u> the camera and saw the building clearly.

6. The diver went into the water at one end of the pool. Swimming underwater, she <u>emerged</u> at the other end.

MOMENTS

All your life you are learning and changing.
Things that you do and see can cause you to feel
angry one moment and happy the next. Your experiences can make you change your mind about something or think about something completely new. All
your experiences work together to make you who and
what you are.

Thinking About "Moments"

1. What experiences caused Antonio to change his
   mind about Coyote?
2. What made Betty Marie Tallchief feel better about
   falling on stage?
3. How did Emma Lazarus's visit to Ward's Island help
   her to understand the meaning of *freedom*?
4. Why didn't Anna share her thoughts and feelings
   about her new glasses with her father?
5. What did Felix see in Rusty that reminded him of
   himself?
6. What experience have you had that made you change
   your mind or feel differently about something?
7. Choose an interesting snapshot or magazine photograph.
   Write a paragraph that tells what was happening at the
   moment the picture was taken.

PARTNERS

At all times, in all places, human beings have relied on animals. Animals have always provided food for people. Animals have also served people as companions and workers. Some animals have come to rely on people.

In "Partners," you will explore the history of our relationships with animals. You will read about ancient cave drawings which show animals that disappeared thousands of years ago. You will read about how the first friendship between a boy and a dog may have taken place long ago. You will also read about some of the ways people have used animals in the past.

As you read, think about the ways we use animals today. Ask yourself what we can do to protect animals now and in the future.

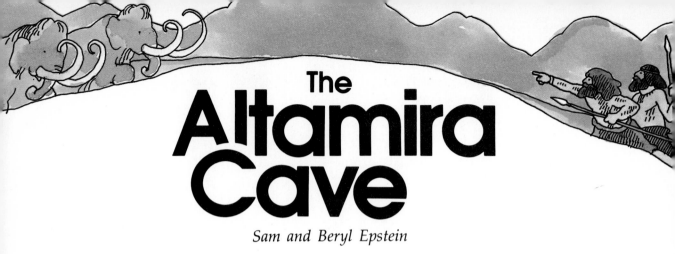

The Altamira Cave

Sam and Beryl Epstein

In the late 1800's, there lived a Spanish noble named Don Marcelino de Sautuola. His hobby was searching for clues to the lives of people who existed thousands of years ago. Don Marcelino knew that prehistoric homes had been found in caves nearby. He also knew of a cave called Altamira close to his farm. He wondered whether prehistoric people might have once lived in this cave. To find out, he began to visit the cave to dig through the deep soil on the cave floor. Over the centuries, this soil had piled up, raising the floor and making the cave dark and cramped. As he dug, Don Marcelino carefully searched each shovelful of dirt. He did not want to overlook even the tiniest scrap of bone or chipped stone. Don Marcelino finally succeeded in unearthing some ancient spearheads. He excitedly brought them home to show his family and friends. That was when his young daughter, Maria, asked to go with him the next time he visited the cave.

At first Don Marcelino shook his head. He felt sure Maria would quickly grow tired of trying to amuse herself in a dark cave. But he was very fond of his little daughter, and it was hard for him to refuse her anything. So he finally agreed to take her into the cave if she promised not to disturb him at his work.

Of course Maria was just as disappointed in the cave as her father had known she would be. She couldn't find anything that was fun to do. It certainly wasn't much fun to watch her father patiently scraping away in the dirt. After a time, with a candle in her hand, she crept into the low passage.

Soon the little corridor grew broader. But it was still so low that Maria had to be careful not to bump her head on the rough ceiling as she moved along.

Suddenly, glancing up at that ceiling, Maria stopped still. The candle wavered in her hand. All around her, in the flickering yellow light, there seemed to be animals—huge beasts with curving horns and staring eyes.

"Father!" Maria screamed. "Bulls! Bulls!"

Her voice echoed and re-echoed against the stone. Don Marcelino dropped his tools, snatched up a candle, and crawled into the little tunnel.

"Look, Father!" Maria cried. "Look!" She was pointing at the ceiling.

At first Don Marcelino couldn't understand where he was supposed to look. Twisting about to peer up at the ceiling, so close above his own head, he could see at first only some black lines and some splotches of red and yellow.

Then slowly, one after the other, the splotches and lines took on shapes. Shifting this way and that, and finally lying flat on his back in order to see more clearly, Don Marcelino at

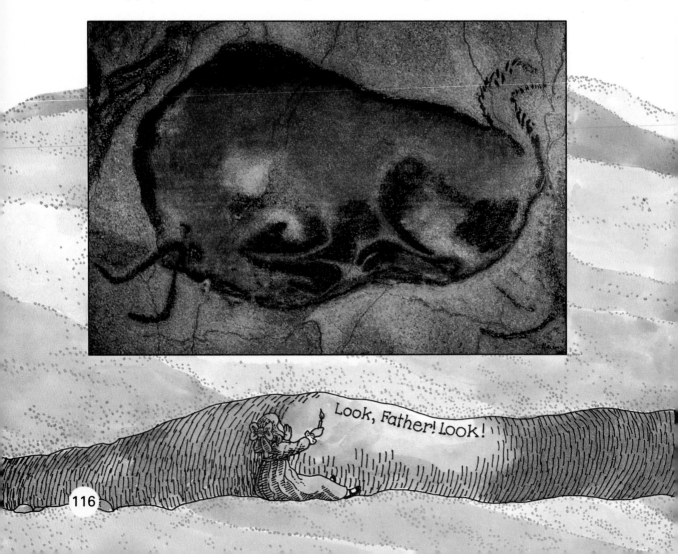

Look, Father! Look!

last realized why Maria had shouted out that startled word "Bulls!" Some of the shapes did look like bulls—huge staring beasts with curving horns.

Don Marcelino blinked his eyes. The more he stared, the more real the animals seemed. He realized that he was looking at paintings so skillfully done that the red and black and yellow creatures appeared to be alive.

There was one great beast, with head down, hind legs crumpled under it, as if it had been struck a mortal blow the very moment before Don Marcelino first saw it.

Not far away was a red horse, with a black mane and a black tail. It looked as if it had just touched the ground after a leap through space.

Utterly amazed, Don Marcelino looked from one picture to another. Red animals had been painted over animals outlined in black. A red creature was half covered up by another animal. The second one was painted in black and yellow, with its legs drawn together as if it were about to spring.

How had these paintings come to be made on the ceiling of a passage so low that a grown man couldn't sit upright in it? Who had made them? And when? Don Marcelino was certain that no one but himself, and a few of the men who worked for him, had entered the cave since the opening had been discovered a few years earlier.

Even as he tried to puzzle out an explanation for the remarkable figures leaping and striding across the rock vault over his head, he began to see that the ones that looked like bulls were not really bulls at all. He studied them more carefully. Then suddenly he caught his breath in excitement. The bull-like animals were actually bison,

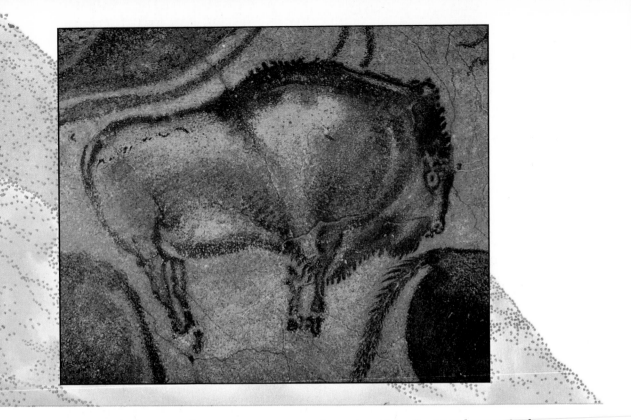

horned and humped creatures that had disappeared from Europe thousands of years before.

Don Marcelino realized that the other figures on the ceiling were prehistoric animals, too. There were wild horses, long-antlered reindeer, and huge wild boars of a kind no living person had ever seen.

Don Marcelino then understood the importance of little Maria's discovery. That very evening he wrote a long letter about the cave paintings to sci-

entists in the Spanish capital, Madrid.

He wrote that the paint on the ceiling of the cave looked fresh and new and that a bit of the red even came off on his finger when he touched it. But, he said, no one skillful enough to paint these figures had ever entered the cave since its discovery a few years earlier. Besides, he wrote, the animals were prehistoric animals, and none of Don Marcelino's Spanish neighbors knew how these animals looked. He ended his letter by saying that he felt sure the amazing pictures had been painted at the time when bison roamed the Spanish hills. They had been painted, he said, by the same people who hunted those bison—by the cave dwellers of prehistoric times.

Maria de Sautuola had discovered the clue that proved beyond a doubt that some of the greatest artists of all time were cave dwellers who lived among bison and mammoths in the prehistoric period called the Ice Age.

Eventually, the Spanish government took over responsibility for the cave, so that its precious paintings, some of the greatest art treasures of Spain, would always be protected. Every year,

Altamira becomes more famous, and more people go there to study and admire the pictures little Maria first saw by the light of her candle.

119

Life in the prehistoric world was hard and full of danger for people. People had to stay together in order to live. It must have been hard for Nal, the boy in this story, to get along by himself. But he does find a way to live, with the help of a new friend. This story is fiction, but keep in mind that it could have happened.

Laurence Swinburne

Nal and the Wolf

As Nal ran through the trees, he thought about the great trouble he was in. It had been a long time since he had seen another person. An earthquake had destroyed his village. Only Nal, who had been out hunting, was left alive. But his sorrow at losing his family and friends had dulled quickly. He had to be alert every moment just to keep alive.

How would he get food? He could not live on berries and roots forever. Yet it took many people working together to hunt successfully. When they found a herd of reindeer, one group would creep around to the far side of the herd.

Then, on a signal, the other group would dash toward the animals. The frightened creatures would run away—right into the hunters hidden on the other side. The deer would be killed as they passed.

But a lone hunter could not hunt like that. And now chances of joining another tribe were poor. "Wandering bands do not welcome strangers," thought Nal bitterly.

Suddenly, somewhere ahead, he heard a chorus of howls. He knew well what those sounds came from—wolves! He had no use for wolves. He wasn't afraid of them, but they weren't good to eat. Also, they hunted the same animals that people did.

Nal was curious, though. It sounded as if the wolves had trapped some creature. He wondered what it was. He went forward slowly until he could see into a clearing.

Nal frowned, puzzled. A wolf pack had caught another wolf. He didn't understand this. Why should they attack one of their own? He looked at the trapped wolf care-

fully. It stood with its back to a high rock. Its hair stood on end, and it was snarling at the ring of sitting wolves. It did not look quite like the other wolves. Its head and body were the same, but it was a little smaller than the average wolf. Its coat was lighter in color, almost white. And it had a large black spot on the center of its back.

The sitting wolves grinned evilly at their prisoner. Now and then a wolf would leap from his place and charge the wounded animal. There would be a yelp, a flash of teeth, and the attacker would limp away.

The tired animal was growing weaker at each charge. Sooner or later it would die. The death would come sooner if all the wolves attacked at the same time. But they preferred to torment the lone one.

Nal shook his head. Something about the single wolf stirred him. The animal was brave, ready to fight to the death. He was a lot like Nal—alone in a cruel world.

With a sudden fury, Nal picked up a rock and hurled it at the wolves.

Yelling, he rushed into the clearing, waving his spear.

The startled wolves were frozen with fear for a moment. Then they scattered, yelping as they ran. All except the wounded one. He stood bewildered as he stared after the retreating pack.

Nal gave the wounded wolf a short glance. The boy suddenly felt foolish. Why was he bothering himself with the affairs of wolves? He had no time for that. He should be searching for food. He spun around and left the clearing.

He had gone a few steps back into the forest when he heard a sound behind him. He whirled, his spear held high and ready. But it was only the small wolf, limping after him.

"Go away," growled Nal. He tossed a small stone at it. The wolf retreated a few steps, sat, and watched Nal.

When Nal went on, the wolf followed. When Nal stopped, the wolf stopped. The boy became angry.

"I haven't any time to fool with wolves," he shouted at the animal. It sat and wagged its tail.

Nal decided to run. After all, the wolf couldn't follow him too far. One of his legs was badly wounded. Nal jogged for many miles. At first the wolf kept up, but slowly it fell behind until it was lost from sight.

When Nal thought he had rid himself of the wolf at long last, he halted. Immediately he had a stroke of good luck. A rabbit ran right across his path. Nal killed it and almost danced with joy. He was very hungry.

He piled dry twigs upon a rock. Then he placed a stick upright in the center. He rubbed it back and forth quickly between the palms of his hands. The stick twirled faster and faster. Suddenly sparks shot out from where the stick and stone met. At once the twigs caught fire.

Nal cooked the rabbit happily. He still felt sorrow from the loss of his whole family and tribe. But that was behind him. Right now he had food and that was good.

Suddenly a chill crept up his back. As a hunter, he knew when something was watching him. His hand crept toward his spear. He stopped when he saw the big eyes of the wolf staring at him from across the fire.

Nal laughed. "Why did you follow me?" he asked. The animal looked at the rabbit eagerly. Nal understood the look. "Why should I feed you, you evil creature? Who ever heard of a hunter giving food to a wolf?"

He felt a little stupid, talking to an animal. He wondered whether animals understood human language or not. The wolf kept on staring at the meat that Nal was now eating. Nal tried to pay no attention, but he felt uneasy. Finally he threw a piece of meat to the wolf. One mighty gulp and the meat was gone.

"Think you'll get some more, do you?" growled Nal. "Well, you won't!"

But he was lying, and he knew it. He tossed the wolf some more meat.

Soon the rabbit was gone. "You've had half the food," said Nal bitterly. "I'm still hungry and you're still hungry. A lot of good you are. And a lot of good I am, too. A hunter feeding a wolf!"

In fury, he hurled a stick at the wolf. It missed. The animal limped after the stick, got it, and brought it back to Nal. He seemed to think it was some sort of game.

Nal knew he should have driven the wolf away. Instead he dipped leaves in a stream and washed the clotted blood off the wolf's leg.

"You can go now," he said. "It's dark and time for me to sleep."

But the wolf didn't go. When Nal lay down, the wolf lay beside him. Nal knew this was silly, a wolf and a man sleeping side by side. But somehow he didn't feel quite so lonely anymore.

For the next few days, the pair traveled together. The wolf gained strength quickly. In a week, its

limp was almost gone. Now it could
run through the woods, barking
happily. Nal was glad for the companionship.

But as the wolf's strength in-
creased, Nal's vigor sank. Roots and
berries alone were not enough to
keep the boy healthy. His legs
ached, he could hardly jog, and he
was tired all the time. The wolf
seemed to know this. Once he
brought Nal part of a dead mouse.

"Bah!" snarled Nal, flinging it
away. "That isn't fit for a man."
But he was sorry immediately. He
patted the wolf as an apology.
To his surprise, the wolf rubbed
its cold nose against Nal's leg and
wagged its tail. Nal laughed. His
unhappiness melted away. The
wolf looked up and seemed to
laugh, too.

The next day, they left the forest
and entered the large plain. They
had not gone far when Nal saw a
small herd of reindeer about a half
mile away.

Nal started to run toward them.
He stopped after a few steps. He

was out of breath, and his legs would take him no farther.

"I'll never be able to get near enough to throw my spear," he said to the wolf sourly. "I'll starve to death while the animals run away."

The wolf cocked its head and listened to Nal. He looked at the boy as if he understood. Then he turned and ran away. He did not run toward the deer, but circled far around them.

Nal watched him go sorrowfully. "But I can't blame you," he said. "No use staying here to watch me die. Good luck, wolf."

Exhausted, he sat and put his head in his hands.

In a few minutes, he heard the wolf's sharp bark in the distance. Startled, he looked up. To his surprise, the deer were running toward him. Then he understood. The wolf's barking had frightened them. The animal had gone to the other side of the herd and made them run in the boy's direction.

Nal rose and moved out of the path of the thundering herd. As the deer passed, he hurled his spear into the side of a deer with the last of his strength. The deer staggered on for a few steps, then fell dead. The wolf returned, yelping loudly.

That night Nal patted his well-filled stomach. The wolf lay in the center of a circle of well-gnawed bones and gave a happy moan. He and Nal looked into the fire.

"Together we will make mighty hunters," said the boy. "It is strange that a wolf and a man should be friends. I never heard of such a thing. But perhaps you're not a wolf at all. Perhaps you're something else, though I don't know what." He turned and stared down at the wolf. "You ought to have a name, though." He thought for a moment, staring at the large black spot on his friend's back. "I know what I'll call you," cried Nal brightly. "I'll call you 'Spot.'"

Then the boy reached forth his hand and patted the head of his new friend.

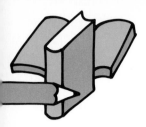

Turning the Tables

Tables and graphs are two ways to show information. A *table* is an arrangement of facts in columns and rows. The heading at the top of each column explains the facts in the column. Look at the following example:

BUS SCHEDULE

Leave Smithtown	Stop at Elm St.	Stop at Main St.	Stop at River Rd.	Arrive Brookside
8:30 A.M.	8:37 A.M.	8:48 A.M.	9:02 A.M.	9:30 A.M.
8:55 A.M.	9:02 A.M.	9:13 A.M.	9:27 A.M.	9:55 A.M.
10:15 A.M.	10:22 A.M.	10:33 A.M.	10:47 A.M.	11:15 A.M.
12:05 P.M.	12:12 P.M.	12:23 P.M.	12:37 P.M.	1:05 P.M.
4:40 P.M.	4:47 P.M.	4:58 P.M.	5:12 P.M.	5:40 P.M.

This table shows the schedule for buses from Smithtown to Brookside. Each bus makes three stops on the way. For example, the first bus leaves Smithtown at 8:30 in the morning. (A.M. stands for *before noon*; P.M. stands for *after noon*.) This bus stops at Elm Street at 8:37. It stops at Main Street at 8:48 and at River Road at 9:02. The bus arrives at Brookside at 9:30 A.M.

ACTIVITY A   Use the table to answer the questions. Write your answers on your paper.

1. At what time does the 10:15 A.M. bus from Smithtown stop at River Road?

2. When does the last bus leave Smithtown each day?

132

3. If you had to be in Brookside by 11:00 A.M., which is the latest bus you could take?

4. If you missed the 8:30 bus from Smithtown, how long would you have to wait for the next bus?

5. How long is the ride from Smithtown to Brookside?

A *graph* is a way of showing information in picture form. Reading a graph helps you compare facts. Look at the bar graph below. It shows the population of some major world cities. Notice that the numbers at the bottom of the graph stand for *millions* of people. For example, Tokyo has a population of 11 million people.

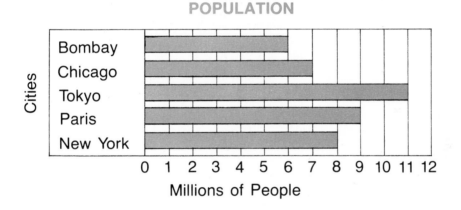

ACTIVITY B Use the graph to answer the questions. Write your answers on your paper.

1. What is the population of Paris?

2. What is the population of Chicago?

3. Which city on the graph has the largest population?

4. Do fewer people live in Chicago or New York?

5. Do more people live in Bombay or Paris?

6. Which city on the graph has the smallest population?

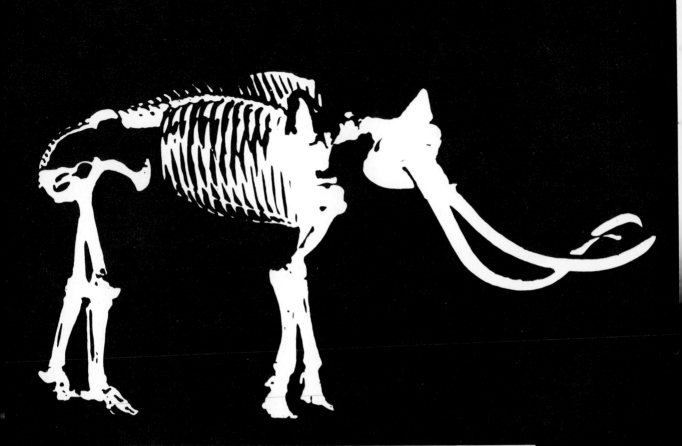

Mammoths were the ancestors of our modern elephants. They were the largest members of the elephant family. They had long, curved tusks, and their bodies were covered with hair.

Scientists do a good job of telling us what an animal that no longer exists looked like. They do this by studying the animal's bones. But just think how exciting it would be to find a prehistoric animal. A man named Ossip did. This is one writer's account of how it may have happened.

MONSTER IN THE ICE

Laurence Swinburne

Ossip made his way slowly across the grassy plain toward the big hill. His eyes scanned the **high** grasses for an elk or bear. Ossip was a hunter, one of the best in all of Siberia. But today he had no luck. He had seen no game all morning. Now he was about to give up and start back to his village. Suddenly Ossip heard a great noise from the top of the hill. That was his only warning. Huge boulders came tumbling toward him. There was no time to run. Ossip threw himself to the ground. He covered his head. In a few minutes, all was quiet.

Slowly Ossip got up and brushed himself off. He was not frightened. Landslides were nothing new to him.

Only then did he notice the huge cave the landslide had made in the side of the hill. Ossip ran forward to get a better look. But what he saw stopped him in his tracks. There, staring out at him from a great block of ice, was the most fearful thing he had ever seen. It was an animal so huge that the sight made Ossip rigid with terror. For a long moment they faced each other—Ossip the hunter and the huge, great-tusked monster. Suddenly Ossip could take no more of those great red eyes looking down at him. With a scream of fear, he turned. He began to run. He was certain that the hairy red beast was coming after him.

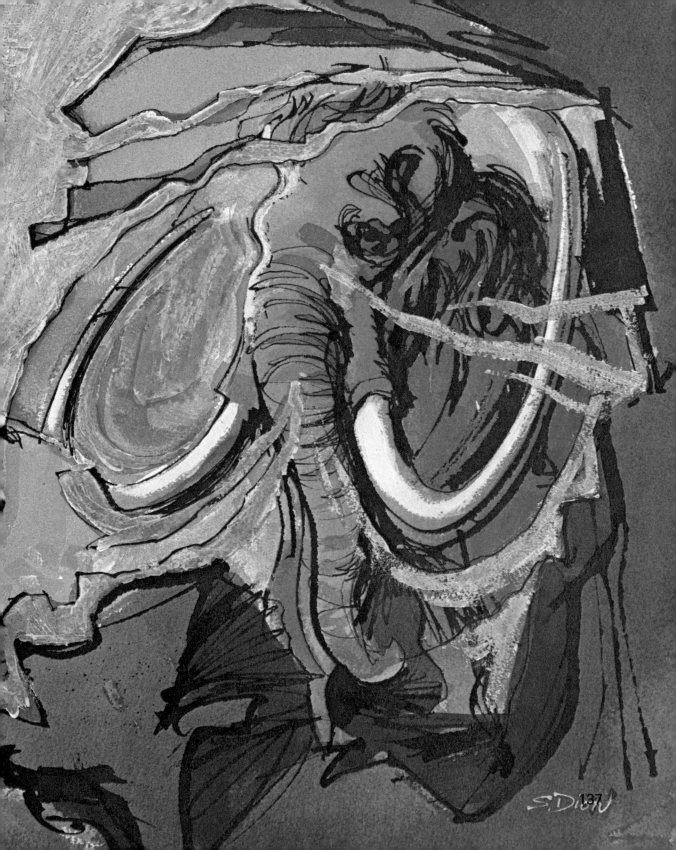

S. Dion

137

Everything had been peaceful in Ossip's little village that afternoon. Some people were napping or sharpening their spears for the next day's hunt. Others were preparing food for the evening meal. The children were playing happily. Even the dogs were quiet. Into this tranquil scene came Ossip. He was screaming in terror.

"Come quickly! We must prepare to fight or we may all be killed!" he cried. "A monster is coming!"

He ran to the chief's house. "A monster is coming!" he cried. "It is bigger than our whole village. It has horns growing out of its mouth. It will kill us all."

The chief ran out of his house. There stood Ossip, the bravest and calmest hunter in the village. Only Ossip did not look brave or calm. He looked terrified.

"Ossip, my friend, what is it?" asked the chief.

"It is a monster. I have seen him. He is chasing me. Hurry, we must prepare to fight him!" Ossip cried. By this time, everyone in the village had come out to see what was going on. The hunters had their spears ready. But so far, no monster had appeared. Some people looked frightened, and a few children were crying.

The chief put his arm around Ossip. He knew of many cases in which the loneliness and cold of the plains had driven people crazy. Many hunters no less brave than Ossip had lost their minds in the wild lands of the north. He hoped this had not happened to his friend. He spoke gently to him. "Ossip, I do not believe there is such a monster. You know that sometimes hunters see strange things on the plains. I think this is what has happened to you."

Ossip looked at the chief with disbelief. "So you think I am crazy," he shouted. "Very well, then, go and see for yourself. But don't blame me for what happens."

The chief stood up very tall beside Ossip. "I am not afraid," he said. "But you must come to show us the way." The chief saw that Ossip was afraid. Then he motioned to his hunters, "Come, we are going to see Ossip's make-believe monster." The chief felt Ossip stiffen beside him. Ossip was angry with him, he knew. But secretly the chief was pleased. "It is better for Ossip to be angry with me than afraid of the monster," he thought.

The group tramped over the grasses of the plains in silence. They walked many miles. Finally Ossip seized the chief's arm and pointed. "There's the hill. The monster was in the cave on the other side. This is as far as I will go. You must look for yourselves."

The chief smiled and shook his head. "All right," he said. "But when we return and tell you that we saw no monster, will you then believe it was just a trick of your mind?"

"Yes, I will believe," muttered Ossip.

The chief and the hunters marched ahead. For many minutes, Ossip stood as still as stone. He held his spear and bow tightly in his hands. He narrowed his eyes as if he were trying to see right through the hill.

Suddenly around the hill came the hunters of the village, running as fast as they could. Ossip raised his spear, "Run!" he yelled. "Run all the way to the village. I'll hold off the monster until you're safe."

One man ran over to Ossip. "The chief is still back there. You are the only one who can save him!"

Ossip did not wait a second. With a roar, he dashed ahead. His fear was gone as he thought of the danger his old friend faced. Why, even now he might be dead.

But the chief was far from dead. Ossip saw him as he rounded the hill. The chief was standing right in front of the cave of ice. His arms were folded. He was staring at the monster.

"Run before it breaks out and kills you!" shouted Ossip. "I'll stand guard while you escape."

The chief smiled. "You were right. It is indeed a monster, Ossip. But I do not think it is alive. It is frozen inside that ice."

Ossip came closer. "Are you sure?" he asked.

The chief stepped forward and rapped on the ice with his spear. "The ice is thick and strong. I do not see how it could get out if it is alive. Not if it had all the strength in the world. It looks dead to me."

He stepped back a few paces and looked at the hairy beast. "No, I do not think it can harm us. Now let us go back to the others before all our people run away in fear."

The news of the large beast spread slowly through the plains of northern Siberia. There, villages were far apart. It was only when hunters met on the plains that the tale was passed along.

So it was little wonder that it took two years for the story to reach the Russian area called the Yakuts, fifteen hundred miles south. The people there laughed. They thought it was an amusing tale. But one man, Vladimir Boltunov, did not laugh. He knew the hunters of the north.

"Maybe they can't read or write," he said, "but they tell the truth. I know. Many is the time I have traded furs with them. They are honest people. There must be something to the story."

Boltunov traveled the long distance. However, he did not see the monster in the same condition that Ossip had first seen it. The ice around the body had melted. The wolves and other animals of the plains had eaten parts of it. But much of it was left.

Boltunov knew he had found something special. He paid well for the animal's body, and it was carted away. He gave it to a museum.

What was the monster that Ossip had discovered? It was a mammoth. This elephant-like animal roamed throughout much of the world thousands of years ago. The people of the Ice Age hunted it for meat. Since Ossip found the first "monster," thirty more mammoths have been discovered, preserved in ice, in Russia.

A World of Languages

It has been estimated that there are nearly 3,000 different languages spoken in the world. The chart below lists thirteen of the most widely spoken languages. It also lists some of the countries in which these languages are spoken. The languages spoken by the largest numbers of people are at the top of the chart. Can you speak or do you know anyone who can speak more than one of these languages?

LANGUAGES	COUNTRIES	MILLIONS OF SPEAKERS*
Mandarin	China	555
English	United States of America, Great Britain, Canada, Australia	350
Hindustani	India, Pakistan	230
Spanish	Spain, Mexico, Argentina, Bolivia	220
Arabic	Algeria, Iraq, Saudi Arabia, Tunisia	150
Russian	Union of Soviet Socialist Republics	140
Portuguese	Portugal, Brazil	110
Japanese	Japan	107
German	Germany, Austria, Switzerland	105
Bengali	Bangladesh, India	95
French	France, Belgium, Switzerland, Canada	80
Italian	Italy	65
Javanese	Java	55

*Estimated figures

PEOPLE DOMESTICATE ANIMALS

To domesticate an animal means to train it to live with and be of use to people. No one knows for sure when people first began to domesticate animals. Scientists have found clues all over the world which tell us that animals have lived near people for thousands of years. Learning about these animals helps us to learn more about the people's lives.

The dates on this map are approximate. They are based on the oldest examples of these animals that have been found so far.

Domestication of animals was one of the first things people did to change the world around them. They domesticated animals so they could raise them for food, and so they could use them to work. Some animals became friends to people, as well as helpers. One such animal was the dog.

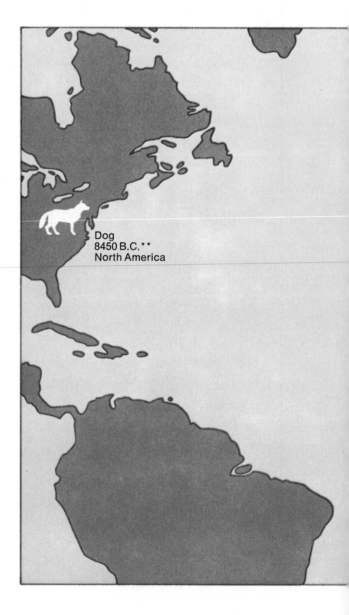

Dog
8450 B.C.**
North America

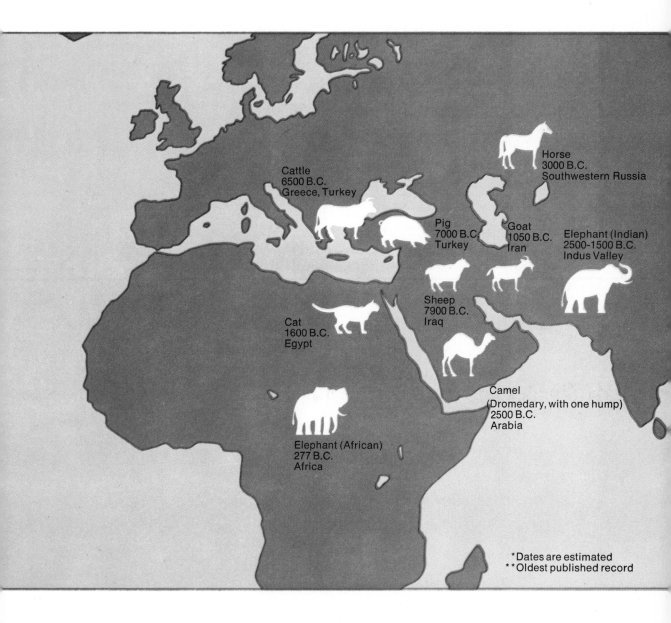

Horse
3000 B.C.
Southwestern Russia

Cattle
6500 B.C.
Greece, Turkey

Pig
7000 B.C.
Turkey

Goat
1050 B.C.
Iran

Elephant (Indian)
2500-1500 B.C.
Indus Valley

Sheep
7900 B.C.
Iraq

Cat
1600 B.C.
Egypt

Camel
(Dromedary, with one hump)
2500 B.C.
Arabia

Elephant (African)
277 B.C.
Africa

*Dates are estimated
**Oldest published record

The dog was one of the first animals that people domesticated. Early people had to hunt for their food. Wolves probably stayed around the hunters' camps because they smelled food. The hunters may have tamed the wolves by throwing food scraps to them. Once they had tamed them, they used them to hunt other animals. The story "Nal and the Wolf" shows how this may have happened. Later, people used dogs to herd sheep and goats and to protect their crops.

In very early times, people did not live in just one place. They were always moving in search of food. Later on, people stopped moving from place to place. They used the land to plant and grow their food. Once people began to settle in one place, they began to domesticate animals. Some of the first animals kept in herds were goats and sheep. These animals were easy to care for. They ate wild grass and other plants. They provided people with milk and meat and hides for clothing.

The size of settlements grew. And people had new problems. Now that they lived in one place, they wanted materials, such as wood, brought to them. For this work, people needed animals that were strong and large. So people began to domesticate elephants and camels.

Cats were probably domesticated when people began storing grain from year to year. Rats and mice would eat the grain. Since cats eat rats and mice, the farmers found the cats very useful.

Horses were among the last animals to be domesticated. For a long time, horses were used only for hunting and war. One reason may be that early harnesses did not work very well on horses. They forced the horses' heads up too high, and they could not pull heavy carts or plows.

These are some of the ideas about how and why people started to domesticate animals. By continuing to study the domestication of animals, we can learn more history.

Alexander and Bucephalus

Alice Gall and Fleming Crew

"Say no more, Orestes. My mind is made up. The horse shall be sold," said Philonicus.

It was a summer day more than two thousand years ago. The speaker, a rich man of Thessaly in Greece, was talking to his slave. They stood by a field looking at a number of horses.

Philonicus was used to being obeyed. When he had spoken, he turned away.

But the slave put out a hand. "Master," he said earnestly, "there is not another horse like Bucephalus."

"I know that," the rich man answered. "His buyer will pay a great deal for him. I mean to sell him to Philip of Macedon."

"King Philip," his slave repeated, amazed.

"Yes," replied Philonicus. "King Philip knows horses. His army rides into battle on the best he can find. It is said that he would rather lose six generals than one good horse. He will find use for Bucephalus."

"Master," Orestes begged, "you would not sell Bucephalus as a war horse? He has been trained gently. He has never felt the sting of a whip. Do not sell him to King Philip."

"I will," Philonicus answered. A greedy look came into his eyes. "King Philip is very rich. I mean to make him pay well."

Orestes stood looking sadly after him. Then he whistled softly. From far across the field, Bucephalus trotted over to Orestes. Then the beautiful dark bay horse lowered his head, so the slave might stroke his nose. Suddenly he gave Orestes a playful shove and was off down the field like the wind, with his head held high and his tail streaming straight out behind him.

This was a favorite trick of Bucephalus, but today the slave could not laugh. His heart was too sad. Orestes had looked after Bucephalus since the horse was a colt. It was Orestes who had trained him and taught him to carry a person on his back. Bucephalus had not liked this at first, but Orestes had been so kind that soon the horse gladly carried the slave.

What would the horse's life be? Orestes wondered. King Philip was a powerful king who had conquered much of Greece. Now he wanted to conquer the rest of Greece and more.

One morning late that summer, King Philip walked through the palace gardens with his sixteen-year-old son, Alexander. They were on their way to the parade grounds when a guard ran after them and stopped them.

"Sire," the guard said. "A stranger from Thessaly would like to see you. He wants to sell you a horse."

"A horse!" King Philip thundered. "Am I a stable boy? If the horse is strong, let him be bought."

"The horse is a good one, sire," the guard said. "But the price is very high. The stable officers won't buy him without your permission. The price is thirteen talents."

"Thirteen talents!" the king exclaimed. "Twenty horses could be bought for that price! Tell the owner to go. Tell him King Philip is no fool."

"Thessaly is a land of splendid horses," Alexander said. "Let's take a look at him, Father. Who knows? He may be better than all the horses in your stables."

King Philip laughed. "All right. We shall see the horse." He turned to the guard. "Have this man bring his horse to the riding field, and tell my horse trainers to come."

In a few minutes Philonicus was kneeling before King Philip on the riding field. "You shall see for yourself, oh King," the rich man said. "He is not like any other horse. I know my price seems high; however, you would not part with him for many times that sum."

Just then Bucephalus came out of the stables with the slave Orestes on his back. Alexander and his father stood looking in admiration. "He is indeed a fine animal," exclaimed the king at last.

"Look, Father," said Alexander, "at the fine legs and the long body. And he has a narrow, well-shaped head."

"Ay," his father answered, and he turned to Philonicus. "We shall pay your price if my trainers cannot find anything wrong with him."

Two trainers stepped forward and held the bridle while Orestes dismounted. He stood for a moment with his hand on the horse's neck. "A good friend you have been, Bucephalus," he said softly, and then he stepped to his master's side.

The King nodded to one of the trainers. "Get on his back and test him." But this was easier said than done. For when the trainer got ready to mount, the horse jerked his head angrily. The strength of the two trainers was barely enough to hold him. Suddenly he reared straight up on his hind legs, almost pulling the two men off their feet.

"Easy! Easy, good horse!" called Orestes, as he hurried forward. "I will quiet him," he said to the trainers.

"Stay where you are, slave!" the king ordered sharply. "I must learn how much of a temper this horse has."

But the trainers were not equal to the task. Bucephalus lunged and reared, kicking and biting at the trainers. At last the king waved his hand in disgust. "Take him away! The horse is crazy. I do not want such a beast!"

The boy Alexander had watched carefully, and now he stepped forward. "Wait!" he called. He looked at the two trainers. "They'll lose a fine horse just because they don't know how to manage him!"

King Philip turned sharply on his son. "Why blame those who are older than yourself," he said, "as if you knew more and were able to manage the horse better than they do?"

Alexander answered boldly, "I could manage him better."

Then he waved the trainers away and took the reins in his own hands. First he turned

Bucephalus around so that he was facing the sun, for Alexander had noticed that the horse seemed to be frightened at seeing his shadow on the ground. The king's son stroked the horse's neck and talked gently.

Little by little the horse grew quiet. There was something in the touch of the boy's hand, something in the sound of his voice that gave Bucephalus confidence. He knew that here was someone he could trust.

With a quick leap Alexander was on the horse's back. The animal threw his head up sharply. He quivered with surprise. But his fear was gone. He pawed the ground, eager to be running free over the plain with this boy on his back. Now Alexander spoke a word of command. Bucephalus bounded away, and the boy did not try to stop him. Giving him his head, he urged Bucephalus to even greater speed. The king and the others looked on, fearing that Alexander might be thrown to his death.

But Orestes smiled. "The lad knows horses," he said. "Bucephalus is in good hands."

At last the horse slowed his pace, and Alexander turned him and came back. His face was beaming with triumph. King Philip of Macedon was prouder at this moment than he had ever been before.

As Alexander got down, the king threw his arms about the boy's neck. "My son, you have great courage. Soon you will have to find yourself a kingdom! Macedon is too small for you!"

These words would come true sooner than the king thought. Within four years Alexander, mounted on Bucephalus, would leave Macedon at the head of a great army. This army would conquer half the world.

How quickly the four years passed. As the days went by, Bucephalus grew to love the boy Alexander more and more. He looked forward to the times when he could run with the boy upon his back. They understood each other, these two. They were friends.

But when the four short years were gone, Alexander was no longer a carefree boy. He was a king. For King Philip was dead, leaving his dream of a great empire unfinished. His son must finish it for him. Alexander and his army rode off to conquer a world. Into far lands they went, and always there was fighting. Alexander's army conquered all before it.

King Philip's dream had come true. Alexander was the greatest ruler in the world. His fame reached every land. Alexander the Great and Bucephalus!

At first the horse had been frightened by battle. The noise had filled him with terror, but his master's

hand always quieted him. The sound of Alexander's voice urged him on, and at last he grew used to war. Through years of bitter fighting the horse served his master well.

But it takes a long time to conquer a world, and the life of a war horse is hard. There came a day when Bucephalus could no longer go into battle. He was growing old.

Alexander was forced to leave him in camp behind the fighting lines. Here the horse was well cared for and happy. Daily the king came and talked to him and stroked his nose. Sometimes the horse would give King Alexander a playful shove with his nose, as he had once done with Orestes.

Back in Thessaly, the horse was not forgotten, and tales were told of the days when he was a colt.

"Orestes," said Philonicus one day, as he and his slave stood again at the edge of the fields. "Do you remember the horse I sold to King Philip?"

"Yes, master," answered Orestes. "I shall not forget Bucephalus."

"Who would have dreamed," went on Philonicus, "that he would become the most famous horse in all the world? He is now almost as famous as the great Alexander himself."

"Bucephalus was always a good horse," said Orestes.

"Ay, a good horse," Philonicus turned away. "And thirteen talents was a good price, too."

For a long time the slave stood silent, and then he walked slowly across the wide field. "A good price indeed," he said softly. "But if you had been mine, Bucephalus, not all the gold in Macedon could have bought you."

Galloping

The rushing, the brushing, the wind in your face
The thudding of hooves and the quickening of pace
Not so clear is your gaze, blocked and dulled by a haze
You feel the horse in a kind of a daze.

You are numb to the feel of the ups and downs
The twists and turns, the curves and the rounds
You feel only the thud of the galloping hooves
And the regular jolt of the horse as he moves.

—Cordelia Chitty, Age 11

Animal	Household Gear
Buffalo 	Horns for drinking vessels. Leather for cups, bags, pouches. Hides for beds. Bones for needles. Straps for tying. Tallow for candles and stone lamps.
Bear	Hides for beds. Fat for light.
Elk, Deer, Prairie Antelope 	Leather for pouches. Hides for blankets. Bones for needles.
Beaver 	Beaver fat for skin oil.
Eagle, Parrot, Other Birds 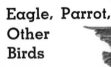	Bones for pipes for spraying paints.

NORTH AMERICAN INDIANS

Hermann Dembeck

Clothing	Food
Hides for robes. Soft leather for moccasins, trousers, and leggings.	One buffalo provided 1,000 pounds of meat and 100 pounds of tallow, which was used in their winter diet.
Claws and teeth for bracelets and necklaces.	One bear provided 100-200 pounds of meat and 30-40 pounds of bear grease.
Various kinds of leather clothing, such as hunting shirts of antelope leather. Women liked dyed leather as clothes.	The elks provided 400-600 pounds of meat and a great deal of tallow.
Caps. Hides to decorate outer clothing. Tails for men's clothing.	One beaver provided a few pounds of meat.
Feathers as ornaments for men's clothing. Also used as headdresses. Warriors wore 1-3 eagle feathers in their headbands.	The American Indians used birds for food. They did not kill for sport.

KEMI

Mary and Conrad Buff

Hundreds of years ago, many different groups of American Indians lived in Southern California. Some lived along the shore, while others lived inland. Often the groups traded with each other for things they needed.

Kemi and his cousin, Tonla, are two boys who might have been part of one of the inland groups. In this story, Kemi and Tonla have gone to the sea for the first time. They have traveled with Kemi's father and other villagers so that they can trade with another group of Indians at the seashore.

Just before dawn Kemi awoke with a sudden start. He heard a strange sound. Where was he? He sat up and then he remembered where he was. He was at the sea.

Once again he heard the strange sounds that had awakened him. He looked up-shore and saw a long, dark thing in the breaking surf. It looked like a huge smooth rock. The strange sounds seemed to come from that rock. As he watched he saw dark moving animals. What could they be? They sounded like grizzly bears.

Kemi was frightened. He shook his cousin. "Tonla, wake up! Listen! Do you hear bears growling?"

Tonla listened. "Where are the bears, Kemi?"

"See that big rock at the water's edge way up there? See those dark animals moving around the rock? They *must* be bears. We must wake up Father!"

Kemi stumbled in the darkness. He found Father and gently touched his shoulder. Father was a light sleeper.

"Why do you waken me in the middle of the night?" he said angrily. "I'm tired. *Now* what is the matter?"

"We are afraid, Father. There are

animals along the ocean. They growl like bears. Come and see."

"There is a dead whale over there in the surf!" Father exclaimed. "The bears have come from their lairs in the river we crossed yesterday." He became excited. "There is enough whale to feed all the villagers along the coast. I will wake up Tula. He is a Headman. He will know how to drive the bears away."

Father entered the Headman's hut. Meanwhile the boys listened to the angry bears and shivered with fear. Kemi heard Tula say, "We will drive the bears away with fire. They fear only fire."

The Indians gathered dry reeds and made torches. Then the most courageous men walked slowly along the seashore toward the great bulk of the whale. They shouted and yelled and sang as they marched with their flaming torches. The bears were still tearing greedily at the dead whale.

Kemi and Tonla sat on a sandy hill and watched. They were afraid to get too close to the terrible beasts. As the Indians who held

torches came near the whale, the bears backed away. Snarling and angry, they ambled toward the tangled riverbed which was their lair.

This whale was the largest the Indians had seen stranded in the sand for many years. The Headman of the villages called the Dividers of the Food to come with their sharp stone knives and sharp reeds to cut the whale to pieces and divide it equally among all the people.

Now the Indians started fires along the shore and before their huts. People brought nets and skins to drag hunks of meat to fires. Whale meat must be cooked quickly, for it soon spoils.

By afternoon nothing remained of the great whale but towering white ribs and bones. From these bones the Indians would later carve spears, ornaments, and tools to pry shellfish from rocks, or even use the ribs for starting a new hut.

Now the tide was going out. The tide left water in holes among the rocks. These were tide pools. Kemi and Tonla spent much of the

afternoon exploring the tide pools.

They found a new friend, Yoko. Yoko was the son of a Headman of a village. He had lived all his life along the sea. He knew about shells, birds, and the dangers of the great ocean.

"Look! There!" said Kemi, pointing at a purple flower growing under the water in a tide pool. The flower had long feelers swaying in the water.

"What a funny flower," said Tonla, "growing under the water."

"That's not a flower," laughed Yoko. "That's an animal."

"It *can't* be an animal," said Tonla stoutly.

"You just watch," said his friend. "Watch that tiny fish there.

If it touches one of those swaying feelers see what happens—"

They watched, hardly daring to breathe. A tiny fish touched a waving feeler of the flower. At once all of the other feelers wrapped themselves around the fish. Soon the fish disappeared in the mouth of a sea anemone. The inland boys were amazed.

Yoko showed them another strange animal shaped like a star. It moved along slowly under the water. It had a rough red skin. "That's a starfish," said their friend. "There are lots of them in the pools. They are many colors, too. They can live out of the water or in the water." Yoko felt proud of his knowledge.

Then on a rock where huge waves broke furiously they saw a strange bird. It had a long bag under its bill. It was a pelican.

They watched the pelican dive into the sea and catch a fish. It flew back to a rock and *seemed* to swallow the fish. But the fish really slipped into the bag under its bill. "When the pelican gets very hungry," said Yoko, "it coughs up a fish and then really swallows it. The bag is just a place to store it."

By now the boys were tired. Much had happened since early morning. They lay on the sand and just looked.

After resting they swam out to a big rock high above the breakers

and climbed on it. The late afternoon passed away. The sun was
setting, making the ocean as red as
if it were burning up.

Feasting went on for hours and
hours. After the feasting was all
over, the time came to honor the
friendly swordfish. The Indians believed that swordfish had driven
the whale to its death. They believed that the swordfish was their
friend. Only one dancer celebrated
the dance of the swordfish. But
everybody watched, clapping,
stomping, singing, and chanting.

The costume of the swordfish
dancer was beautiful. The dance
was more like the swimming of a
fish than dancing. It was an exciting
dance to watch. The songs the Indians sang in honor of the swordfish were beautiful. Slowly, as the
night wore on, one child after
another fell asleep. At last even
Kemi and Tonla could not stay
awake.

American-Indian Names

There were once many different American-Indian languages in North America. Some of those languages have disappeared. Others have changed a great deal. So it is difficult to find out the *exact* meaning for some American-Indian names for places.

Rivers, cities, and states with American-Indian names and their accepted meanings are listed below. Do you know any American-Indian names of places in your state?

Names of Rivers

Ohio
"beautiful water"

Susquehanna
"crooked water"

Wabash
"shining white"

Names of Cities

Chattanooga
"rock rising
to a point"

Milwaukee
"rich land"

Pasadena
"crown of
the valley"

Names of States

Arizona
"place of a
few springs"

Massachusetts
"great hills"

Michigan
"great water"

Minnesota
"cloudy water"

Texas
"friends"

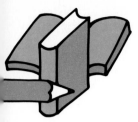

Don't Jump to Conclusions

Suppose you go to a movie. You search every row in the theater for an empty seat, but you can't find one. Then you say:

All the seats in the theater are taken.

This statement is a generalization. A *generalization* is a statement that draws a conclusion. A generalization is based on facts. A reliable, or true, generalization is based on a complete set of facts. The above generalization is true because you checked the entire theater before you concluded that all the seats were taken.

Now suppose you had made the above generalization after checking only three rows. Then you would have made a faulty generalization. You would not have gathered enough facts to support your conclusion. There might have been seats in another part of the theater.

Generalizations are sometimes made about people.

All store owners in this city are tall.

This statement draws a conclusion about all owners of stores. Unless you have seen all the store owners in the city, you cannot say that all of them are tall. If you have not seen all, your conclusion is faulty.

When you are judging whether or not a generalization is reliable, or true, ask yourself this question:

Is the generalization based on a complete set of facts?

If the answer is *yes*, the generalization is true.

ACTIVITY A   Read each group of facts. Then read the generalization. On your paper, write whether each generalization is true or faulty.

1. **Facts:** Both my sister and my brother like cereal. My friends Susan and Gregory like cereal, too.
Generalization: All children like cereal.

2. **Facts:** Four months of the year have thirty days each. Seven months have thirty-one days each. One month, February, has twenty-eight—and sometimes, twenty-nine—days.
Generalization: All months have at least twenty-eight days.

3. **Facts:** The pay telephone on this corner is broken. The pay phone on the next corner is also broken.
Generalization: Pay phones are always out of order.

4. **Facts:** The Petersen family has four members. Mr. Petersen likes baseball. Mrs. Petersen likes golf. Their two children enjoy tennis.
Generalization: Every member of the Petersen family likes a sport.

ACTIVITY B   Read each generalization. On your paper, write whether the generalization is true or faulty. Then write the reason for your decision.

1. All cooks like to eat spinach.
2. All bus drivers like to meet new people.
3. All the names for days of the week contain the word part -*day*.
4. All two-digit numbers that end in 0 can be evenly divided by 10.
5. All the generalizations in ACTIVITY B are true.

171

When the Burke family moved to Texas, they hoped Pa would recover from his illness there. Instead, Pa got worse; but he still made plans to support his family. He bought a small herd of Texas longhorns to sell in Chicago. Then he, his wife, and their six children set out to take the herd home to Illinois.

On the way, Pa died. He left fourteen-year-old Emma Jane, the oldest child, in charge. Easter Ellen and Martin, the two next-oldest, helped with the herd. Ma drove the wagon. Martha helped Ma take care of Phoebe, who had been deaf since she was two, and Matt, who was only five years old.

Emma Jane and her family really lived in the 1800's. After many exciting adventures, they did reach Chicago safely. "Red River Crossing" tells about one of their adventures.

RED RIVER CROSSING

Marjorie Filley Stover

A week dragged by. From the rocky hill, Emma Jane stared across the roiling waters. Moodily she traced a pattern with her finger on Star's neck. The water was down some, but the low, gentle slope on the other side, which made it easy for the cattle to come out, was still licked by the flood. Once again she measured the distance with her eye. Her fingers drummed on the saddle pommel as she studied the turbulent river. The ferry was going again, making a dent in the backed-up traffic. But to swim a herd—

173

A horse reined up beside her. In the saddle sat a man with a bright red beard and hair to match. He gave a low whistle. "The Red's big swimming, I see."

Emma Jane snapped the ends of the reins across her open hand. "Been that way the past week. Rains up the river keeping it full, I guess."

The man pushed back his hat and studied the sky. "We may get a few more bucketfuls tonight."

"Could be." Emma Jane snapped the leather ends of the reins so hard that they reddened her hand, but she didn't notice.

The newcomer rubbed his red beard and sucked speculatively on his lips. "It's full, but I've been across worse."

The restless snapping of the reins stopped. Emma Jane's look focused squarely on man and horse. "You aiming to swim a herd across, Mister?"

"Yep. Got seven hundred critters coming up the trail an hour behind me."

Emma Jane didn't wait to think twice. "If you're aiming to cross, Mister, would you let us crowd our herd of eighty-two longhorns in behind yours? We'd sure like to get traveling again."

"*Your* herd?" Bushy red eyebrows lifted in surprise.

"Yes, sir. Our whole family is going back to Illinois. We aim to sell the longhorns in Chicago."

The bushy brows pulled together. "Well, I can't see as there'd be any harm shoving your steers in behind mine—as long as you've got a good hand following them. That river's not going to be any child's play."

Emma Jane's eyes gleamed. "Thanks, Mister! Thanks a heap!"

She stopped by the herd to get Martin. He would have to be on the other side to help her. Emma Jane planned as they rode. "Hightail it to the boat landing as fast as you can. Alone on horseback you ought

to make the next ferry."

Martha and Phoebe were playing under an oak tree. Martha jumped up. "Has the Red gone down? Are we leaving?" Phoebe heard nothing, but she took her cue from Martha and jumped up after her.

Matt abandoned the anthill he was watching. "Are we going? Are we going?"

"We're leaving Texas," said Emma Jane, as Ma hurried from the tent. Even while Emma Jane's excited words spilled out the story, Ma was reaching into an inner skirt pocket for the black leather purse.

"Wait a minute, don't go yet," she told Martin as she handed him a coin. "You'll need a packet of food." Ma was stuffing corn pone and dried beef into a clean salt sack. "It'll be good to get going again. Here, Martin—be careful now." They waved him off.

Camp was nearly broken. Ma was yoking the oxen when Emma Jane put her foot in the stirrup and swung into the saddle.

By the time Emma Jane joined Easter, she could hear the bellowing and trampling of the approaching herd. She deliberately kept her own cattle back from the trail. It would be better, she figured, if she did not talk to that trail boss again on this side of the river. When he spotted her, he gave a beckoning wave, showing that they would join the drag of his herd.

Emma Jane and Easter watched until the drag came into view. Then they turned their longhorns toward the trail. They swung in at the tail of the big herd.

A lanky cowboy blinked at the girls from under sandy lashes. His crooked teeth flashed. "Thought your trail boss was going to follow them across."

Emma Jane leaned forward, pretending to pull a cocklebur from Star's mane. "Sure thing. Everything's all set. We're still half a mile from the riverbanks."

The cowboy shrugged. There was plenty of time for the trail boss of this pint-sized herd to join them. He turned back to his own cattle.

Down between the sides of the rocky chute went the Burke eighty-two. Emma Jane had counted on the fact that the cowboys ahead would be too busy watching their own cattle to pay any attention to her, and she was right.

The water was colder than Emma Jane had expected, and swifter as they neared the middle of the channel. Star swam like a veteran, steadily and strongly. Emma Jane watched her herd with pride as they unwaveringly answered the challenge of the river. Soon they were climbing, dripping and snorting, out on the other side. It had all gone as smoothly as a greased sourdough biscuit.

For a moment, Star's foot slipped as she scrambled up the slippery bank. In an instant she found firm footing, and they were safe on the other side. They were across!

Emma Jane turned and waved to Easter, watching from the top of the hill. Giving herself a shake, she turned back to the herd. She found herself looking directly into the glaring blue eyes of the man she had met by the river. His red beard shook with indignation as he thundered, "*Where* is your trail boss? Of all the silly things I ever saw, this beats them all—to let a mite of a girl like you swim across a swift rough river!"

The water was still running in muddy streams down Emma Jane's pants. Her shirt and face were spattered, but she pulled herself tall in the saddle and met his gaze straight on. "*I'm* the trail boss, Mister."

"*You're* the trail boss!" Emma Jane had heard that same note of surprise before. But your pa—you told me your whole family was going back to Illinois!"

"That's right." Emma Jane was meekly polite. "Ma's driving the covered wagon with the little ones.

Martin, Easter, and I take care of the herd—and *that's* all the family we've got now, Mister!"

He stared at her in open-mouthed amazement. "Well, that beats all. How far you come like this?"

"Waco. We left Waco in mid-April."

"Clear from Waco—and planning on going clear to Chicago—well, I'll be—! This is no job for a mite of a girl!" The roar rose again and the red beard flashed. "You can't do that!"

"Oh, yes I can! I'm *doing* it, Mister!"

For a moment the red beard shook in fiery agitation. Then the quivering thatch of red quieted. A look of admiration swept away the anger in the man's face.

"By the great horn spoon, I guess you are! You've got plenty of spunk. With a bit of luck you may make it at that. You just may make it at that!"

"Thanks, Mister. Pa said he *knew* I could do it. And I guess I will!"

Wilderness Rivers

There are rivers
That I know,
Born of ice
And melting snow,
White with rapids,
Swift to roar,
With no farms
Along their shore,
With no cattle
Come to drink
At a staid
And welcoming brink,
With no millwheel
Ever turning
In that cold,
Relentless churning.

Only deer
And bear and mink
At those shallows
Come to drink;
Only paddles
Swift and light
Flick the current
In their flight.
I have felt
My heart beat high,
Watching
With exultant eye
Those pure rivers
Which have known
No will, no purpose
But their own.

—Elizabeth Coatsworth

People and Places

Did you know that the continents of North and South America are named after a person? In 1497, Amerigo Vespucci, an Italian merchant-explorer, landed on the continent now known as South America. When he returned to Europe, he wrote about his discoveries. In 1507, the name of the New World, as it was then called, was changed to *America* in honor of Amerigo Vespucci.

Many cities in the United States are named after people. The map below shows some of these cities.

Did you know that there are more than twenty-five cities in the United States named in honor of George Washington? There are ten cities named after Thomas Jefferson, twenty-one named for Abraham Lincoln, and twenty-nine that honor the name of Columbus. What cities or towns in your state are named after famous people?

Connie's New Eyes

Bernard Wolf

The partnership between a blind person and a seeing eye dog is truly wonderful. The dog acts as eyes for the person, guiding and protecting its master.

A seeing eye dog spends its first year with a loving family. The family, chosen through the 4-H Club, cares for the dog and begins training it. At the end of the year the dog goes to a school for special training, such as The Seeing Eye in Morristown, New Jersey. Three months later, the dog is ready to meet its master.

At The Seeing Eye, blind people are taught how to communicate with their dogs. Teachers take the place of the dogs at first, so the blind people can learn how it feels to be led by a dog. Blind people also learn how to tell the dogs what to do.

For years Connie David has dreamed of owning a guide dog. She has come to The Seeing Eye from Iowa to make her dream come true. With the dog's help, Connie will be able to be independent. She has been offered a challenging job teaching handicapped children. When this story begins, Connie is meeting her dog for the first time.

Connie hears approaching footsteps and leans forward in her chair.

"Here she is," Doug says. "Her name is Blythe."

"What a lovely name!" Connie exclaims.

"Why don't you take Blythe to your room and get acquainted with her?" Doug suggests. He follows them to the room, then leaves them alone.

Connie tenderly turns Blythe's face away from the door. Again and again, she runs her fingers through Blythe's coat. Then, pressing her face to Blythe's, Connie murmurs, "Oh, Blythe, I'm so happy I've found you, girl. You're going to make such a difference in my life. We're going to do good things together, you'll see. I'll take care of you, I promise I will." Blythe seems to sense Connie's need. With a soft whine, she gently licks her face.

Later, Doug returns to Connie's room, bringing a pan of dog food. "Hi," he says when Connie tells him to come in. "How are you two getting along?"

"She's wonderful!" Connie exclaims.

"Yes, she is," Doug replies. He tells Connie, "This is about the time I feed Blythe every day, and I've brought her dog food with me. From now on, you'll be the one who looks after her. Feeding her is a good way to start." Connie takes the pan from Doug and puts it in front of Blythe. She listens with satisfaction as Blythe eats.

That evening, Doug shows Connie where to walk Blythe after her meals. He gives Connie a leather shoulder pouch containing a metal comb and a brush and shows her how to groom Blythe.

Next morning, he teaches his students how to put the harnesses on their dogs. Then Doug has his students trace the routes they will take today on a large wooden relief map of a section of Morristown. The name of each street is marked in braille.

With Blythe's guidance, the streets seem to flow past Connie. She is enjoying this new sensation so much that, at the far side of a crossing, she forgets to turn right. Blythe, who has been given the command "Forward," strides straight ahead.

"Oh, gosh," Connie says when Doug reminds her about the turn. "I guess I got carried away."

"No harm done," Doug reassures her. "The important thing is, *you're* the one who must direct Blythe. You have to know where you want to go. Let's try it again."

At the far side of Madison Street, Connie gives another right-turn signal. Blythe leads her clear of the signpost. "Atta girl, Blythe!" Connie says enthusiastically.

Blythe is having a good time too. She likes her work and she loves the praise she is getting.

Toward the end of their route, there is a huge gap in the sidewalk paving. A fall here could cost Connie a sprained or broken ankle. Blythe swerves to her left, giving herself just enough room to avoid the fence, while allowing Connie plenty of clearance. Doug tells

Connie what Blythe has done. Connie gives her a big hug. "Blythe," she says, "I know you're a good girl, but I'm just beginning to find out *how* good you really are."

With each passing day, Connie and Blythe work more and more like a smoothly coordinated unit. Their routes begin to take them closer to the center of Morristown.

On one trip, Connie and Blythe are about to cross a street when an automobile suddenly swings around the corner in front of them. Blythe pulls up in mid-stride and veers sharply to the right, almost knocking Connie off-balance.

"What's going on?" Connie cries, alarmed.

"It's all right," Doug tells her. "Blythe has just saved you and herself from a dangerous situation. She used what we call 'intelligent disobedience.'" He explains what has happened.

Connie exclaims, "Thank you, Blythe! You're the best girl there is."

Doug has Connie walk into a small park where he sees a flock of pigeons on the path. Blythe sees no reason to walk around the pigeons, but as she advances, they take off almost under her nose. For once, Blythe is startled enough to lose her self-control. She pulls back, yanking the harness out of Connie's hand.

"What do I do now?" Connie asks, hanging tightly onto Blythe's leash.

"For your own safety, you've got to discipline her," Doug replies. "Give her leash a sharp snap. Let her know you're displeased."

Doug suggests that they wait until the pigeons settle back down, and try again. This time, when the birds fly up in front of her face, Blythe flinches nervously but keeps on walking.

"That's a good girl, Blythe," Connie tells her.

All is well in Blythe's world again.

Soon it is Connie's third week at The Seeing Eye. She is ready for a solo route through the shopping district of Morristown on a busy Saturday. Doug will watch from the other side of the street. He will not interfere in any way.

Blythe is in top form today. She leads Connie through crowds and obstacles at a brisk pace. Her confidence must be catching. Connie soon relaxes and enjoys the trip. They finish the route without mishap. Today's trip has been an important turning point for Connie and Blythe. Soon they will leave The Seeing Eye.

During Connie's final week of training, her daily working trips are designed to give her and Blythe maximum practice with everyday life situations. Connie is now making many of the decisions about where to go each day.

Near the end of the week, she decides to buy some gifts for her family. She's amused by Blythe's reaction to the revolving door at the department store. Blythe doesn't find the situation at all funny. She's afraid of getting her tail caught and starts to whine. She crowds close to the glass pane, eager to get out. The instant she can, she shoots into the store, pulling Connie behind her. Connie makes a mental note that they will have to practice some more with revolving doors.

Next day they go to the railroad station. For the past week, Connie and Blythe have been practicing using public transportation. They have made short bus trips. Tomorrow they will take a train to another town.

When the train clatters up to the platform, Blythe calmly responds to Connie's "Forward" command. She leads her up and down the steps of a coach.

Doug knows Connie has always enjoyed being in the country. That afternoon he takes her and Blythe to the beautiful Morristown Historical Park. As they come to the end of a trail, they find themselves on top of a steep hill with a lush grassy field far below. Doug describes the scene to Connie.

"Let's run down," says Connie.

"Are you sure you want to?"

"You bet I do!" And before Doug can say anything else, Connie is running down the slope.

ON SAFARI IN KENYA

Robert Bell

If you had to pick the most interesting animal in the world, what would it be? The giraffe, with its long neck? The rhinoceros, with its armored body and curved horn? How about the elephant with its long trunk?

You could see these, and many other strange animals, in Africa. Africa is a continent of many wonders. The cheetah, the fastest animal on land, lives there. The Nile River, the world's longest river, is in Africa. So is the Sahara, the largest desert on earth. Africa is a land of contrasts—of mountains and plains, of heat and cold, of dryness and wet.

If you wanted to see animals in Africa, you might choose Tsavo National Park in Kenya for your visit. Tsavo has more large land animals than any other park on earth. It was set up, like the many other parks of Africa, to protect African animals.

Kenya is less than a day away from the United States by jet. Your plane lands at Nairobi International Airport

AFRICA

Equator — Kenya

Atlantic Ocean

Indian Ocean

191

in Nairobi, Kenya's capital. If you think of Africa as a land of mud huts and jungles, Nairobi will surprise you. It is a modern city of skyscrapers and highways. Its busy airport easily handles the flood of tourists and business people who come to Kenya.

Kenya is on the equator. Most of the land is above sea level, so the weather is hot and dry during the day and cool at night. As your airplane lands, you see the dry, open grassland that surrounds the city. Two hundred miles southeast across that grassland, or savanna, lies Tsavo National Park.

Tsavo is so big (over eight thousand square miles) that it is divided into two parts. Tsavo West is a beautiful land of hills and plains with Mt. Kilimanjaro on its border. Kilimanjaro is Africa's highest mountain. Tsavo East is flatter.

The Park Headquarters is at Voi between Tsavo East and Tsavo West. Here you find information about Tsavo's animals, trees, plants, and terrain. At the entrance to Tsavo East, you hire a guide. The guide will ride with you and show you the best places to see animals. People can also join groups that tour the park in small buses driven by guides.

Your guide reminds you of the safety rules of a safari. The midday sun in Kenya is so hot that you must dress to protect yourself. Many people wear light brown safari suits and hats. In the hot, dry weather, you will also perspire a lot. You should have supplies of water and salt handy.

It is even more important to protect yourself from the animals. The large ones—elephants, lions, or rhinoceroses—can be dangerous if they are frightened

In contrast to the modern surroundings at Nairobi
Airport are the horned rhinoceros with tickbirds
on its back, the spotted cheetahs, and the lion
pride resting in the grass.

Weaver birds' nests hang in an acacia tree.

or angry. Some of Kenya's snakes are poisonous and can be equally dangerous. Your guide tells you to stay in the car at all times, unless you are told it is safe to leave.

At last, your safari can begin. Your guide directs you onto the road to Lugard's Falls through the broad savanna of Tsavo East.

The trees draw your notice first. Acacia trees, with their spreading branches and flat tops, stand up from the plain. There are also the odd-looking baobab trees, with their thick, soft trunks. You stop beneath one tree while your guide points out hundreds of weaver birds' nests hanging from its branches like fruit.

On the savanna, you see herds of gazelle and wildebeest and zebra. Many kinds of animals—water buffalo, impala, eland, lesser kudu, bushbuck—graze peacefully side by side. Suddenly though, they all lift their heads and then scatter wildly. Your guide, whose sharp eyes are used to the terrain, points out the distant lion that frightened the herds.

194

Lions are not usually on the move during the heat of day. They prefer to sit in the shade and gaze with sleepy eyes around them. They will usually let your car come quite close without becoming disturbed. As their great yellow eyes look into yours, you may wonder: What do the lions see? What do they think of me, who has come all this way to see them?

Other animals are shyer than lions. Giraffes feed from trees near the road. Your guide tells you to stop long before you reach them. At first, they freeze and stare at you. They slowly relax. Then you can move closer for a better look. The gerenuk, one of Africa's many antelopes, is one of the hardest animals to see at close range.

Lugard's Falls, on the Galana River, is well known for its crocodiles. Large groups of them lie on the shore below the falls or glide through the water. Your guide directs you east along the Galana. There you see herons, storks, flamingos, and other colorful birds.

Tsavo has a huge number of elephants. You come upon a herd crossing the river. They keep tightly together for protection. Elephants on the outside of the herd keep guard. Baby elephants are kept in the middle. Elephants seem to care more strongly about each other than many animals do.

Water is vital to this dry country. You see many animals come to the river to drink. The sullen rhinoceros appears. Tickbirds perch on it and keep it free from pests. Water buffalo graze in sight of the river. They are dangerous creatures that are best left alone. In places where the river grows into a pool, you are surprised to see great hippos rise to the surface and open their huge mouths in yawns.

At Sobo, you turn south across the savanna again. Ostriches cross the road ahead of you. Your guide stops you beneath another tree. Looking up, you see a leopard lying across a branch. Overhead, vultures glide through the air. They watch a pack of hyenas close in on a running zebra.

The hyenas and lions may seem cruel to us, but they really are not. The life of Tsavo shows a great balance at work. The hyena, the lion, and the leopard feed on the grazing animals. Without these wild hunters, the herds of zebra, buffalo, and antelope would grow too big. They would eat all the food they could find and destroy their grazing ground. Thousands would die of hunger. The wild hunters actually help to keep Tsavo from becoming a wasteland.

A spotted cheetah rests on a tree limb, water buffalo surround a watering hole, and zebras stop for a drink of cool water.

You reach Aruba, tired, hungry, and dazzled by the sun. You will be staying here in a banda, a comfortable, two-room hut. After dinner, you spend a few hours at the lake nearby. Animals come to the lake to drink as the sun sets. Elephants plod up to the shore and into the water. Lions, no longer sleepy, come to drink before starting the night's hunt. Alert zebras and gazelles come nervously to the water.

The African night is noisy. Birds call, insects buzz and hum, and lions roar. The smaller animals dash and squeal. A whole new cycle of life begins in the cool hours of night. The hunters and hunted of the day relax and sleep. The night's hunters and hunted begin to roam.

As you fall asleep on this, your first night in Africa, you wonder: What *is* the most interesting animal on earth? Can you decide? Or are the many amazing animals you have seen equally strange—and equally wonderful?

Carmen  Miranda
AND

Alice Schick and Sara Ann Friedman

Wally Kennedy knew something had to be wrong. He entered the elephant enclosure, carrying a hose and a broom, with a bottle of neat's-foot oil sticking out of his pocket. Normally the two Indian elephants would take it as a sign to begin their mock protest. Carmen would lower her head and lazily swing her trunk back and forth. Then, when Wally was least expecting it, the elephant would extend her trunk. She would grab the hose and pull, engaging him in a futile tug-of-war against her three tons. On a successful day, she would also knock the broom out of Wally's hand and the bottle out of his pocket. She would even knock Wally himself to his knees. Whatever Carmen did, Miranda did too.

Eventually both elephants would allow themselves to be caught. They would stand patiently while Wally went through his weekly routine. First he would spray them with water, then rub their huge sides with the broom. Finally he would oil their skin to keep it from drying out.

Today, however, Carmen just stood still—as if she didn't care what happened to her. At first Wally thought it was a trick. But when she continued to stand passively, he knew it wasn't. Waving her trunk in the air and stamping her foot, Miranda appeared equally bewildered. Without someone to imitate, she didn't know how to behave. "What's wrong, girl?" Wally asked as he whacked the broom against Carmen's tough hide. Examining her ears, her trunk, and as much of her body as he could while rubbing her down, Wally found nothing

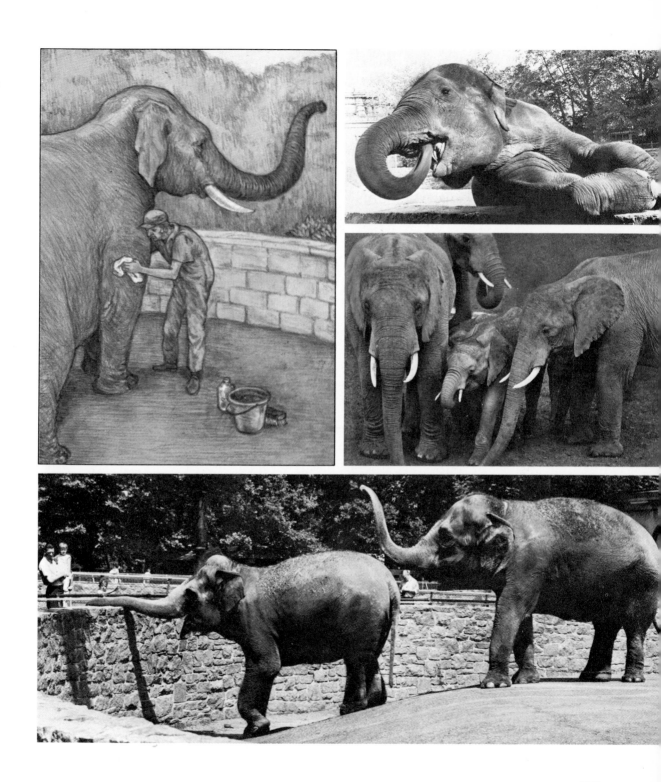

wrong. "Well, I guess after thirty-five years you finally admitted who's boss."

Wally decided he would look foolish if he reported that Carmen was ill when there were no symptoms. Still, Wally remained uneasy. He knew his elephants better than he knew anyone else. The three of them had been together at the Metropolitan Zoo for thirty-five years, and for five years before that at the circus.

Soon after Wally and the elephants had come to the zoo, they were familiar favorites with thousands of zoo visitors. People loved watching Carmen and Miranda, whatever the elephants were doing: getting a bath, learning new tricks, or rolling in the mud after a heavy rain.

Recently, the zoo had bought four new African elephants. Carmen and Miranda were now used only as riding elephants for children during the summer months.

At Wally's suggestion, young Rose Cooper had been hired to work with the new African elephants. During high school, Rose had worked at the zoo in a special program for gifted science students. She had been taking zoology courses since then, hoping for a paying job at the zoo.

Rose respected and admired Wally. But she often questioned his methods. Rose had been well trained not to think of animals in human terms. Whenever Rose would try to tell Wally that the elephants did not really have feelings, his favorite response was, "Who says so?"

Two weeks had passed since Wally had noticed the change in Carmen's behavior. Now she had physical symptoms as well. Her appetite was poor, and Wally had discovered a lump in her belly. Rose stood outside the enclosure and watched as Dr. Neil Goldman and Wally knelt, probing the elephant's abdomen.

Dr. Goldman stood up. "There's something there, Wally," the doctor said. "I'll take some blood samples."

"Rose," Wally called, "you distract Carmen with some carrots. I'll help the good doctor here." To keep Carmen's mind off the doctor's work, Wally walked around the elephant. He began slapping her side as hard as he could. The doctor inserted the needle into a vein in Carmen's ear. Rose concentrated hard on her own task.

Dr. Goldman found that Carmen had an infection. He gave her medicine. Carmen got better for several days, then got worse again. A white foamy substance dribbled from her trunk. She was given more medicine. For the next several weeks, the seesawing went on. Each time the symptoms returned, they were worse. Carmen began to have difficulty standing up without help. Wally would come to work in the morning and find her leaning against the wall. Some days she would lean her head against Miranda, apparently for moral as well as physical support.

"Come on, girl," Wally pleaded as he felt the heavy weight of her head in his arms. "We're a threesome—Carmen, Miranda, and Wally. Don't let us down now." He looked over at Miranda. She was standing in a corner rocking her head back and forth, back and forth.

Suddenly Wally heard a loud roar from behind him, and then a scream. Rose! He looked over. There was Rose pinned into a corner by Murphy, the little male African elephant. He had grown quite a bit since his arrival, but up until now he had been relatively docile.

Murphy's bluffing charge had startled Rose. "Stand up and face him," Wally ordered in such a stern voice that Rose obeyed instantly. "Now tell him 'Steady.' Keep your voice firm, no matter how scared you are. Hold your hook up so he can see it, but don't use it unless you have to." Wally continued his orders in a slow, firm voice. "OK. Fine. Now you back *him* up. Stare him down." Terrified, Rose did as she was told. So did Murphy.

"Thanks, Wally," Rose said later. "I'm sorry. I know how upset you are about Carmen, and I had to go and upset you more."

"It was a good lesson," Wally consoled her. "I'm glad I was there. Don't ever let an elephant know you're afraid, or you're sunk."

Carmen grew worse daily. She became weaker and weaker, hardly able to stand even with help. Then one day, before he even saw her, Wally knew. All the animals in the Elephant House were pacing nervously, but it was Miranda who told him. The elephant stood next to the prone body of her companion. Lowering her head, Miranda took a step back. Then, edging forward, she used her trunk and forefeet in an attempt to make Carmen stand. Carmen did not move. Miranda tried again. When there was no response, she stepped back. She raised her trunk and made a noise Wally had never heard before—a pitiful, heartrending groan that meant utter grief.

"She's dead, Miranda," Wally almost whispered. "I don't want to believe it either."

The Elephant House remained closed all day, with only zoo staff permitted inside. Wally spent most of the day with Miranda, trying to calm her. Rose went about her duties silently.

Miranda refused to be calmed, even by Wally. She had been

chained inside the building. When Carmen's body was removed later, Miranda could not follow it. She began to trumpet, tug on her leg chain, and bang her head against the wall. Stamping and trumpeting she went on rocking back and forth. She gained momentum until it looked as if she would tear the wall apart.

After forty years together, Miranda seemed lost without her friend. She couldn't take pleasure in her favorite foods. Miranda was old. Perhaps she would never adjust to her loss. Wally Kennedy was devoting a lot of time to Miranda. He was convinced he could help her overcome her grief. If anyone could work such a miracle, it was Wally.

However, one day Dr. Goldman walked into the Elephant House and Miranda was dead. "I found her like this when I came in," Wally said, making no effort to hold back his tears.

"What did she die of, Dr. Goldman?" Rose asked. "She didn't act sick at all."

"I suppose you could say she died of grief," Dr. Goldman said.

With both his elephants gone, Wally Kennedy saw no reason to stay at the zoo. Now he could look forward to retirement. Wally's last day was spent doing ordinary chores. He left the four little elephants pretty much to Rose while he fed the other animals and cleaned their enclosures.

At quitting time, Wally got his coat, planning to slip away unnoticed. But before he could get out the door, Rose called to him from the elephant enclosure. "Wait a minute, Wally. We want to show you something."

Directing them with verbal commands, Rose marched the four young elephants around her in a circle. Then she lined them up in a row, facing Wally. She tapped her hook gently against each flank. Each elephant raised its right foreleg and held it in the air. "Come on, you guys," she said in a voice loud enough for Wally to hear, "let's show Wally how we feel about him!" She whispered a command. Four elephants raised their trunks and trumpeted together.

Choked up, Wally turned away quickly. "I thought 'elephants didn't have feelings,'" he said over his shoulder.

Not sure whether to laugh or cry, Rose called back, "Who says so?"

Where in the World Are the Animals From?

Where in the world are the animals from?
From where in the world do the animals come?
Why in the world do they live where they do?
Where do they live when they're not in the zoo?

They come from all over. No matter how hot
Or cold a place is, something lives in that spot.
(It may be a mere little worm of small worth,
But someone's alive everywhere on the earth.)

They live where it suits them, which often depends
On whether their neighbors are foes or are friends
And whether the food supply's fit for their feed
And whether the weather's the weather they need.

Some are quite fussy and only can thrive
In a special location, while others survive
In a number of places; and then there are those
Who seem to live everywhere anyone goes.

Where in the world are the animals from?
From where in the world do the animals come?
Why in the world do they live where they do?
Where do they live when they're not in the zoo?

—by Mary Ann Hoberman

Word Magic

Have you ever watched chemists at work? By combining two substances, they can form a completely different and new substance. It's almost like magic! You can perform similar feats with words.

A *prefix* is a word part that is added to the beginning of a base word. The prefixes *in-, un-, il-, ir-, dis-,* and *non-* all mean "not." By adding one of these prefixes to a word, you can form a new word with an opposite meaning. Read the following example:

$$un + true \Rightarrow untrue$$

Adding the prefix *un-* to the word *true* forms the word *untrue*. The word *untrue* means "not true." The words *true* and *untrue* have opposite meanings. Words with opposite meanings are called *antonyms*. Here is another example:

$$dis + loyal \Rightarrow disloyal$$

Adding the prefix *dis-* to the word *loyal* forms the new word *disloyal*. The word *disloyal* means "not loyal." The words *loyal* and *disloyal* are antonyms.

ACTIVITY A   Read these sentences. On your paper, write the prefix in each underlined word. Then write the meaning of the whole word.

1. The rocky road ahead is <u>unsafe</u> for travelers.
2. The time for our meeting is still <u>indefinite</u>.
3. It is <u>illegal</u> to drive through a red light.
4. The hours she works are <u>irregular</u>.

5. This magazine has <u>nonfiction</u> articles.

6. That was not a <u>dishonest</u> statement by the press.

Sometimes the prefixes *un-* and *dis-* mean "to do the opposite of." Read the following examples:

$$un + pack \Rightarrow unpack$$
$$dis + appear \Rightarrow disappear$$

Adding the prefix *un-* to the word *pack* forms the word *unpack*. The word *unpack* means "to do the opposite of pack." Adding the prefix *dis-* to the word *appear* forms the word *disappear*. The word *disappear* means "to do the opposite of appear."

ACTIVITY B   Read these sentences. On your paper, write the prefix in each underlined word. Then write the meaning of the whole word.

1. The campers will <u>unfold</u> the tent this afternoon.

2. We plan to <u>discontinue</u> the program after a week.

3. Please <u>untie</u> the boat.

4. The soldiers wouldn't <u>disobey</u> the command.

ACTIVITY C   Use the prefix in parentheses at the end of each sentence. Replace the underlined words with one word that uses the prefix. Write the new sentence on your paper.

1. The work you have given me is <u>not complete</u>. (in-)

2. Please <u>do the opposite of lock</u> the door. (un-)

3. Driving over the speed limit is <u>not legal</u>. (il-)

4. The judge's decision was <u>not reversible</u>. (ir-)

5. Rain and snow <u>do the opposite of please</u> me. (dis-)

PARTNERS

For thousands of years, people and animals have shared the earth. We have hunted animals for food, trained them to work for us, and relied on them for companionship. Often we have used animals to make our lives better. Sometimes we have made life worse for the animals. Many people are working to make life better for both people and animals.

Thinking About "Partners"

1. What caused Don Marcelino's daughter, Maria, to crawl into the passageway where the cave drawings were painted on the ceiling?
2. What are some reasons why Nal and the wolf became friends?
3. What were some of the animals Kemi and Tonla learned about on their trip to the sea?
4. What qualities do Emma Jane Burke and Connie David have in common?
5. Why is it important for Connie and Blythe to work together?
6. Compare some of the ways we use animals today with the ways people have used them in the past.
7. Imagine that you were on the safari trip in the Tsavo Game Reserve. Write a paragraph telling about the animals you saw on the second day of your trip.

SIGNALS

From the time we are born, we are concerned with communication. Even before we can talk, our facial expressions, sounds, and gestures convey our feelings and thoughts to others. From the time animals are born, they also communicate. Animals send messages to each other using touch, smell, sight, and hearing. But communication among people is special. Only human beings have the ability to use words to convey messages.

By reading "Signals," you will find answers to the following questions: How do animals "talk" to each other without using words? How did people begin to write? How is a television show put together? What kinds of communication can be misleading? What new methods of communication might there be in the future?

As you read, think about how communication has developed and how it might change in the future. Think of all the ways you communicate with people and animals.

The Animal's Point of View

Millicent E. Selsam

Animals communicate with each other all the time. How do they do it? This essay presents some fascinating facts about the ways animals "talk" to each other.

Animals do not have a language like ours. They do not talk to each other in words and sentences. In fact, most animals cannot say a single word. But we only have to watch them to see that they communicate with each other by signals of some kind.

A school of minnows comes close to shore, and as we approach, their silvery bodies flash in unison. The whole school goes off together in another direction. Flocks of starlings come in to roost on a winter evening and shift and turn and dive together with the greatest precision. The monkeys in a zoo, the dogs on a street, the chickens in a barnyard, the minnows, the starlings, and most other animals have ways of communicating with one another.

But how can we find out about their secret worlds? How can we be sure of what an animal sees, hears, tastes, or smells? It is easy enough to imagine that their worlds are just like ours. We find it natural to think that they see what we see, hear what we hear, and smell the same odors we do. But if you think this way, you are bound to make mistakes.

Once, as a young teacher-in-training, I was asked to get down on the floor and sing to a turtle. My supervisor was sure that turtles loved music. I asked her if she thought they preferred classical or jazz. "Classical," she said. So I got as close as I could to the turtle and sang a theme from a Beethoven symphony. The turtle wagged its head back and forth, "almost in time to the music," my boss said. But somebody should have told us that it could not possibly hear anything, since a turtle is deaf.

A snake is deaf, too. But you can read stories and see pictures of snake charmers in Indian bazaars playing music to charm their deadly poisonous cobra snakes. If you watch such a performance, it looks as though the snake is listening and responding to the music. But a scientist became interested in this response and did some tests. He blindfolded the cobra. Then he beat on tin cans and blew bugles near the cobra. There was no reaction. When the blindfolds were removed, the experimenter waved his arms around. The cobra immediately raised its head and spread its hood. So we found out that snakes are charmed not by the sound of music, but by the movements the snake charmer makes while playing.

Imagine yourself sitting in a living room with a dog beside you, a bird in a cage, and a fish swimming in an aquarium. Each is in its own world. The dog can't see colors and in general can't see as well as we do. But it can smell the faintest odors and hear much higher sounds that we can. The bird has keen eyes but hardly any sense of smell. The fish is nearsighted in its watery world, but has taste organs in its skin that make it sensitive to chemicals or dissolved food in the water. If we want to find out how fish communicate with fish, or dogs with dogs, we must find out what their particular worlds are like. We must look at animals from the animal's point of view.

Animal communication is a relatively new branch of science. Much information has only recently been discovered. Some ideas we now think are true may change with further experimental work. But that is the very nature of all science —ever-changing and developing.

Afterword

Scientists continue to study animal communication through carefully planned experiments and observations. Scientists now know that animal communication by odor is the most common form of communication. A rabbit, for example, will rub its chin on twigs and stones in passing. This rubbing will leave an odor. Other rabbits then "read" the odor to learn what animals have used the path earlier.

Some ants give off a special alarm odor. This odor serves two purposes at once. It warns nearby ants of danger. At the same time, it attracts distant ants that will come to the rescue.

Touch is also used by animals to communicate. One kind of spider plucks the rim of its web in a special rhythm. This plucking communicates the spider's presence to another spider resting within the web.

Animals send messages by sight and sound, too. A fish may flick its tail or spread its fin. Other fish see and respond to this message. Many of the sounds of animal communication are familiar: dogs bark, birds chirp, lions growl. Other sounds too high for humans to hear are used by bats, moths, whales, and porpoises.

What might be learned in the future about animal communication? What kinds of nonverbal signals might people be sending out? Do animals respond to them? How? What can we learn about the world by "listening in" as animals communicate? These and other questions may someday be answered as scientists continue to study and experiment, observe and record, the communication of animals.

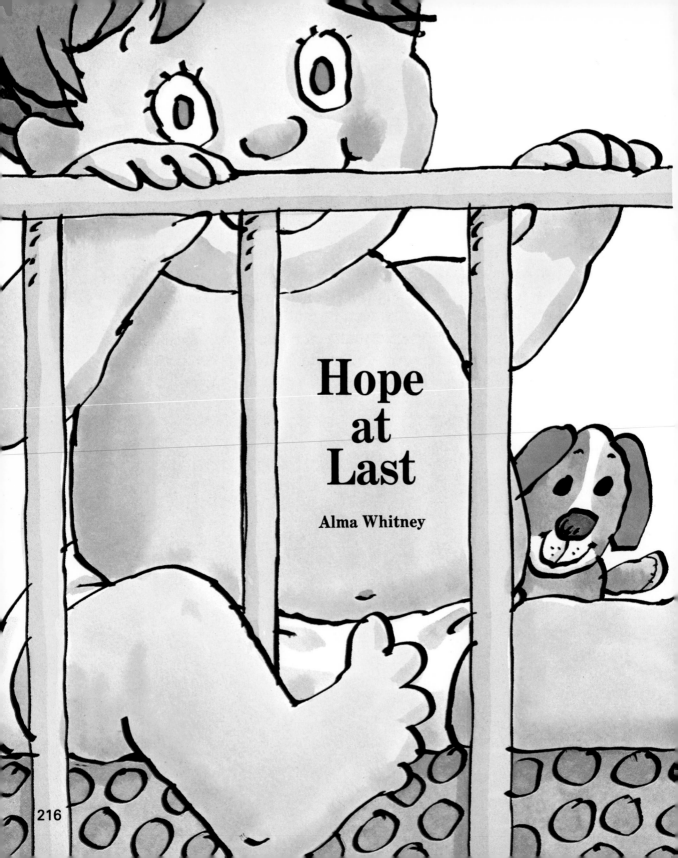

Hope
at
Last

Alma Whitney

You think you've got problems? Well, listen to me. Up until a few days ago, I didn't think there was any hope for me. But then something happened to make me think maybe, just maybe, there is some hope, after all. But I guess I have to tell you what's been going on. Then you'll understand.

Each day, I would lie here in my crib. The most unbelievable things would happen. Grownups, large people, would keep walking by and looking down at me.

"A boo-boo-boo," would say the one with the blond hair. She's my mother.

"Wutch-um, wutch-um, wutch-um," the one with the whiskers would say. He's my father.

And every so often, the top of a smaller person's head would go by. That would be my big brother, Fred. He wouldn't say much at all. Just "ugh" and "ick," sometimes.

I was really getting worried. "How will I ever learn to talk right at this rate?" I kept thinking. I knew people didn't talk to each other the way they talked to me. For example, my mother would say, "Walter, is it time for the news on television yet?"

And my father would answer, "In a few minutes, Agnes."

Not one "a-boo" or "wutch-um" that time.

And of course, the people on the television didn't say "hozum babee." They'd say really terrific things like "traffic report" and "this evening's presentation."

Just the other day I was having my lunch. According to my mother, the menu was eggsies and pearsies. But when Fred asked my mother if he could have eggsies and pearsies, my mother said, "Don't talk like that, Fred. That's baby talk."

In my whole life, which happens to be about six months, I have never said anything like "eggsies" or "pearsies." As a matter of fact, I have never said much at all. That is, until a few days ago. But I must say that, when I did finally speak, what I said made quite a commotion.

I was lying on my back. I was looking up at my bird mobile when my mother decided to peek down at me. Now I usually make a lot of different sounds. But that day I said "ah-ah" right to my mother's face.

"Walter," my mother called. "Walter, come here. The baby just said 'mama.'"

My father came running into the room. He looked down at me. Since it seemed to make everybody so excited, I said it again. "Ah-ah."

"Nonsense," my father said. "The baby just said 'dada.'"

MAMA
DADA
WATER
DOG
SPAGHETTI

"Mama," said my mother looking down at me.

"Ah-ah-ah-ah," I answered.

"Da-da-da-da," said my father.

"Ah-ah-ah-ah," I said again.

Since then, I've said "ah-ah" quite a bit. My mother has decided that it also means "water" and "dog." At least, I think she has. Every time she brings me a bottle of water, she says "whaaah-terrr." And when she gives me my little pink dog, she says "dahg." I say "ah-ah" to these things. And does she get excited!

Frankly, I think my father still believes I'm saying "dada." He keeps sneaking by my crib and whispering "dada." When I answer "ah-ah," he grins and says "a very intelligent baby!"

So you see, there seems to be some hope for me now. I haven't gotten it quite right yet. But I'm working on "ab-ab-ab" and "boo." I can't wait to hear what they think I'm saying then.

What I'm really looking forward to is the day when I can say fantastic words like "spaghetti" and "chocolate syrup." You've got to admit, they're pretty terrific. But for now I would really settle for "Please ma, don't make me eat that squash again." I hate spitting the stuff out and crying. But that seems to be the only way I can make myself understood.

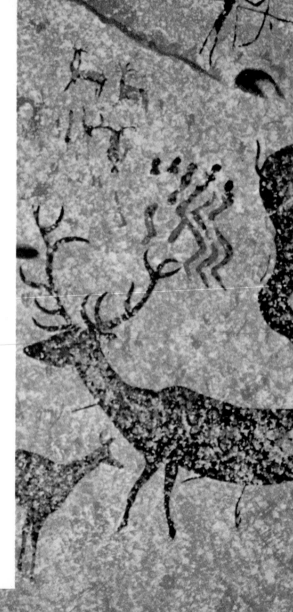

WRITE IT DOWN!

Sam and Beryl Epstein

The invention of writing happened very slowly, and it took place so long ago that no one really knows much about it. You can guess why it happened, though.

People could speak their thoughts. They knew how to put their thoughts into the sounds we call words. But they didn't know how to keep the thoughts.

You know that if you tell somebody something, the person may forget it. If you put your thought into written words, however, the person can look at the words again and again. Whenever the person looks at the words they will say the same thing.

When your words are written down they can't be forgotten.

All writing is just a way of keeping thoughts. Newspapers and magazines and books are thoughts written down so that people can read them, whenever they want to, so that they can keep the thoughts forever and even hand them down to their children's children.

The first kind of writing was what is called picture-writing. Today in America if we want to write about a dog, we write *DOG*. People who did picture-writing made a picture of a dog, instead, like this:

After a time, people found that they couldn't always make a picture that looked like the thing that was in their minds. They could make a picture that looked like a dog, but they couldn't make a picture that looked like "good" or "comfort" or "true." If people wanted to put down thoughts such as "good" or "comfort" or "true," they had to think of special pictures that would express those ideas. When people make pictures that express ideas, they are said to be writing *ideographs*. *Graph* is from an ancient Greek word that means "writing." You can see that *ideograph* means "idea-writing."

Left: Cave painting found in Bicorp, Spain

Right: Cave painting found in Caballos, Spain

221

The Chinese still use ideographs when they write today. Some of the ideographs are so simple that they are almost picture-writing. When the Chinese want to talk about a tree, for example, they say the word *mu,* which means tree or wood in Chinese. But when they want to write about a tree they don't write the letters *m* and *u.* Instead they draw a little picture of a tree, like this: 木 . If they want to write about trees, they don't add a letter *s* to their word, as English-speaking people do. They make a picture of two trees, like this: 木木. The picture of the two trees means "more than one tree," or "forest."

Probably when people first used picture-writing they made whatever kind of pictures they wanted to make. After a while, all the people in one part of the world agreed that certain pictures would mean certain things. Then they could understand each other's writing.

In the ancient land of Phoenicia, about three thousand years ago, people who wanted to write down the idea of an ox made this little picture: ⌣ , which looked to them like the horns of an ox. If they wanted to write "door," they made this picture: ⌢ . Their word for ox

Text and drawing on manuscript page by Chinese author/artist Tsen Yen-Tung

was *aleph*. Their word for door was *daleth*.

The Phoenicians had to learn a new picture for every single word. It took a long time to learn the pictures for all the words. So, after a while, the Phoenicians began to work out a new method of writing. Instead of using the picture  to mean *aleph*, they used that picture for the first sound in the word *aleph*—the sound of *A*. Instead of using ⌒ to mean door, or *daleth*, they used it for the first sound in the word *daleth*, the sound of *D*. If the Phoenicians had wanted to write the English word *AD*, they would have written it like this: ⌣⌒

The Phoenicians were the only people in the world ever to develop a true alphabet—a system of signs to represent sounds.

After a time the Greeks borrowed most of the signs the Phoenicians were using. They changed some of them to suit themselves. They turned the sign for *A*, ⌣ , upside down, for example, and made it like this: ⌒ . They also added a few new signs of their own, because the Greek language had some sounds in it that the Phoenician language didn't have.

Phoenician writing on The Nora Stone found in Nora, Sardinia

223

Then the Romans began to use many of the signs the Greeks were using, and they changed the signs too. Finally the signs the Romans used, plus a few others, were used for the writing of English words. The old Phoenician sign for ox had become the letter *A*, and the old sign for a door had become the letter *D*. The other letters of the Roman alphabet developed in the same way from those long-ago signs first used in picture-writing.

Greek writing on stone tablet from 480 B.C.

Roman coin

The Phoenician word for	The Phoenician sign was	Greeks changed this to	Romans changed this to	
ox was aleph	⊀ or ▽	▷ then to A	A	A
house was beth	⋑ or ℘	B then to B	B	B
camel was gimel	∧ or ∧	⌐ then to Γ	C	C
door was daleth	◸ or △	△	D	D
window was he	⋙	⋞ then to E	E	E
hook was vau	Y or ⋔	⋀ then lost	F	F
		⌐ then to Γ	G	G
fence was cheth	⊟ or ⊞	⊟ then to H	H	H
hand was yod	Z	⪴ then to I	I	I
				J
palm was kaph	Ψ or Ҝ	Ҝ then to k	K	K
rod was lamed	L or ∟	↑ then to ∧	L	L
water was mem	⧢ or ⩊	M then to M	M	M
fish was nun	⅄ or ⅃	⅄ then to N	N	N
eye was ayin	○	○	O	O
mouth was pe	⌐ or ⌐	⅂ then to Π	P	P
knot was koph	Φ	Φ then lost	Q	Q
head was resh	⊲ or ⋖	⊲ then to P	R	R
tooth was shin	W or ⋃	Σ	S	S
mark was tahv	T or X	T	T	T
		V then to V		U
			V	V
				W
support was samekh	⟊ or ⋔	⟊ then to ☰	X	X
			Y	Y
weapon was zayin	I or ⋁	I then to Z	Z	Z

225

Say It With Symbols

The idea of a world-wide system of communication based on symbols rather than words has interested people for many years. One such system has been developed by a man named C.K. Bliss. This system is called *Semantography*, which means "writing for meaning." Most of the symbols are drawn to look like the things they name. So it is easy to remember what the symbols mean. Here are some examples:

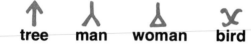

Of course, you need to be able to show actions as well as the names of things. In Semantography, actions are shown by placing a ʌ above a symbol. Here are two examples:

⊙ is the symbol for eye

⊙̂ is the symbol for seeing

⋏̱ is the symbol for legs and feet

⋏̂ is the symbol for walking

In Semantography, symbols are combined to mean different things. Here are some examples:

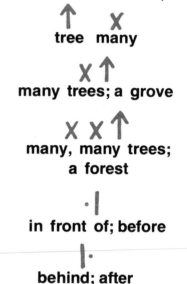

Here is a sentence written in Semantography. Can you read it?

Now try writing this sentence in Semantography: *The man sees a bird behind the tree.*

Would you like to create your own system of symbols? If so, remember to keep your symbols simple. Use as few symbols as possible, and keep your system easy to read.

What Do You Know About NEWSPAPERS?

Any time you want to find out what's happening around the world or around the block, turn to a newspaper. You couldn't have done that in America in 1690 because there was only one newspaper, and it ran for only one issue. But in our world today, it's easy to turn to a newspaper. More than 62½ million papers are sold every day in the United States alone. It's hard to imagine life without a newspaper.

Glance at the front page of a newspaper. The first thing you are sure to notice is the paper's name, or *logo*. As you start reading, you will find many *headlines*, the attention-getting titles of news articles.

If you want to know who wrote a story, you can sometimes find the writer's name in a *byline*. To learn more about a photograph, just read the description, or *caption*, under it.

You might be confused when an article seems to be cut off in the middle of a sentence. Don't worry! You'll see the *jumpline*. What is a jumpline? It's a note telling you where to find the conclusion of the story.

To take a close look at the form of a newspaper, just turn the page . . .

Morning
Edition

The Daily Banner

Weather:
Sunny
and
clear.

20 cents   Saturday, June 1, 1985   *Vol. CCCXL*

A LONG WAY FROM HOME: Explorer reaches North Pole.

How Sweet It Is

Madison, Wis. (AP) — The honeybee buzzed in yesterday as Wisconsin's state insect. In a ceremony, the governor approved a bill to make the honeybee the state insect. Honeybees in the state last year made more than 10.2 million pounds of honey. This gave the state fifth-place honors in honey production.

Solo to the North Pole

Tokyo (AP) — A Japanese explorer became the first person to reach the North Pole alone by dog sled. The 500-mile trip took 57 days.

First word of the deed was sent to the Smithsonian Institution in Washington, D.C. It was sent through an automatic device the explorer was carrying. This device sent a beam to Washington by way of a satellite.

Two photographers were flown to the North Pole to take the explorer's picture. At the same time, the photographers also picked up the diary he had been keeping. He is expected to stay in the North Pole area for several days. He started his trip from the Canadian Arctic.

To place a classified advertisement, call 988-1138 between 9:00 A.M. and 5:00 P.M.

U.S. plans another space flight to ringed planet, Saturn.

Space Flight

It has been announced that the United States is planning another space flight to explore Saturn, the sixth planet from the sun.

Saturn has long been of interest because it is surrounded by rings. With every flight, scientists hope to discover more about Saturn's hundreds of rings.

No further information on the nature of the flight has been made public.

Metrics Move Ahead
From Inches to Centimeters

By Ed Meagher

The United States is moving closer to the metric age. Many grade school youngsters are studying metric measurements for the first time.

Some experimental classes in metrics have already been held. Entire schools have also been introducing metrics on their own. Nationwide, more and more people are beginning to learn and use metrics.

Some teachers still do not feel that the schools or the nation is ready for metrics teaching. They say that textbooks are not in agreement on how metrics should be taught. They also feel that some schools will teach metrics, but others may not.

But the change to metrics is surely happening. The nation decided to change when the Metrics Conversion Act was passed in

(Continued on Next Page)

Metrics Move Ahead

(Continued from Previous Page)

1975. As a result, Americans in years to come will increasingly use meters, kilometers, grams, and so on. Good-by to pints, quarts, and ounces.

UNDER THE BIG TOP: Circus plans two-week stay.

Circus Comes to Town

By Nancy Weldon

With the words "Ladies and gentlemen and children of ALL ages . . ." the circus began on Thursday. Glittering and in some cases death-defying acts followed. They were led by a performer's breath-taking wire walk 200 feet above the floor.

The entire performance was full of thrills. One highlight was the trapeze act, which received plenty of applause and cheers. The biggest problem the crowd of thousands had was deciding which ring to watch.

During the second half of the show, the houselights were dimmed. Trainers put the big cats through their act. The "children of all ages" had a good time.

Statewide Baseball Scores

Columbus 4 . . . . Loomis 2
Wright 3 . . . . Eugene 0
Everett 5 . . . . Pacific 4
Louis 1 . . . . Randolph 0
Rockwell 5 . . . . Drummond 2

Sports Today

Blue Jays vs. Bears at Main High School, 6:00 P.M.

Summer Sports Program Announced

This week the mayor outlined the city's summer sports program. Training will be offered in tennis, jogging, swimming, and other activities.

The classes are free and open to the public. However, the mayor encouraged anyone interested to sign up for classes as soon as possible to avoid disappointment.

The program is to have a staff of five teachers. There are still two positions to be filled. Mayor Andersen said that anyone who has had sports training experience could apply at Town Hall.

The program will start in the middle of June and last until the end of August. So sports fans — pick up your rackets, start running, and dive in!

Skateboards Get Winterized

By Ross Atkin

In some northern countries, skateboarders can practice their sport year-round in indoor skateboard parks. But why go indoors when Old Man Winter arrives? Ask Swiss youngsters. They are changing their skateboards into skiboards. By replacing wheels with small runners, they turn their boards into mini-sleds. Then they can skiboard down snow-covered hills. The idea for skiboards may have come from skiers, who keep training during the summer by using skis on wheels.

231

The Daily Banner

Founded in 1851

Charles Brooks, *Publisher*

Metric: Yes or No?

The debate about whether America should go metric continues. The case for giving up inches and gallons for meters and liters is based on several ideas. The metric system is more efficient and practical. Also, it is now the way of the world. Only the United States and some small nations cling to the old measurements. Fully 90% of the world's population enjoys the ease of metrics. We have argued for years in favor of the metric system.

Letters

Editor:

What in the world is going on? I thought that we had changed to metrics in this country. But everywhere I look — even in this newspaper — I still see the old measurements. Don't send me this newspaper anymore!

Elizabeth Kendall
Schlesinger

Editor:

I agree with your editorial of last Sunday on litter. Let's have the police give out more tickets to litterers. Maybe a $25 fine would help some people break their bad habits. Those of us who use public trash cans support you completely.

I. M. Tidy

Editor:

Increase police ticketing of litterers? Ridiculous! Our police have more important things to do. We can all help. When was the last time you picked up a piece of stray litter to deposit it in a trash can?

Lee Tucker

Editor:

We feel a traffic light is needed on the corner of Bergen and Sixth Avenue. Children have to cross that street to reach Bergen School. Traffic is heavy, and the cars and trucks travel rapidly. Let's put up a traffic light *before* a child is hurt.

S. Lopez
R. Smith

Editor:

I agree with your recent editorial on city parks. These parks belong to all of us. Everyone should help keep them clean. Who wants to picnic or stroll through a dirty park? Down with litter!

Anna Choy

Doggy Alibi Flops

Parkersburg, W. Va. (UPI) — A young man told the judge he could not have been going 45 mph in a 35 mph zone. A dog was chasing his car at the time. The driver argued that no dog could run that fast. He said the encyclopedia proved he was right. It says that the fastest dog, the greyhound, can only run 35 mph. The dog chasing his car was just a common breed. But Judge Anne McDonough found him guilty anyway. She fined him $40.

Town News

- Chatham — Last minute decisions were made to hire two more police officers and four more firefighters.
- Boylston — The Fire Department will get a new pumper. A new heating system will be installed in the town library.
- Weymouth — The Fore River will be dredged. The vote for this project was 100 votes for and 38 against.
- Spring Valley — Everyone is invited to the annual pancake breakfast on Saturday. Doors open at 8:00 A.M. and close when the batter is gone.

Classified Advertisements

HELP WANTED: Babysitter. Weekdays. $1.50 an hour. Call Mr. Drake. 366-1128.

HELP WANTED: Stock person. Williams Department Store. Experienced only. 722-8815.

HELP WANTED: Someone to care for yard while owner is on vacation. 776-4242.

HELP WANTED: Salesperson. Kim's Flower Shop. Apply in person. 310 South Main St.

FOR RENT: One bedroom apartment. Call 788-3040.

FOR SALE: Drums. Like new. Best offer. 388-4910.

FOR SALE: Piano. Just tuned. Best offer. Call 905-2336.

FOR SALE: Used boy's bike. Blue. $40. Call 331-9801.

LOST: Black dog. Answers to Daisy. Reward. Call 744-5627.

FREE: Kittens. Have shots. To good home only. 314-8972.

Daniel Craig

Elizabeth D. Squire

One day in the mid-1800's, a stubborn man boarded a steamship as it neared Halifax, Nova Scotia. In his hands was a basket of carrier pigeons. In his coat pocket was hidden another pigeon. The man was Daniel Craig, and he wanted to be first with the news.

In the 1800's, no radios or telephones existed, and all the news from Europe came by steamship. The ships made their first North American stop in Nova Scotia. Then they sailed down to the large eastern cities of the United States.

Daniel Craig wanted to get stories to newspapers in Boston and New York before the steamships did. He had learned how pigeons could be trained to return to their home roosts with messages strapped to their legs. He decided these birds could be used to carry news.

So, with pigeons in hand, Craig would take a boat out to meet the ships from Europe before they arrived in Halifax. After boarding a ship, he would write up the most important news: wars which had started or ended; kings, queens, or heads of state who had come to power or died. Then he would attach his news report to the leg of a pigeon and send the bird flying off.

The pigeon would fly to its home on the roof of a newspaper office. The newspaper then bought and used Craig's news.

Some rival newspapers wanted to stop Craig. They tried to persuade the ships not to allow him to bring his birds on board. For this reason, Craig began carrying a bird in his pocket each time he boarded a ship.

Once, Craig and his basket of carrier pigeons boarded the ship of a strict captain named Byrie. Captain Byrie took Craig's basket of birds. He said that they would not be returned until the ship reached Boston. But Craig attached the news to the leg of his hidden bird. Then he went up on deck, stood right next to the captain, and released the bird.

The angry captain ran for his rifle and tried to shoot the bird. But by the time he could take aim and fire, the carrier pigeon was already a mile in the air. It was on its way to Boston. Craig again was first with the news.

When the rival newspapers found they could not beat Craig's news, they hired him. The rooftops of their buildings then became landing areas for pigeons.

Prior to this time, a new kind of printing press was invented. The old presses had been able to print only a few hundred pages an hour. The new press was a steam-driven press that could print 2,000 pages an hour. Later, it was improved so that it printed 4,000 pages an hour.

With the new press, newspapers made more money, and soon there was an increase in the number of new newspapers. Each wanted to get as many readers as possible. However, the cost of getting the news was still expensive. Boats were hired to meet ships in the harbor and rush the news to shore. Pony expresses were hired to carry the news overland.

Finally, in 1848, the six most important New York newspapers decided that an agency should be formed to collect the news and get it to the papers. The agency was called the *Associated Press*. Daniel Craig was hired to send the news from Halifax to the *AP*.

By the time Craig went to work for the *AP*, the telegraph had been developed. Poles carrying telegraph wires reached as far north as Portland, Maine. But there was only one wire for use in sending messages. The reporter who got to Portland first got his story through first. As always, Craig meant to be first.

Here's what he did. First, Craig's news reached shore at Halifax. There, an express rider was ready to gallop off to the Nova Scotia port town that was nearest Maine. A few miles

outside of this town, Craig placed a man with a cannon. The man would fire the cannon when the express rider was in sight. This sound signaled the captain of another steamship to get up steam and go to shore to pick up the news. The ship carried the news full steam down the coast of Maine to Portland and the single telegraph wire.

By 1849, the telegraph wires reached Halifax. Even then, Craig had to be clever. Another man wanted to sell foreign news, as Craig was doing. Once, this man managed to get to the telegraph wire in Halifax first and to block Craig's news. After that, Craig sent a friend to the telegraph office as soon as a steamship was sighted. The friend handed the operator a book and asked him to start sending the first chapter as *AP* "news" to New York. This "news" kept the wire busy until the "rest" of the *AP* news arrived from the ship. It was an expensive way to reserve the line, but Craig meant to be first.

Finally, one day in 1851, Craig received a telegram calling him to New York to see the publishers who employed him. The publishers asked Craig to become the general agent in charge of the *AP.* The *AP* had begun selling news to newspapers in many parts of the country. Thus, Craig now had to report a story in such a way as to make it useable by a Northern paper as well as a Southern paper. It also had to be useable by a Democratic-Party or a Republican-Party paper. Therefore, the *AP* news service had had to stick to the facts and get the facts as correct as possible.

Most newspapers at that time did not report the facts as accurately as possible. News stories were full of the opinions of the editors. They printed good news about the people they liked. They often published anything bad they could find about their enemies. They frequently failed to check the facts.

Craig made all his newspeople get the facts of a story exactly right. If they discovered a mistake, they had to send a second wire correcting it.

While he was the general agent of the *AP,* Craig saw many changes occur that helped to speed the news. One was the Atlantic cable, completed in 1866. This cable made it possible to receive news from across the ocean on the same day it occurred.

Craig left the *AP* in 1866 and started his own news agency. But he was not able to compete with the *AP* and soon retired from newsreporting.

Nevertheless, while Craig was in charge of the *AP,* the agency formed two important guides for news-gathering: get the news fast, and get the correct facts.

What's New?

Almost everyone likes to learn the latest news. One way to learn the latest news is by reading the newspaper. A newspaper informs you about important events. It also entertains you. A newspaper has many parts:

News articles give information about world, national, or local events. In the selection "What Do You Know About Newspapers?" you read news articles about an explorer reaching the North Pole, a governor approving a bill, a planned space flight, a circus performance, and a summer sports program.

Editorials are essays that tell the opinions of the newspaper's editors. In *The Daily Banner,* you read an editorial in which the editors gave reasons why Americans should use the metric system.

Letters to the Editor are written by people who want to express their opinions. In *The Daily Banner,* you read letters in which people told how they felt about litterbugs, the metric system, and the town's new traffic light.

Advertisements are notices written by store owners, manufacturers, and others. They tell about products or goods for sale or use. In *The Daily Banner,* you saw advertisements for a movie and a sale.

Classified Ads (or Advertisements) are placed by individuals or by businesses. They may announce job openings or items for sale. Some of the ads in *The Daily Banner* announced apartments for rent, musical instruments for sale, and jobs available for a babysitter, and a stock person.

A *weather report* gives the predicted weather for the day. Some reports give predictions for later days.

Cartoons and comics entertain the reader. A cartoon is usually one funny picture. Comics may be a series of pictures that tell a funny story.

Entertainment listings give information about TV and radio programs. They may also tell what movies are playing in town.

ACTIVITY A   On your paper, name the newspaper part that would answer each question.

1. Is it supposed to rain tomorrow?
2. What's on television tonight?
3. What was the score in yesterday's ball game?
4. Does anyone have a used trumpet for sale?
5. Is Winkles Store having a sale this week?

ACTIVITY B   On your paper, name the part of the newspaper that would give the following information.

1. The mayor takes a trip around the world.
2. Apartment for rent: 3 rooms, $350 a month.
3. Charlie Brown and Snoopy lose a ball game.
4. People give reasons for wanting a new park.
5. It will be sunny today and cloudy tonight.
6. Dress shoes at Shoe World are on sale: $15 a pair.
7. Business leaders meet to discuss world problems.
8. The editor explains the need to raise taxes.

RADIO

Before television, people used to listen to the radio. They listened to many kinds of programs for entertainment the way people watch television today. There were mysteries, spy stories, and westerns. And there were programs about science fiction and make-believe worlds.

While you listened to the radio, you might have heard Clark Kent change into Superman and take off after some robbers. How could you have heard him change into Superman? Well, the people who produced the radio shows made you hear it by using sound effects. The actors read their parts from the script. And the sound-effects people supplied the sounds needed. Using different props, they made the listener hear thunder crashing, bombs exploding, or horses running. They made whatever sound was necessary to make the program seem more realistic.

Radio also depended on the listener's imagination to make programs believable. When a character was described as a beautiful, young princess, that's what the audience imagined. It's like reading a book that has no pictures.

Here is a script from a radio show for young people. The program was *Let's Pretend.* It was very popular from 1930 to 1953.

Each week *Let's Pretend* dramatized a well-known story for young people. The script you are going to read is for "King Midas and the Golden Touch." It was first presented on February 12, 1944.

You will see that along with the parts for the characters, there is also a part for sound. Each time you see this part, there will be a suggestion for a sound effect that should be created in that place.

If you have a tape recorder in your classroom, you may wish to record the script with the sound effects. And then you can present your own *Let's Pretend* show.

KING MIDAS AND THE GOLDEN TOUCH

Nila Mack

CHARACTERS:

Announcer

King Midas

Catalan, the king's advisor

Professor Messor, the king's scientist

Marygold, the king's daughter

Aurum, the spirit of gold

Landers, the king's servant

Leandra, the king's maid

Announcer: Once upon a time, there lived a very rich king whose name was Midas. He had a little daughter whom he named Marygold. He'd chosen this name especially because it had *gold* in it. Gold was the thing he liked best in all the world—next to the little princess herself. King Midas had great quantities of gold in his treasure room, but he was always trying to figure out ways to get more. Right now he's talking to his advisor, Catalan.

Sound: *Happy music* (5 seconds then fade out)

Midas: War ... that's one way to get gold, Catalan. But if I declared war on some country, some of my soldiers would surely perish.

Catalan: There are plenty of kings who wouldn't let that stop them. You have a heart of gold, Your Majesty. You don't want your subjects to suffer.

Midas: Heart of gold! Can I put *that* in my treasure room? Can I weigh it? Feel it in my hand?

Catalan: Well, no, sire, but . . .

Midas: And that scientist, Professor Messor! Is he making any progress turning brass into gold?

Catalan: He's trying, Your Majesty. He's always working with those chemicals and potions. So far, there's been nothing, but . . .

Sound: *Dull explosion* (drop a heavy book on the desk)

Catalan *(as explosion dies out):* . . . explosions.

Sound: *Door opens, hurried steps* (hold shoes in your hand and use them to make running sounds on the table)

Professor: I'm sorry, Your Majesty. It was just a slight mistake.

Midas: I hope you weren't hurt.

Professor: No, Your Majesty.

Midas: And I take it you're no closer to finding a magic formula for making gold than you were yesterday—or a year ago.

Professor: Sire, we seek to unlock the riddle that has puzzled people for centuries. We can't hope to find an answer quickly.

Midas: I'm beginning to wonder if we can find the answer in a lifetime.

Professor: I'll get back to work at once, sire. *(Fading)* Have faith, Your Highness!

Marygold *(fading in):* Are you busy now, Father?

Midas: Never too busy for a "good morning" from my little Marygold. How are you today?

Marygold: Fine, Father. I've brought you a present from the garden! Buttercups and daffodils!

Midas: Very pretty, little one . . . the color of gold. Just think. If they really were gold, they'd be worth a king's ransom.

Marygold: But Father, you don't need to be ransomed from anybody. What use is more gold?

Midas: Child, you talk of things you don't understand. Now run along and play.

Marygold: Couldn't you come out with me for a while?

Midas: No, Marygold. It's time now for me to go to the treasure house with Catalan. I have to count my gold, little daughter. It's for you I'm collecting it. . . . So you'll always have everything you want.

Marygold: The only thing I want is to spend more time with you.

Midas: Just wait, Marygold. When I've finally collected enough, we'll be together all the time.

Marygold *(sighs):* It just seems like you'll never have enough. *(Fading)* Goodbye, Father. Goodbye, Catalan.

Sound: *Fading footsteps*

Catalan: Goodbye, little princess.

Sound: *Door closes*

Midas: Well, then. Come along to the underground vaults and help me count what's there.

Sound: *Happy music* (5 seconds)

Sound: *Clink of metal bowls*

Catalan *(fading in):* That's ten thousand and fifteen golden bowls.

Midas: And how many bags of gold did you say?

Catalan: Two million, sire.

Midas: A goodly number, but it's not enough.
All right, Catalan. Take those tally sheets into
the next room and come back as soon as
you have the totals.

Catalan *(fading):* Yes, sire.

Sound: *Fading footsteps, door shuts*

Midas: Golden bowls, bars of gold, gold in bags,
and gold in boxes. But it's not enough. It's
hardly a handful compared to what I might
have. Oh, I want all the gold in the world!
All of it!

Sound: *Tambourine shakes*

Midas *(startled):* What was that?

Sound: *Cymbals crash*

Aurum: Greetings, King Midas.

Midas: Who is this? Is it a dream?

Aurum: No, King Midas, it is not a dream. I am
Aurum, the Spirit of Gold.

Midas: The Spirit of Gold! No wonder you appear
so golden. Why have you come to me?

Aurum: I know that you have much gold, King Midas. But I know that you do not think you have enough. What would satisfy you, my king? Perhaps I might help you.

Midas: You might? Oh, my, I'd better think of a really worthwhile wish. I . . . I . . . I have it! Aurum, Spirit of Gold, I wish that everything that I touch be turned to gold!

Aurum: Are you quite sure this will make you happy?

Midas: How could it fail?

Aurum: Very well. Tomorrow, with the first rays of the rising sun, you will find yourself gifted with . . . THE GOLDEN TOUCH.

Sound: *Tambourine shakes, then cymbals crash*

Midas: He's gone. Can what he promised be true? Tomorrow at sunrise will I have THE GOLDEN TOUCH!

Sound: *Happy music* (5 seconds), *rooster crows in distance* (have someone crow like a rooster)

Midas *(yawns):* Oh that roo . . . oh my goodness! Today's the day. Landers! Confound that man . . . never around when you want him! Landers!

Sound: *Running steps fade in*

Landers *(fading in):* Sire! Is something wrong?

Midas: Of course not. Why aren't you properly dressed?

Landers: But, sire . . . it isn't even daylight yet. The sun . . .

Midas: Never mind. Let me touch something. The bell cord! It would look very fine if it were gold.

Sound: *Little bells ring in distance five times*

Leandra *(fading in, breathless):* Yes, Your Majesty?

Midas: It didn't work. Why are you two staring
at me?

Landers: Sire, you've never been up before the
sun before.

Midas: The sun isn't up yet. That's what it is.
All right, girl. You can run along now.
Landers, fix my shaving things.

Sound: *Water splashing* (splash water in a large
bowl)

Midas: I'll busy myself shaving. Any sign of the
sun yet, Landers?

Landers: It's just barely visible at the horizon.

Midas: Soon, soon! I'll know soon.

Sound: *Splash is suddenly followed by ring of
metal* (splash water and hit empty metal bowl
with wooden spoon)

Midas: By all the powers, it's happened. Landers!
Look! The water's turned to gold!

Landers: Sire?

Midas: Bring me the china pitcher!

Sound: *Pitcher rattles followed by ring of metal*
(tap two china cups together and hit empty
metal bowl with wooden spoon)

Landers: What's happening here?

Midas: Can't you see what's happening? My
clothes, Landers! Bring them to me quickly.

Landers: Your shirt and trousers, sire.

Sound: *Rattle of aluminum foil*

Midas: My shirt and trousers are gold!

Landers: Heavens above us!

Midas: My boots, Landers. Bring me my boots!

Sound: *Clump of boot followed by ring of metal*

Midas: Gold boots. But is it real gold? The scientist! Professor Messor! He will know. I'll show my boots to him right now. Oh, wait until Marygold sees what I can do.

Sound: *Running footsteps with a clanging sound*

Midas *(panting):* Professor Messor! Look at my boots!

Professor: Why, they are gold, sire.

Midas: Real gold, Professor? Test them. Scratch them. Do whatever you do!

Professor: I don't have to do anything. I can see they are real gold. Pure gold, but . . .

Midas: It's happened! It's happened! Anything I touch turns to gold!

Professor: But, sire, how? . . .

Midas: You don't believe I can do it? Well, just look. I'll pick up this wooden stool.

Sound: *Scrape of wood followed by clang of metal*

Midas: It's pure gold. I have only to touch anything, and it's pure gold! It's the golden touch!

Professor: You have only to touch things and they're transformed! What will I do? I've been working my whole life to change brass to gold. What do I do *now*?

Midas: I don't know, Professor. But I know what I'm going to do. I'm going to find Marygold and show her what I can do.

Sound: *Hurrying steps*

Midas *(fading out):* Marygold! Marygold!

Sound: *Happy music (10 seconds)*

Sound: *Clink of china being set down*

Leandra: His breakfast is here, but he is not. Oh, what is going on this morning?

Landers: Come here, Leandra. Look out the window and see for yourself.

Leandra: Why he's racing from flower to flower. And he's touching each one.

Landers: And laughing like a crazy man. But he's coming this way now. You'll soon see for yourself.

Leandra: What will I see?

Landers: Shhh—here he comes.

Sound: *Door opens*

Midas *(fading in, excited):* Marygold? Is she here?

Landers: No, Your Majesty. She just went out into the garden.

Midas: I must have just missed her. Well, she's sure to be along for breakfast very soon. I'm starving. Bring on the eggs, Leandra.

Sound: *China being set down on table*

Midas: Ah eggs! I'm starving.

Sound: *Metal dropping on plate* (drop coins into empty metal bowl)

Midas: Ow!

Leandra: Your Majesty! What happened?

Midas: I've burned my fingers to the bone on that hunk of molten metal—that's what! My goodness! I turned that egg into gold. *(Frightened a little)* But what am I going to eat? I'm hungry! Will every bite of food turn into gold before I can. . .?

(MARYGOLD *fades in crying*)

Marygold, what is it?

Marygold: Oh, Father, a dreadful thing has happened. My garden—my beautiful garden is ruined. Something awful has happened to every flower.

Midas: Not *awful*, Marygold.

Marygold: All the flowers are hard metal. There's no fragrance. The petals scratch me. What could have happened?

Midas: Marygold, don't cry. Look! Isn't this a beautiful golden rose?

Marygold: It isn't. I hate it that way.

Midas: Marygold! Please, dear! Oh, I hate to see you so unhappy. . . . Come here to your father.

Marygold *(sobbing):* Oh, Father, change them back.

Midas: Come here, dear.

Sound: *Cling of a big metal object being tapped, then thud of a heavy object being set down*

Midas *(shocked):* Marygold! What have I done! My daughter has turned to gold!

Sound: *Funeral music (10 seconds)*

Midas: I shall be in my room all afternoon, Landers. Please see that I am not disturbed.

Landers: Yes, Your Majesty.

Sound: *Fading footsteps, door closes*

Midas: Great Aurum, I would do anything to have my little girl alive. I would give everything I have.

Sound: *Tambourine shakes*

Midas *(pleadingly):* Aurum, do you hear?

Sound: *Cymbals crash*

Aurum: Well, Midas?

Midas: Aurum? You're here. Oh, Spirit of Gold, help me.

Aurum: King Midas with the golden touch. How can *you* need help?

Midas: The golden touch has cost me everything that was worthwhile.

Aurum: Then you have made a discovery?

Midas: Oh, I have learned too well . . . and too late.

Aurum: Let me see. Which of these two things do you think is worth more—the golden touch or a crust of bread?

Midas: A piece of bread is worth all the gold on earth.

Aurum: The golden touch or your little daughter?

Midas: Oh, my child. Restore her to me! Help me, Aurum. Have pity! Help me!

Aurum: You are wiser than you were, my king. At last you seem to see that the commonest things are more valuable than riches. Tell me, do you really wish to be rid of your golden touch?

Midas: Oh, yes. With all my heart.

Aurum: Then go to the river that glides past the bottom of your garden. Plunge into it. Take with you a vase and fill it with river water. If your promise is true, if you have really cleansed your soul of greed for gold, you will be able to undo this tragedy.

Midas: And bring Marygold back to life?

Aurum: Sprinkle the water over her, and she will be restored. If you are honest within yourself, she will have no memory of what has happened.

Midas: Aurum, with all my heart I thank you.

Sound: *Cymbals crash*

Leandra: Where was he going when he rushed out of here with that vase, Landers?

Landers: "To the river," he said. Oh, my poor king. No wonder he is distraught. Look at the little girl princess. Just look at her.

Leandra: A golden statue. The poor child.

Landers: Shh. Here he comes back again. The vase is full of water!

Sound: *Footsteps hurry in*

Midas: Landers and Leandra. See to it that whatever happens in the next few moments you keep to yourselves. I ask this, not as your king, but as a father who loves his child.

Landers and Leandra: Yes, Your Majesty.

Midas: And now, Spirit of Gold, if honesty is the test, let my child be restored.

Sound: *Swoosh of water* (empty pitcher of water all at once into empty metal bowl)

Marygold *(coughs and sputters)*: Father! What on earth are you doing? You've splashed my new dress, and I just put it on this morning.

Midas: Forgive me for spoiling the dress, my child. We'll get another one. We'll play like today is your birthday. We'll have a real celebration. How's that?

Marygold: Terrific! What shall we do first?

Midas: Well, first we can take this vase of water and go sprinkle all the flowers in the garden. We'll change them back from golden flowers to the soft kind you love.

Marygold: How wonderful, Father.

Midas: Then we shall order the carriage and drive through the streets. You shall throw gold pieces from my treasure room to everyone you see.

Marygold: Father, really? We've never done anything like that before!

Midas: No, but we will from now on! Landers, order the carriage.

Landers: Certainly, sire. Anything for our little princess! She's worth her weight in gold.

Midas: What did you say?

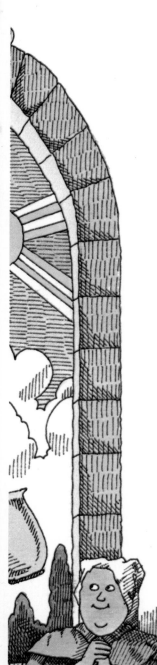

Landers: Why I only said she's worth her weight in...

Sound: *Metal crashes* (drop metal bowl on the table)

Landers: Ow!

Sound: *Door slams*

Marygold: Father, you threw a gold bowl at Landers. You almost hit him. What's the matter with you?

Midas: Well, somehow, I just don't like that expression any more . . . worth her weight in gold.

Sound: *Door opens*

Professor *(fading in):* Oh, Your Majesty, here you are. Oh, what *am* I going to do now that you can turn anything to gold with a touch.

Midas: Professor Messor! I'm happy to tell you I have lost my golden touch and you can now resume your search for a way to turn brass to gold.

Professor: Sire, really?

Midas: Really. And you have my permission to spend the rest of your life looking—in vain.

Sound: *Triumphant finale music* (ten seconds)

ZOOMING IN ON ZOOM

A. Whitney

Have you ever stopped to think about what goes into preparing a television show? We thought it would be interesting to find out, so we went to station WGBH in Boston. That's where the program *Zoom* is taped each week. We chose *Zoom* because the material for the show is written almost entirely by the youngsters who watch it. There have been many programs for young people since television became popular. But *Zoom* is the first to be written by young viewers.

Like all television shows, *Zoom* started out as an idea. Chris Sarson, who has worked in television for many years, wanted to give young people a chance to have a show that was really their own. It took three years of work and planning before the first *Zoom* program went on the air in January 1971. Since then, *Zoom* has been viewed on television stations all over the country.

265

Most television shows have script writers who write the material that will be used. The "script writers" for *Zoom* are the show's viewers. They supply all the material used on *Zoom* except the musical production numbers. These are prepared by a musical director and a choreographer.

Each day between 1,500 and 20,000 letters arrive at the *Zoom* mailroom. Youngsters from all over the country send riddles, games, plays, recipes, experiments, and stories that they would like to see presented on the show. Many fan letters are received in the mailroom, too. A staff of volunteers reads through each letter and decides which ones contain material that might be presented on the show.

The producer, director, and editors of *Zoom* read through the material sent them from the mailroom and decide which things will be used.

The seven youngsters who perform on *Zoom* each week are called "Zoomers." They rehearse after school two afternoons a week at the WGBH studio.

Like most television programs, *Zoom* is not performed at the time that you see it. *Zoom* is recorded on video tape. That is why the same program can be seen at different times and on different days all over the country.

On a typical taping day, the production schedule for *Zoom* begins several hours before the Zoomers arrive from school.

At one o'clock the people who work the lights arrive. They have to make sure that all of the lights are working, and that they have the lights they need in the right places.

At two o'clock another group of people arrives at the studio. They check the three television cameras to be used that day. Then they place the microphones where they belong and make sure that the scenery to be used is all together and looks right.

By 3:30 the Zoomers arrive at the studio. They rehearse their musical number a little more to smooth out any rough spots. While this is going

on, *Zoom's* director rehearses the camera crew so that they know which cameras will be used at certain points during the show. The lighting director makes sure that the proper lighting has been arranged.

At four o'clock the cameras are ready to roll! The first item to be taped is a musical number. The Zoomers take their places. Lights, camera, action. The number has been taped. But wait. A couple of Zoomers were out of step. Better try it again. The Zoomers go through the number again before the cameras. It usually takes between two and six "takes" to get a final product that is perfect.

As the Zoomers dance, they move their lips to look like they are singing. But they aren't. The song is taped separately from the dance so the Zoomers sound clear and not out of breath. This song tape is then played along with the dance tape so it looks like the Zoomers are singing and dancing at the same time. This way of taping is common in television.

At five o'clock, the Zoomers and the crew eat supper. They still have several hours to go before this week's production work will be finished.

At six o'clock the Zoomers and the crew are back in the studio. While the performers rehearse the play they will tape, the crew sets up the scenery needed for the play.

Seven o'clock. Time to tape the play. The Zoomers take their positions. Lights, camera, action. A "take" is made. Then, another and maybe another, just to be sure.

At 8 o'clock the crew and cast take a break. But not for long. Because at 8:15 everybody is back at work again. There are many other things to be taped: riddles, games, experiments, and recipes, to name a few. The cameras and people work until 9:30. Then, between 9:30 and 10 o'clock, the cameras and lights are unplugged and the scenery is removed. In the morning, the studio may be used to tape a different show.

The day in the studio is over. About three hours of tape have been made. But there is still one more step before *Zoom* can go on the air.

This next step in preparing the television program is called editing. Editing is the way in which the best scenes from the video tape are selected for the final production.

In editing, the pieces that were taped are viewed, and it is decided which ones will actually be used on a telecast. Only one "take" of the musical number and the play will be used. And, for example, some of the games or experiments that have been taped may be shortened. So although the cameras have worked for about three hours, the final product is a *Zoom* program thirty minutes long. So there you are. Now *Zoom* is ready to go on the air.

Next time you turn on your favorite television program, think of all the steps and the people that are needed to produce one show. Now you know it's not as easy as it looks.

Prove It!

You probably see and hear many advertisements each day. They are on television and on radio. They appear in newspapers and magazines. To be a smart buyer, you must study ads carefully. First, decide if each statement is a fact or an opinion.

A *fact* is a statement that can be proven true or false. You can check facts by looking in reference books or by seeing for yourself if they are true. The statement, "A box of *Golden Pancake Mix* costs thirty-nine cents," is a fact. You can check its truth by looking at the box.

An *opinion* is a statement that tells someone's belief about something. It cannot be proven true or false. The statement, "*Golden Pancakes* taste good," is an opinion. To some people, this statement may be true. Other people may not agree that *Golden Pancakes* taste good.

ACTIVITY A   Read each statement. Write **Fact** if the statement is a fact. Write Opinion if it is an opinion.

1. *Dento* toothpaste comes in three different sizes.
2. *Dento* toothpaste has a delicious flavor.
3. This toothpaste smells good, too.
4. *Dento* toothpaste is selling at halfprice this week.
5. *Dento* contains a compound called *hexifloride*.
6. The design on the tube is beautiful.
7. The Dento Company also sells toothbrushes.
8. The tube is printed in white and blue.
9. *Dento* is the best selling toothpaste in the country.

An advertisement can offer two types of opinions. *Personal opinion* is a belief based on one person's feelings about something. *Expert testimony* is the opinion of an expert in the field. You should trust expert testimony more than you trust personal opinion.

Suppose you saw two car advertisements. In one ad, a movie star said that a car was safe. In the other ad, a driving teacher said that a car was safe. You should trust the second opinion more than the first. The driving teacher is an expert in handling cars.

ACTIVITY B   Imagine that each statement below appears in an advertisement. Read each statement. Then read the descriptions of the two people who might have made the statement. On your paper, write the description of the person whose opinion is the most trustworthy.

1. *Growrite* vitamins are good for you.
   a. a doctor of medicine
   b. a doctor of engineering

2. *Pepso* chewing gum is fine for your teeth.
   a. a famous baseball player
   b. a dentist

3. *Dudso* detergent is best for washing clothes.
   a. the owner of a laundry
   b. the owner of a shoe store

4. *Tracto* tires are dependable in bad weather.
   a. a taxi driver
   b. a well-known comedian

5. *Saf-T* toys are the safest toys for babies.
   a. a small child
   b. a nursery-school director

May 1, 1972

Dear Senator Moss,

My name is Dawn A Kurth. I am 11 years old and in 5th grade at Meadowlane Elementary school in Melbourne Florida Recently I was selected by my teachers to do a project in the Talented Student Program in Brevard.

My project is the study of deceptive advertising towards parents through children. Recently I have received a copy of your bill and I read It with interest

I thought you might be interested in seeing a survey I made on children's reaction towards T.V. commercials (I inclued the survey in with this letter)

I recently met Mr. Robert B. Choate and he told me your committee would be holding hearings about advertising and children in May. I was wondering If you would like me to come and give a child's veiw of the whole thing and tell the committee about my survey.

Thank You Dawn A. Kurth

274

Commercials and you

Dawn Kurth

When Dawn Kurth was in the fifth grade, she decided that TV commercials were often misleading and even harmful.

Dawn drew up a questionnaire about TV advertising. She wanted to see if other youngsters shared her views. She learned that many youngsters buy products advertised on TV to get free gifts. And she learned that many youngsters are very disappointed with the gifts they receive.

Then Dawn heard that the United States Senate was holding a special hearing about TV commercials. She went to Washington to tell her story. You will read about it on the following pages.

My name is Dawn Ann Kurth. On May 31, 1972,
I testified before the Senate Commerce Committee.
I told the Committee about a project I had done. I
had studied TV commercials that are aimed at kids.
I thought my appearance at the hearing would
be the end of my project. But as it has turned out, it
was the beginning of the most exciting thing that has
ever happened to me.

It all started last fall. Our school began a new
program. The program gave kids a chance to do a
project in any field they wanted. I wanted to do a
project that would maybe help the world be a little
better for people. At the same time, my sister Martha
had a problem. She had asked my mother to buy a
certain brand of cereal. It had a free record on the
back of the box. My mother finally bought the cereal.
But when Martha got the record, it wouldn't work.
She was really upset. She asked my mother to buy
the cereal again to get another record that might work
better.

I began to think about what was happening. It really made me mad. I had seen the commercial that advertised the record. It really worked well on TV. People were laughing and dancing to it. I knew it wasn't right that my sister had been fooled. I felt that maybe lots of other kids had the same problem. That is when I decided to investigate commercials shown on kid's TV programs.

The first thing I did was to sit down and keep a record of all the commercials shown on Saturday morning. There were so many, my mother had to help me write them down. Then I began to think about the messages that the commercials were giving to kids. Many of the commercials were misleading or told kids things that didn't make sense.

Some of the commercials were dangerous. They were advertising vitamin pills by telling kids how good they were. They were comparing vitamins to chocolate cookies. I knew that if my three-year-old sister were to get a bottle of those pills, she would eat them all. I felt it was wrong to advertise something to kids that said on the bottle, "Keep out of the reach of children."

My next step was to find out if kids really believed the commercials. I surveyed 1,540 kids. I tried to find out how they felt about commercials. When I got the results of my survey, I knew that TV commercials influence kids a lot. So I decided to do what I could to make them better and more truthful.

I began writing letters. I wrote to anyone I thought would help. That is how I heard about the Senate Commerce Committee hearing. I wrote to Senator Moss. I asked if the senators would like me to come to the hearing. I said I would like to give a kid's view of television ads directed at kids.

I wrote to the committee. But I really didn't expect to be asked to come to Washington. Then a few days later, my mother got a phone call from the committee. The committee was interested in what I had to say. My mother was very excited. She couldn't wait for me to come home. My mother came to school to tell me!

My mother and I went to Washington the day before the hearing. The next morning, we walked to the Senate Office Building. That's where the hearing was going to be held. In the hearing room, the networks were setting up TV cameras. Reporters were running in and out. Some of them talked to me. And some were surprised to hear that I was going to testify. I was the second witness. I didn't hear too much of what the first one said.

Then my name was called. The senators sat on a raised platform at the front of the room. The witness table was in front of them. There was a typist taking down everything that was said. All the testimony was going into the *Congressional Record*. I sat at the witness table.

Here is some of my testimony:

To begin my project, I kept a record of the number of commercials shown on Saturday morning TV shows. There were twenty-five commercials during one hour, from 8:00 to 9:00 A.M. This is not counting ads for shows coming up or public service ads. I found there were only ten to twelve commercials during shows my parents like to watch. For the first time, I really began to think about what commercials were saying. I had always listened to them before. And many times, I had asked my mother to buy certain products I had seen. But now I was really listening. And I was thinking about what was said.

One type of commercial advertises a free bonus gift if you buy a certain product. The commercial tells about the bonus gift. It says nothing about the product they want you to buy. Many times, the bonus gift is worthless junk or isn't in the package. I wrote to the TV networks. They told me it costs about $4,000 for a thirty-second commercial. Many of those ads appeared four times in each hour. Why would any company spend $15,000 or $20,000 an hour to advertise worthless junk?

These ads I consider misleading. But others I feel are dangerous.

Some vitamin ads say their vitamins taste "yummy."

Let's say my mother were to buy those vitamins. If my little sister found them, I am sure she would eat them as if they were candy.

I do not know a lot about nutrition. But I do know that my mother tries to keep us from eating so many sweets. She says they are bad for our teeth. Our dentist says so, too. If they are bad, why are companies allowed to make children want them by advertising?

I know the people who make these commercials are not bad. I know the commercials pay for TV shows. And I like to watch TV. I just think that it would be as easy to produce a good commercial as a bad one. If nothing good can be said about a product that is the truth, perhaps it should not be sold in the first place.

I do not know all the ways to write a good commercial. But I think commercials would be good if they taught kids something. Something that was true and maybe educational. They could teach about good health. They could tell kids about where food is grown.

People who write commercials are much smarter than I. They should be able to think of many ways to write a commercial that tells the truth about a product. They should not tell kids to eat a cereal because it is the world's sweetest or because it's "shaped like fun." What shape is fun, anyway?

I also think kids should not be bribed by commercials telling of wonderful free bonus gifts.

Kids should not be told to eat a certain product because a well-known hero does.

I think vitamin companies should be more careful. They should never be allowed to say vitamins are delicious or yummy. They should not make the children think vitamins are candy. Perhaps these commercials could teach children the dangers of taking drugs. Or they could teach children to tell a grownup if they find a bottle of pills. And they should tell kids never to eat the medicine.

I want to thank the Commerce Committee and especially Chairman Moss, for letting me appear. When I leave Washington, D.C., I will remember for the rest of my life that people do care what kids think. I know I could have led a protest about commercials through our shopping center. People would have laughed at me. Or they would have thought I needed a good spanking. Or they would have wondered what kind of parents I had that would let me protest. Instead I gathered my information and wrote letters to anyone I thought would listen. Many of them didn't listen. But some did. That is why I am here today. Because some people cared about what I thought. Now I can tell all the kids in America that when they see a wrong that needs to be right, they shouldn't just forget about it. They should not just hope it will go away. They should begin to do what they can to change it. People will listen. I know, because you're here listening to me.

Thank you.

After I finished testifying, the senator called a short recess. A lot of reporters came over to me. They asked me what I wanted to be when I grew up and things like that. There were two more witnesses. Then the hearing was over.

After lunch I met some more senators. We spent the rest of the afternoon touring the Capitol. Then we watched the news on TV. When they talked about the hearing, I was very happy. I knew a lot of people would be watching. Maybe some of them would write letters to their senators or representatives in congress about ads that fool kids.

That night I really slept well. In fact I overslept.
I nearly missed being on a TV morning news program. It
was my first time in a TV studio. I was very busy looking
around. I almost forgot to talk.

After that we visited the senator from Florida and our
representative in congress. Next I visited the Federal
Trade Commission, the FTC. I was very happy to do that.
The people there have the power to correct much of what
is wrong with TV ads. They said they were glad that I came.
They wished everyone would tell them about problems
they have with ads. This is the best way they have of
finding out what needs to be investigated.

When we left the FTC, it was almost time to go to the airport. I was anxious to get home. I wanted to tell the rest of my family about everything that had happened.

Finally the plane landed in Florida. There were lots of reporters and photographers waiting for me. My family was there. My fifth-grade teacher, the principal of my school, and members of the school board were there. And lots of friends were there. I can honestly say it was the happiest moment of my life.

The next day was Friday. I went to school. We didn't do too much studying. Everybody wanted to hear about my trip. All the kids were really interested in everything that had happened. Most of them would like to see ads made better. But some of them are worried.

They are afraid that, if companies stop advertising, we won't have any TV shows. I told them that companies didn't have to stop advertising. They should just make their ads more truthful. And they should give kids useful information. Then kids can make wise choices before they buy something. I think this is important. Kids should learn to be wise consumers.

Since the hearing, I have been on several radio and TV shows. And there have been a lot of things written in the paper about me. It is always exciting and a lot of fun when I'm on a show. But it hasn't changed me. Everyone who knows me treats me just the same. And that is how I like it. Most grownups ask me what I'm going to do next. I think they are happy a kid cares about what is going on. I have received dozens of letters. Most of them are from adults thanking me for my stand. They say they feel the same way I do. Because of all the letters and support, I'm going to keep working for better TV ads. Well, I would keep working for better ads even if I didn't get any support. I think what I'm doing is right. But encouragement from other kids and their parents makes it a lot easier.

In advertising, language is used in two ways. It is used *to state facts* about a product. It is also used *to persuade people* to buy the product.

Here is an example of the way language is used to state facts in an advertisement:

> Garden Juice is good for you. It is made from carrots, tomatoes, and celery. A glass of Garden Juice supplies you with Vitamins A and D.

Here is an example of the way language in advertising is used to persuade people to buy something:

> Drinking Garden Juice will make you first in your class. If you drink Garden Juice, you'll soon be stronger and healthier than you are now.

Now read the advertisement below. Find the sentences that state facts about the product. Then find the sentences that are used to persuade people to buy the product.

Mighty Milk is the best milk in the world. It is rich in Vitamin D. If you drink Mighty Milk, you will become the best player on your team. Mighty Milk is always fresh. It is delivered each day from a near-by dairy.

290

AT HOME
IN THE FUTURE

Alma Whitney

A telephone small enough to wear on your wrist? A trip to the library without leaving your home? A medical examination without a doctor or nurse in the room?

These ideas may seem strange to you. But today work is being done in communication systems that may turn these ideas into realities within your lifetime.

Let's pretend that we can visit the twenty-first century. We will visit a boy named Peter Smith. He has already awakened this morning. But he is not feeling too well.

Mrs. Smith, Peter's mother, wants the doctor to see Peter. That is, it would be a good idea for the doctor to *listen* to Peter. Mrs. Smith brings a set of wires to Peter's bedside. These wires are called sensors. She places one sensor in his mouth and one on his chest. She puts another one around his wrist and one on his forehead. Then she plugs the sensors into a wall outlet. She says the code "TCP. " This means *telephone call placed.* A little light flashes on the wall. This indicates that the Smith's wireless telephone is ready to accept a call.

Mrs. Smith says "2478." That's the doctor's phone number.

From a speaker on the wall the doctor's voice says, "Good morning."

"Good morning, Dr. Cooper," answers Mrs. Smith. "Peter isn't feeling too well this morning. I've hooked him up to the sensors. I wonder if you can examine him now."

"Sure," the doctor's voice says over the speaker. "Well, he doesn't appear to have any fever. And his pulse rate is fine. Now, breathe deeply, Peter."

Peter breathes deeply.

"Just a little congestion in the chest," announces the doctor. "A little cold. Better stay inside today. And take it easy."

"Thank you, Doctor," says Mrs. Smith. "TCC (telephone call complete)." The light on the wall turns off. The phone call and examination are finished.

"Peter," says Mrs. Smith, "as long as you have to stay home, why don't you shop? You could pick out your new bicycle. Your birthday's only two weeks away."

"Great," Peter answers.

To shop for the bicycle, Peter and his mother and father sit in front of one of the visionphones. There are several in their house.

Here is a business executive using a picturephone.

292

293

"TCP," says Peter. The word *ready* flashes on the screen of the visionphone.

"Do you know the number of the bicycle section at the merchandise center?" Mr. Smith asks Peter.

"Sure, Dad. It's 7752," Peter answers, loudly enough so that the call will go through.

"Eastwood Bicycle Shop," a voice says. "May we help you?"

Peter answers. "I'd like to see your line of ten-speed, two wheelers."

In the next few moments, pictures of many models of the bicycles are flashed on the screen of the Smith's visionphone. The price of each bike is also shown. After the last picture, a voice asks, "Is there a particular model that you wish to see again?"

"I'd like to see models 3 and 6," Peter answers. Pictures of models 3 and 6 are shown on the screen. A voice explains the features.

"I think number 6 is the one I really like," Peter tells his parents.

"Do you wish to place an order at this time?" asks a voice.

"Not just yet," says Mr. Smith. "My son's birthday isn't for two weeks. Thank you. TCC."

In the future, messages will be speeded through space by lasers like this one.

ITT Public Relations

The visionphone shuts off.

The shopping is finished. Peter's parents tell Peter they have to go out for a little while. "Why don't you visit the library while we're gone," Peter's dad suggests. "I know they have some new books about basketball."

Peter goes to one of the visionphones. He places a call to the library. He asks to see one of the new books on basketball.

The title, *Basketball Giants,* appears on the screen. "Turn," says Peter. The first page of the book appears on the screen. Peter has read about thirty pages of it. Then he hears his mother's voice coming through a speaker on the wall. Peter turns off the visionphone. He says hello to his mother.

"Where are you?" he adds.

"We're driving on the freeway," Mrs. Smith says. "This is taking a little more time than we thought. Better get some lunch for yourself."

"What are you doing?" Peter asks.

"We'll explain later," she says.

Peter goes to the kitchen. He thinks about what he would like to have for lunch. Pizza! That sounds like just the thing to have for lunch on a day when you're home with a cold. Peter walks over to the menu selector. He presses a button marked p. A drawer containing recipes that begin with that letter slides out of a cabinet. Peter pulls out the recipe for pizza. He drops it into the meal-maker. He turns a dial on the meal-maker to 1, meaning one portion.

While the meal-maker prepares the pizza, Peter takes a look at his treehouse. He's building it in the backyard. He switches on his home television camera and presses a button marked *yard.* Looking at the TV screen on the wall, he sees that the treehouse is in fine shape.

This city of the future will house 3000 people on ten acres of an 860 acre site.

It's just waiting for him to do some more work on it. Maybe tomorrow.

Beep, beep, beep. Lunch is ready. Peter returns to the meal-maker just in time to greet his pizza. It is coming out through a slot in the side of the machine.

The pizza is delicious. It really hits the spot. Peter is feeling much better now. He thinks he'll be well enough to go to school tomorrow. Thinking of school, Peter remembers that there is supposed to be a math test tomorrow. It is a math test for which he could use some studying. It's nice and quiet in the Smith's house now. A perfect time to study.

Peter walks to the home study center. It is located next to the living room. He seats himself in front of a small picture screen. Then he pushes the button marked *connect*. His home study unit is now hooked up to a central computer located 100 miles from his house.

"Hello, this is Peter," he types on the key board beneath the little screen. Peter watches as his message appears on the screen. After a moment his message disappears, and "Hello, Peter, what do you wish to do?" flashes in its place.

"Multiplication. Two-place numbers," Peter types.

An example appears on the screen in front of Peter:

$$72 \times 28$$

Peter sets up his work. He types:

$$\begin{array}{r} 28 \\ \underline{\times 72} \end{array}$$

"You are correct. Proceed to next step," flashes on the screen.

Peter types:

$$\begin{array}{r} 28 \\ \underline{\times 72} \\ 56 \\ \underline{193} \\ 1986 \end{array}$$

More than 98 per cent of the land will remain for agriculture and recreation.

S. S. Tommy, The Cosanti Foundation.

"Error" flashes on the screen. "Review multiplication tables 7 and 8."

Peter groans. He has been getting some of his multiplication facts mixed up lately. But he will practice them now. By tomorrow he should have them all under control.

Peter sits at the home study center for the next fifteen minutes, reviewing the two multiplication tables. When he is finished, he is able to do the original example correctly. A star flashes on the screen when Peter types "2016."

"You have done very well. What else do you wish to do?" appears on the screen.

"That is all for today. Thank you," Peter answers by typing the message on the keyboard.

Peter feels a little sleepy now. He goes to his room to take a nap. He is awakened after a while by a buzzing sound. It is his wireless phone letting him know that someone is calling him.

"TCA (telephone call accepted)," says Peter without getting up from his bed.

"Peter, it's Karl. How are you doing?"

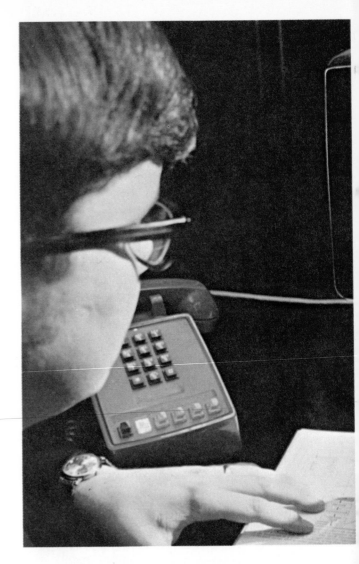

"Pretty well," Peter answers without getting up. "How was school today?"

"Oh, fine," Karl's voice says. "We had a ball game during lunch. You should have been there. We could have used you."

"I'll be back tomorrow," Peter says. "Thanks for calling. TCC."

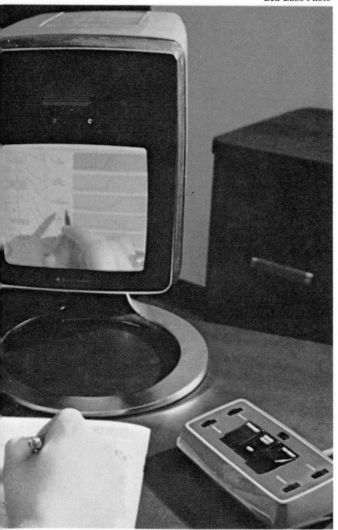

A few minutes later, Peter gets up when he hears his parents come in. They're finally back. And they've got something with them. It's a pretty big box. About the size that could hold, say, a bicycle.

"Here it is," Mr. Smith says. "Model 6."

Peter is excited. And he is surprised to be getting his bicycle so early.

"Wow! Thanks!" he tells his parents. "But why did you go all the way to the merchandise center yourselves? You could have placed the order by phone and had the bicycle delivered."

Mrs. Smith explains. "In the old days," she says, "people actually used to go *out* of the house to shop for things. They went to places called stores. It was kind of exciting, we've heard. You could see and touch all the different things there were to choose from. Oh, sure. It had drawbacks. For one thing, it took longer than visionphone shopping. But we thought it would be fun to try it. So we drove to the merchandise center. We asked if we might be able to go in and pick out your bicycle ourselves. They looked at us as though we were crazy. But they let us in."

"Oh," says Peter, examining the gears on his new model 6. "How was it?"

"Great," says his mother. "It was really fun. Maybe some day soon we'll try it again."

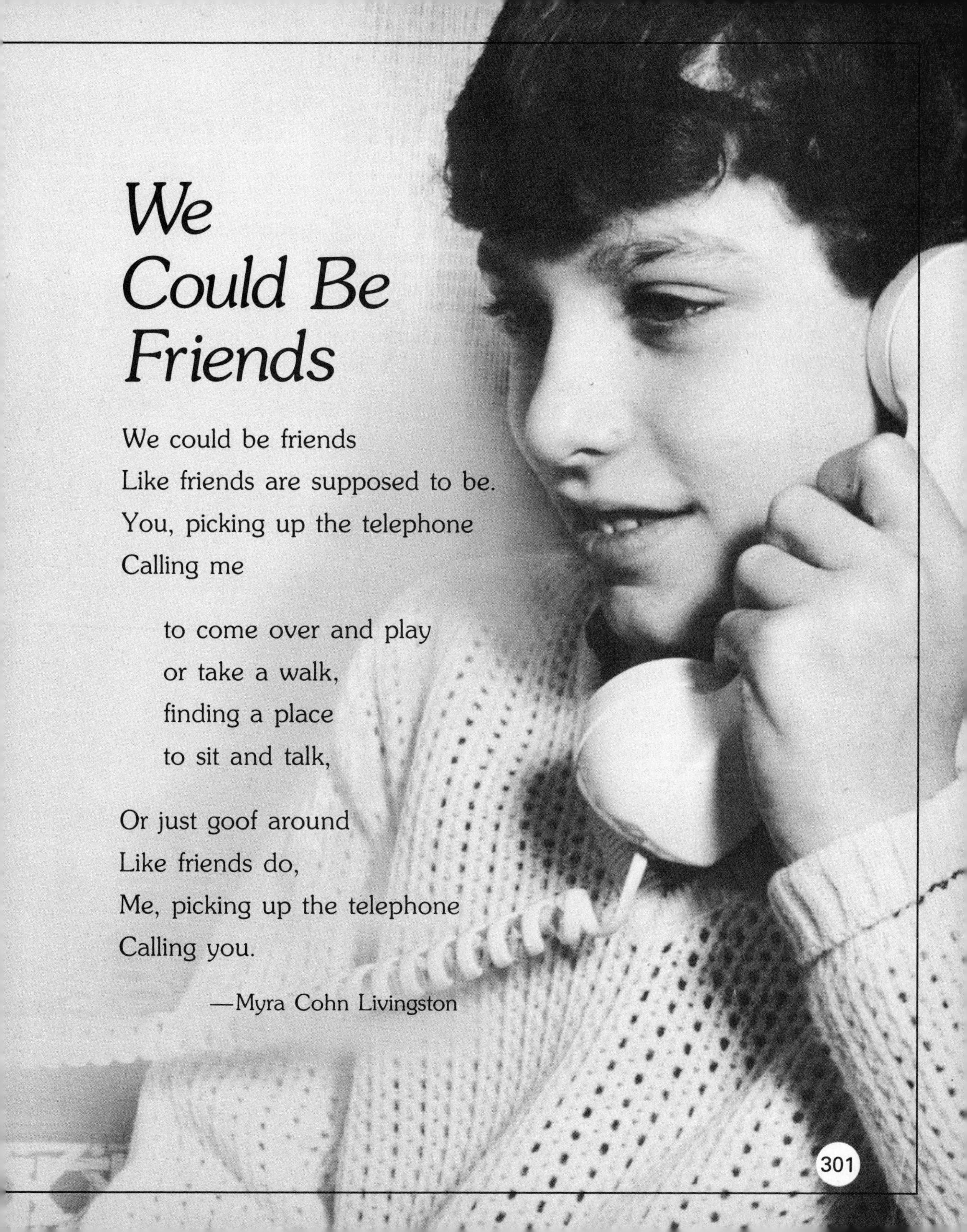

We Could Be Friends

We could be friends
Like friends are supposed to be.
You, picking up the telephone
Calling me

to come over and play
or take a walk,
finding a place
to sit and talk,

Or just goof around
Like friends do,
Me, picking up the telephone
Calling you.

—Myra Cohn Livingston

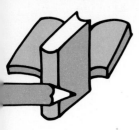

What Do You Mean By That?

Did you hear about the children who wanted a snack? All they had was a calendar. So they ate dates.

That story is funny because *dates* has two different meanings. A *date* can mean "a particular day," such as May 9. A *date* can also mean "a type of fruit."

Many words have more than one meaning. When you read such a word, you need to know which meaning applies. You can usually tell by the way the word is used in the sentence. Read the following sentence:

   I think what I'm doing is right.

The word *right* has more than one meaning. Sometimes, it means "correct." Other times, it means "the opposite of left." In the above sentence, the first meaning applies. You know because of the context clues in the sentence.

ACTIVITY A   Write each pair of sentences on your paper. Then read the two meanings for the underlined word. After each sentence, write the letter of the meaning that applies to the word in that sentence.

1. I am dressing now.
   The dressing tastes good.
   a. a sauce for salads
   b. putting on clothes

2. The rose is pink.
   He rose from the bed.
   a. a type of flower
   b. got up

3. Let's light a candle.
   This package is light.
   a. not heavy
   b. bright

4. A bat flew overhead.
   He swung the bat hard.
   a. an animal
   b. a wooden club

ACTIVITY B   Read each sentence. Then read the meanings for the underlined word. On your paper, write the letter of the meaning that is used in the sentence.

1. We watched the men box for thirty minutes.
   a. a container   b. to fight with gloved fists

2. Duck behind the bushes so the raccoon won't see you.
   a. to bend down   b. a bird that swims

3. The lines of cars created a heavy traffic jam.
   a. a type of food   b. a crowded condition

4. Doctors train their assistants at the hospital.
   a. to teach   b. a line of railroad cars

5. I can fast for ten hours without getting hungry.
   a. quick, speedily   b. to go without food

6. The movie I saw last night was fair.
   a. a carnival   b. not very good, but not bad

7. We left the two-dollar bill as the waiter's tip.
   a. paper money   b. a list of money owed

8. Do you know how to run that machine?
   a. to move quickly   b. operate

9. Sheila broke the point of her pencil.
   a. a purpose   b. a sharp end

10. His sentence didn't have a subject or a predicate.
    a. time in prison   b. words stating an idea

11. She tied her hair in a bun.
    a. a hairstyle   b. a kind of roll or bread

12. She added another coat of paint.
    a. a layer   b. something to wear

13. He felt blue about missing the big game.
    a. in low spirits   b. a color

SIGNALS

Both human beings and animals communicate. Animals send and receive messages by using smell, touch, sight, and hearing. People do not have to rely solely on the senses to communicate. As human beings, we have a special ability to convey messages by using words. We are always looking for new and better ways to convey thoughts and feelings to others.

Thinking About "Signals"

1. How did the Associated Press improve communication among newspaper people?
2. What is the theme of "King Midas and the Golden Touch"? What does it say about money, people, and happiness?
3. How might you use language differently when (a) speaking to a baby, and (b) testifying before a committee of the U.S. Senate?
4. How does the written word make communication easier than using picture writing?
5. How can a television show like "Zoom" help children all over the country communicate?
6. In what ways do you communicate with and without words?
7. Think of something that has happened in your community or school that you are happy about or would like to see changed. Write a letter to the editor of your local newspaper to express your opinion.

WONDERS

For thousands of years, people have wondered about the universe. People long ago made up stories to explain the stars, the moon, and the planets. As time went on, scientists developed instruments, such as the telescope. Then people were able to test old ideas and make new discoveries. More recently, astronauts have visited the moon to gather first-hand information about space.

The selections you will read in "Wonders" are about the wonders of the sky. Some of them are about real people and about events that really happened in the past. You will meet an early Greek astronomer and a girl from Cape Cod, Massachusetts. Both used telescopes to make new discoveries about the heavens. You will learn how slaves guided by the North Star escaped to freedom over a hundred years ago. Other stories describe imaginary characters and events that take place in the future. These stories are not real. Still, as you read them, you may find yourself wondering if the events could ever really happen.

Now, as always, people wonder about the universe. As you read, think of questions you would like answered about the stars, the moon, and the planets.

EARTH, MOON, AND SUN

While the earth spins on,
Turning, turning
Toward the sun,

The moon floats by
In its circle
In our sky.

And while it floats,
Earth and moon, two in one,
Rush on
With the bright planets
In a ring
Around the sun.

And as they rush
And swing
And turn
The gases of the sun
Swirl
And burn.

And all the while these three,
Swirling sun
And moon
And earth,
Spiral in the galaxy.

Spiral in that great wheel turning
With its billion stars
Sparkling,
Burning;

That starry wheel
Where you and I
Night and day
Are riding high,
Riding high!

—Claudia Lewis

Vincent Van Gogh: *The Starry Night*. (Detail) 1889. Oil on canvas,
(Collection, The Museum of Modern Art, New York.
Acquired through the Lillie P. Bliss Bequest)

GALILEO GALILEI

Arthur S. Gregor

This story takes place more than 400 years ago. At that time, much of science as we know it was unknown. For thousands of years, people had many inaccurate beliefs about their world. For example, they had never felt the earth move, so they believed that it was stationary in space. But people were beginning to question and to experiment in order to prove or disprove many of the old ideas. They were beginning to make discoveries about their earth and the skies above them. One of the first great scientists of this new age of science was Galileo.

From the time Galileo Galilei was a boy, he had thought about the stars—and wondered. In 1572, when he was only eight, a new star appeared in the sky. That was real excitement! Everybody in the city of Florence, Italy, where Galileo then lived, rushed to look at it.

But even Galileo's father, who let him stay up late to look at the sky filled with thousands of stars, couldn't answer all his questions. Because Galileo had asked so many questions, he knew the names of many of the stars.

"There's the Milky Way," he cried, pointing to a great white starry cloud that stretched across the sky. "I wonder what it is."

"Who can tell?" said his father. "It is all so far away."

Then Galileo looked at the new—and marvelous—star. "What is it made of?" he cried. "Where did it come from? Will it go away?"

His father laughed. "Always asking questions, aren't you? When you grow up, you will read the books of scholars. There you will find some of the answers."

In the sixteenth century, science was very young, and people usually made no effort to find out for themselves. If you wanted to know about the stars, you looked up a writer named Aristotle, who had lived two thousand years ago. Aristotle was supposed to have known everything that was to be known about nature—and science.

Aristotle had said the earth stood still in space. Well, you've never felt the earth moving, have you? So—Aristotle seemed to make good sense. At least he did until Galileo came along.

Galileo said, "When I grow up, I'd like to know *all* about the stars."

In 1604, Galileo was a grown man and a well-known teacher. That year something happened that changed Galileo's whole life. Another new star appeared in the sky. It glowed yellow, purple, red, and white. It was so bright that it could be seen during the day!

It shone for one-and-one-half years, and then, like the new star of 1572 that had so excited the young Galileo, it faded and disappeared. But while it blazed people wondered about it. What did it mean? Were new wars about to break out? Were plagues to sweep over the earth?

In those days, these were logical questions, since most people believed that the stars foretold the future. Today we know that the Star of 1604, as well as the Star of 1572, were *supernovas*, stars that explode like giant fireworks and scatter their fragments over the sky. There have been only three supernovas in the last thousand years—and Galileo lived to see two of them.

When Galileo announced that he was going to talk about the Star of 1604, vast crowds came to hear him.

"There is no need to be upset about this new star," he said. "The heavens are full of marvels that we can look at every day. What can be more marvelous than the daily rising of the sun? Yet you don't worry about that. The coming of this new star is just as natural as the rising of the sun!"

"But a new star is an impossibility," one of the professors said. "Aristotle tells us that the heavens are unchanging," the professor continued. "The sun is perfect without a single spot on it, while the moon also has a completely smooth surface. The planets and the stars, as well as the sun and the moon, go about the earth every day in a perfect circle. All is perfection in the universe. So Aristotle said."

Galileo took a deep breath. His eyes flashed. "I do not believe," he said, "that the heavens go around the earth. I believe that the earth is a planet that circles once a year about the sun!"

A murmur of voices arose in the room. People turned to each other in amazement. What was Professor Galileo saying?

For two thousand years, people had believed that the earth stood still in the very center of the universe, and once a day, the moon, the sun, the planets, and the stars circled around it. Aristotle had said so.

There was only one thing wrong with Galileo's belief: while it was reasonable, and it answered many more questions about the universe than did the theory of Aristotle, there was no real proof. How could Galileo be certain when the heavens were so far away?

Five years later, Galileo *was* able to bring the heavens closer! Word was brought to him that someone in Holland had invented a simple telescope.

Galileo set to work at once and built his own telescope by fitting glass lenses to the ends of a lead tube.

Galileo's first telescope appeared to bring things three times closer. Later, he built one he called "Old Discoverer," and with it, he brought objects thirty times closer than they could appear to the naked eye.

Crowds of people waited in line to look through Professor Galileo's magic glass. News of it soon reached even the powerful ruler of Venice, who was called the Doge. One morning, Galileo presented one of his best telescopes to the Doge. Thereupon one of the Doge's officers unfurled a long scroll of parchment and read as follows:

"Master Galileo Galilei, in return for your many inventions and especially for your new 'spyglass,' by which far-off things are brought closer, the Republic of Venice is honored to make you a professor for life and to offer you a salary of one thousand gold pieces a year."

Galileo bowed. It was the proudest moment of his life. While the entire city looked on, the noble company paraded across the square and climbed the bell tower.

On the roof, the Doge looked through this new telescope. "I see a great ship in full sail at least fifty miles off," the Doge cried. "With this spyglass we will be able to make out an enemy fleet long before it sees us."

But Galileo had other thoughts. He knew the best use for his invention. Now we would *really* be able to see the stars. That same night, he turned his favorite telescope, "Old Discoverer," toward the heavens.

At once vast areas of the sky that no mortal had ever seen flashed before him. Thousands upon thousands of stars blazed in the heavens. Astronomers had never dreamed of a sight like this!

Galileo made many important discoveries with his telescope. He found that the moon is not perfectly smooth and that mountains and valleys are on its surface. He also found that the moon does not give off its own light, but reflects light from the sun. For these and many other scientific discoveries, Galileo is remembered today as one of history's most important scientists.

Five Degrees From Polaris

Nina Link and Alma Whitney

Maria Mitchell sat in front of the blazing fire, talking with her mother and sister. But her mind was not on the conversation. She was thinking about her father. He was on the roof of the house looking at the heavens through his telescope.

Maria Mitchell's house looks the same today as it did when she made her famous discovery.

Mr. Mitchell was a well-known astronomer on the island of Nantucket in the 1800s. Nantucket was a great whaling community, and many sailors came to Mr. Mitchell for advice. Mr. Mitchell helped the sailors plot their routes by the stars. Sometimes he would even adjust their timepieces according to the stars.

Maria was just eleven, but she had been interested in astronomy since she was very little. She loved to look through her father's telescope and talk about the stars and planets with him.

Now it was Mr. Mitchell's voice that broke the silence in the living room. "Maria, Maria. Come up here quickly. I've something to show you."

Maria jumped up from her chair. She grabbed her coat and hood and a whale-oil lamp. She didn't look back as she raced up the stairs that led to the roof of the house.

Outside, the winter night was cold and windy. Waves pounded against the shores not far from the Mitchell house. And the whaling ships in the harbor groaned as they rocked back and forth. Their tall masts kept time with the sea.

But Maria had no time to think about such things as she made her way across the roof to where the telescope was perched.

"Come quickly," her father said. "Take a look at this. Look right below Polaris. Can you see it?"

Maria moved the telescope slightly until she sighted the North Star. Then she looked just below it. A fuzzy ball of light came into view. And behind it Maria could make out a glowing tail.

"It's a comet, Father, isn't it? I can't believe my eyes!"

"You're on your way to becoming an astronomer," Mr. Mitchell laughed. "I'm proud of you, Maria. That's just what it is. A comet. And right on time, too. Astronomers all over have expected this one to return right about now."

Mr. Mitchell smiled with delight to see how closely his young daughter watched the sky.

"All right, back to work," he said. "Do you know which comets have tails?"

"Big ones," Maria answered. Her eyes were still glued to the telescope.

"Right," said her father. "Smaller comets just look like fuzzy balls of light."

"And the tails of the big comets always point away from the sun," Maria added.

"Maria, you remember everything," Mr. Mitchell said. "Someday you will be a famous astronomer. You'll see."

"Someday you will both catch pneumonia," a voice called from the doorway. Maria and her father turned to see Mrs. Mitchell standing in the doorway, with her shawl around her.

"It's freezing up here on the roof, and this child has been up here for half an hour. Please come down now."

Maria and her father closed up the telescope and walked toward the door.

"Our Maria is quite a girl," Maria heard her father say to her mother. "Quite a girl."

With those words still ringing in her ears, Maria went off to her room to think about what she had seen and learned that night.

As Maria grew, so did her interest in astronomy. She learned not only about comets, but about the sun and the moon. She learned about the movements of the planets and about the different constellations in the sky. In school she worked hard at mathematics because it could help her to study the stars. She read every book she could about astronomy. And as always, her father taught her as much as he could about the subject.

After Maria finished school she taught for a while. Then something happened that made Maria very happy. She went to work as a librarian. Maria loved her job for two reasons. The library was open only in the afternoon. That gave her time to study in the morning and left her nights free for stargazing. And she could read all of the newest books on astronomy that the library got. Many of these books were very hard. New ideas and discoveries were popping up all the time. As Maria read about these discoveries, she never dreamed that one day she might make a discovery of her own.

One October evening in 1847 the Mitchells were entertaining friends at home. Even with all the talk and laughter around her, Maria could not help looking out the window. It was a clear night, perfect for stargazing.

The October air was brisk as Maria stepped out onto the roof and hurried to the shed. The stars shone brightly against their midnight background. Maria set up the telescope and got ready to work. As she looked through the telescope, she found the familiar star groups in the sky.

Maria noted their positions. Time always passed
quickly when Maria was at work. She was not
surprised when she looked at her timepiece and
saw that she had been up on the roof for two
hours. Maria decided she had better go downstairs. She wanted to take one last look through
the telescope before leaving, though.

Maria pointed the telescope toward the North
Star to begin a final sweep of the sky. She
raised the telescope slightly and was about to
move it again when something caught her eye.
Maria blinked her eyes and looked again. There,
in a spot a little above the North Star, was a
small, white haze.

"It looks like a comet," Maria thought, pulling back from the telescope for a second. "But it can't be. There isn't supposed to be a comet in that position at this time."

Maria looked again through the telescope. The white haze appeared to be moving slowly. It was a comet. One that Maria had never seen or heard about before.

Maria raced to the door of the roof and down the stairs to the living room. Her father was talking to a guest when Maria came up to him. "Excuse me, Father," Maria said. Then she whispered in his ear what she had just seen.

Her father looked up in surprise. "Are you sure?" he said.

"Quite sure," answered Maria.

"You'll have to excuse me," Mr. Mitchell said to his guests. "Maria has just found something in the sky that I must go and see."

When Maria and her father got to the telescope, Mr. Mitchell stepped behind it.

"Look right above the North Star and tell me what you think it is," said Maria.

Mr. Mitchell peered through the telescope. "Why it *is* a comet, Maria. And you're right. There is not supposed to be one in this position tonight. You've done it, Maria! You've discovered a comet."

Maria took up the telescope again. "Father, we must note the direction in which it is moving. And the time we first saw it."

"You mean the time *you* first saw it," said Mr. Mitchell. "*You've* discovered a comet!"

"But, Father," Maria said. "Somebody else may have already discovered it, and we just don't know about it yet."

"I don't know about that," Mr. Mitchell answered. "We will report it to the observatory at Harvard University right away. If you are the first to have reported this comet, Maria, you will get the credit for it. And the comet will be named after you. The Mitchell Comet. I rather like the way that sounds!"

That night Mr. Mitchell wrote in his notebook:

On October 1, 1847, at half past ten in the evening, Maria discovered a telescopic comet, just five degrees above Polaris.

Then Mr. Mitchell wrote of Maria's discovery to Professor Bond at the Harvard Observatory.

"We've sent word of your discovery as fast as we could," Mr. Mitchell told Maria as he left to post the letter. "This letter will sail with the next ship in the morning."

But the next day a bad storm moved in around Nantucket. The seas whipped around the island and no ship could leave the harbor. The storm lasted through the next day, too. Finally on October 4, the skies cleared and the letter about Maria's discovery went on its way to Harvard.

But by the time the observatory received the letter, people in Europe had already reported spotting the comet.

"It's not right, Maria," her father said. "If only that storm hadn't come up. Then word of seeing the comet would first have been received from you."

"It's not important, Father. I don't care who the comet is named for," answered Maria.

"But you've worked very hard all these years learning as much as you could. I think you *deserve* the credit for your discovery. The King of Denmark gives a medal and money to people who discover a comet with a telescope. Why shouldn't you have them?"

Other people cared about Maria and her comet, too. Mr. Mitchell wrote to important scientists explaining what had happened to the letter because of the storm. These scientists wrote to the King of Denmark urging him to consider Maria as the comet's discoverer.

Maria forgot about all of the fuss around her. She continued to study astronomy as much as she could and to work at the library.

But one day, in October of 1848, the mail contained a special surprise for Maria. There was a small package that she had not expected. It was from the King of Denmark.

Inside the package lay a shining gold disk. Maria picked it up and read the lettering on the front. It said:

Maria Mitchell—October 1, 1847

Maria turned the disk over and read the Latin, which said:

> *Not in vain do we watch the setting*
> *and rising of the stars*

After Maria's discovery, people began to pay more attention to her knowledge of the stars. Maria moved away from Nantucket to become the first professor of astronomy at Vassar College. She continued to learn all she could. She passed on what she knew to her students in the same way her father had taught her.

The Mitchell Comet was not a very big one. It had no streaking tail, and you could not see it without a telescope. Yet it was something new in the heavens to be studied. It was something to be added to the store of knowledge about comets.

Thoughts from Many Lands

Natalia Belting

Centuries before Maria Mitchell lived, people understood very little about the things they saw in the sky. Often they made up their own explanations for what they saw. Many of these explanations were passed down from generation to generation. We can still read some of them today. Here are a few examples from around the world.

The moon is a white cat
that hunts
the gray mice of the night.
Hungary

The sun is a ball of red feathers
stuck in a pot.
Every morning, the lid is lifted
off the pot.
Every evening, the lid is replaced.
                                    Brazil

Some say the North Star is a nail
on which the heavens are hung.
                              Lapland

329

Once, when the sky was very real,
the earth, a woman hoeing in her
garden, took off her necklace and
hung it in the sky.
The stars are her silver necklace.

Hawaiian Islands

The moon is a crystal ball
filled with silver water.
And the dark patches you see
on it are shadows of the
fishes and turtles that live
in the silver sea.

India

Using Metaphors

A **metaphor** is a special way of comparing two objects. Instead of saying one object is *like* another object, a metaphor says that one object *is* the other object.

Below are two metaphors from "Thoughts from Many Lands."

      1. The moon is a crystal ball.
      2. The moon is a white cat.

The first metaphor compares the moon to a crystal ball. The moon and a crystal ball are alike because they are both round and shiny. What two objects are being compared in the second metaphor? How are these two objects alike?

Read the sentences below. Those on the left are metaphors. Match each metaphor with the sentence on the right that explains what the metaphor means.

1. The ocean is a pool of tears.   a. It is hard.
2. The lawn is a velvet carpet.   b. It is smooth and soft underfoot.
3. This room is an icebox.   c. It is salty and wet.
4. His bed is a rock.   d. It is cold.

Find the metaphors in the paragraph below.

    In winter, it snows. Each tiny flake is a six-pointed flower. It floats gracefully through the air. When the snowflakes reach the ground, they join together. The snow is a blanket that covers the earth.

Fact Finding

A library is a kind of storehouse. It is a storehouse of information. A library has *reference books* that are filled with information. When you look for a particular fact, you must know which reference book to check. Most libraries have the following reference books:

An *encyclopedia* is a book or set of books with articles on different subjects. It has articles about famous people, events, and other topics. You have read a story about Galileo Galilei. To learn more about him, you might look in an encyclopedia.

An *almanac* is a single book usually published yearly. It contains the latest facts and figures on different subjects. It tells of recent events and records. To find out which scientists won the Nobel Prize last year, you would use an almanac.

An *atlas* is a book of maps. The maps show information about different areas. Maps may show countries, states, or towns. They may identify mountains, rivers, and deserts. Some maps show how the world looked years ago. Galileo lived in Italy. To find a map of Italy, you would look in an atlas.

A *dictionary* contains information about words. It tells how a word is spelled and pronounced. It also tells the meaning or meanings of the word. A dictionary may also give the history of the word. The word *supernova* was used in the story about Galileo. To learn more about the word *supernova*, you could use a dictionary.

Read each question. Choose the reference book
you would use to find the answer. On your paper,
write the name of the reference book you would use.

1. What is the meaning of the word *astronomer*?
   a. atlas   b. almanac   c. dictionary

2. How did Albert Einstein contribute to science?
   a. encyclopedia   b. atlas   c. dictionary

3. Where in the United States are the Rocky Mountains?
   a. dictionary   b. encyclopedia   c. atlas

4. Who won the Super Bowl game last year?
   a. almanac   b. atlas   c. dictionary

5. What do mice eat?
   a. encyclopedia   b. atlas   c. almanac

6. What is the correct way to pronounce *Caribbean*?
   a. atlas   b. dictionary   c. almanac

7. Which team won the 1980 World Series?
   a. dictionary   b. atlas   c. almanac

8. Where are the lakes and mountains in California?
   a. dictionary   b. atlas   c. almanac

9. What is the history of the word *sandwich*?
   a. atlas   b. encyclopedia   c. dictionary

10. What were the events that led to World War II?
    a. encyclopedia   b. dictionary   c. atlas

11. Who invented the hearing aid?
    a. encyclopedia   b. dictionary   c. almanac

12. What are the boundaries of Rumania?
    a. dictionary   b. atlas   c. almanac

13. What was the population of China last year?
    a. encyclopedia   b. almanac   c. dictionary

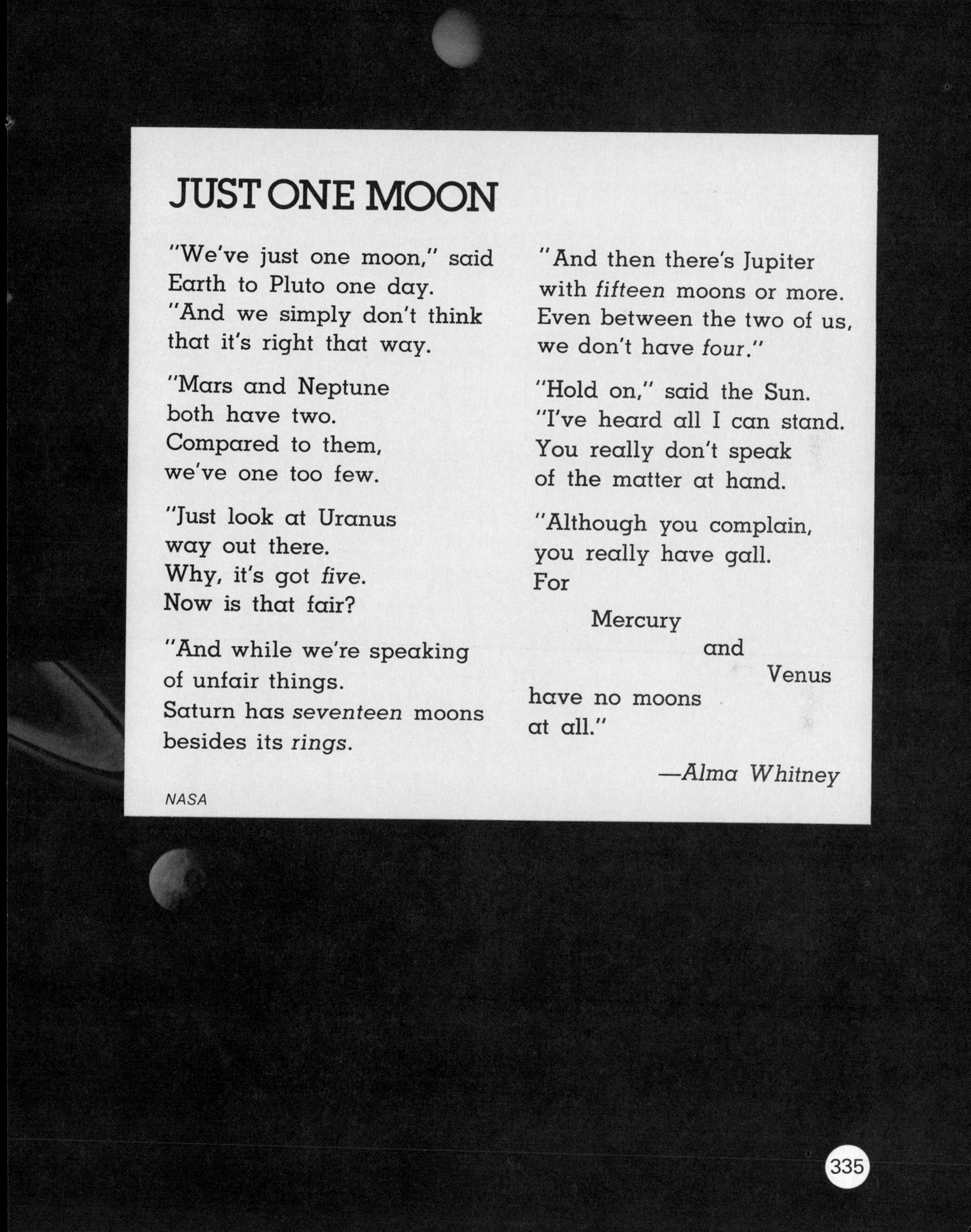

JUST ONE MOON

"We've just one moon," said
Earth to Pluto one day.
"And we simply don't think
that it's right that way.

"Mars and Neptune
both have two.
Compared to them,
we've one too few.

"Just look at Uranus
way out there.
Why, it's got *five*.
Now is that fair?

"And while we're speaking
of unfair things.
Saturn has *seventeen* moons
besides its *rings*.

"And then there's Jupiter
with *fifteen* moons or more.
Even between the two of us,
we don't have *four*."

"Hold on," said the Sun.
"I've heard all I can stand.
You really don't speak
of the matter at hand.

"Although you complain,
you really have gall.
For

      Mercury

              and

                  Venus

have no moons
at all."

—*Alma Whitney*

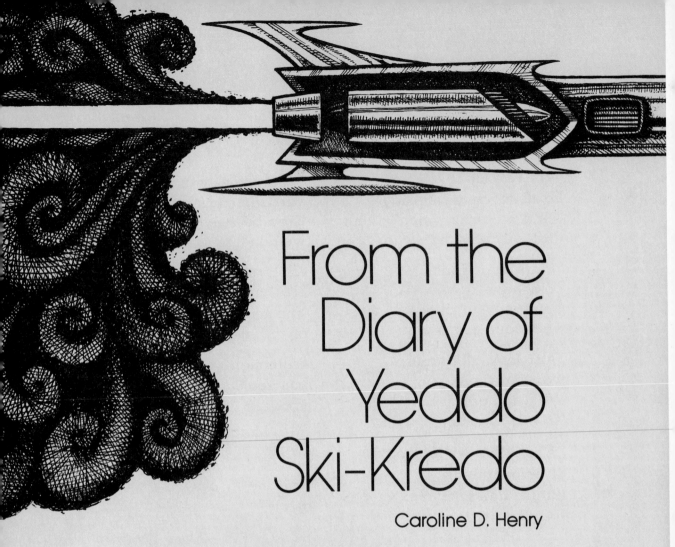

From the Diary of Yeddo Ski-Kredo

Caroline D. Henry

Year 2146, 217th Day, New Calendar

Spent the afternoon in the learning room doing manual-dexterity drills.

It was a sunny spring day. I was tempted to go with Tsadi after school and explore the old meteor crater. The exam for trainee rocket-train pilots is only a few days away. I am determined to be one of the seventeen who qualify, so I shall keep at my studies.

The big item on the televiewer newscast tonight was a report by miners from the Red Hills. They had sighted a

336

strange object in the sky. It was probably a buzzer catching the light in a strange way. Before the rocket-trains, the skies were full of aircraft. Now there are only a few little buzzers. Even so, from the number of reports of Unidentified Flying Objects, you'd think the skies were alive with strange craft.

218th Day

More UFO reports. Only on these private pages can I say how much aliens from space frighten me. No matter how I try to stop it, my mind imagines huge monsters who would crush us without a second thought. We'd be insects to creatures who could leap between the stars.

Enough of that. I've an exam to prepare for, and my math needs work.

If I am admitted as a trainee, the program won't start until the beginning of the year. I will have my first ride in the control room much sooner, though. As soon as I am a qualified candidate, my father will take me on a run with him. You cannot enter the control room of a rocket-train without first proving yourself.

Of course, I've ridden rocket-trains. It's the only way to travel between cities, except for the little buzzer vehicles, but only rich people can afford them. How different it will feel to ride in the control room of a rocket-train.

219th Day

Tsadi urged me to take the day off and go to the mountains with him in his uncle's buzzer. I had to remind myself that it's only two days until the exam. My whole future lies there.

Tsadi says I'm "taking the wrong train." He quotes Traz, the mad physicist. Traz says we are a nation of soil-bound dirt farmers. We may have many new inventions, but he says we are still living in the past. He feels we moved backward when the rocket-train systems replaced aircraft. I can't make sense of the space-warp theory that he says makes space travel possible.

I think the distant stars must remain distant. At least I hope they will.

220th Day

More UFO rumors. I had nightmares last night. They were about monsters with long slimy tentacles. They sprayed the planet with an atmosphere which was sweet to them but poisonous to us. It's not only the UFO rumors bothering me, but also my worries about the exam.

I brought up the subjects of UFO's and life on other planets with my father. I asked him what he thought the sightings were. Maybe the reports were being exaggerated.

In the cool, careful way of a good rocket-train pilot, he answered: "Nothing must be thought impossible, but I think that travel between the stars is unlikely. The question of life on other planets or in other galaxies is another thing. Our astronomers assure us it is highly likely."

"But what would it be like?"

"The possibilities are endless. Different worlds might require different life-forms. But I think intelligent beings of any kind would be able to communicate with other intelligent beings."

Nightmare monsters stayed in the back of my mind. It's hard for me to imagine kinship with them. Tsadi is my closest friend, but we are different. If you told him he was going to meet a native of the Giant's Eye Galaxy, he'd jump at the chance.

221st Day

The exam was tough. Results? I just don't know.

224th Day

Good news came today! I'm one of the seventeen. Tsadi's giving a party for me.

My father says he'll take me on a really important run, and it will be in a few days.

Excitement and celebrations! I'm in a hurry. Tsadi's waiting.

226th Day

Tomorrow is my day in the control room of my father's rocket-train. It is a special run. We are picking up officials here and in the capital. We then take them to a special meeting at the City in the Desert.

The streets are full of rumors. If they are true, I would rather not go to the City in the Desert tomorrow. But I

must. I hope I don't become a shaking mass of fear. I don't want to be unfit to handle a job that means the safety of hundreds.

Tsadi is delighted but afraid. He doesn't dare believe the rumors.

Has a starship actually made contact? In spite of the rumors, there is not a word in the news.

My father says our trip is important. He can't tell me the exact nature of it until we leave. This journey in celebration of becoming a trainee no longer seems as sweet as it did. It is touched by fear. The rumor of contact with aliens is probably true. What will they be like?

My diary will go with me. Whatever happens, it will be a momentous day.

227th Day

I was somewhat prepared. On the rocket-train, my father told me there was, indeed, to be an alien landing, and we were about to witness it.

When I saw the white and silver craft glide slowly down from the desert sky, my heart pounded. I wondered if it were the end of our world.

The spaceship touched down with a thud that shook the ground. A cloud of desert dust rose around it. We watched from the rocket-train station at the edge of the city's dome. The crew was present along with the vice-president, a half dozen city chiefs and their aides, the great linguists Middo and Tsimli, and a few scientists, including Traz.

The aliens came out of the spaceship wearing protective suits and helmets. One of them carried a box which seemed to be for testing the atmosphere. After studying the box carefully, they took off their helmets. They breathe oxygen as we do. Their heads are about the same size as ours, with a larger brain area. Beings who solved the riddle of space travel would, of course, be highly intelligent.

Our linguists and mathematicians will develop a workable language with them. The beginnings of communication are there.

Their senses are very similar to ours. There are two ear cups at the side of their head and a pair of eyes. Below the

342

breathing cavity, which is smaller than ours, is a mouth that is used for speech. It also looked as if it had the proper structure for taking in food. But I don't know their eating habits yet.

Perhaps we can learn from these strange beings. Perhaps Tsadi is right, and the future is in the stars.

There are some dramatic differences between the aliens and us. My fears were laid to rest. These beings from space are not ugly, evil giants ready to smash us in an instant. In fact, I had to remember my father's warning against rudely laughing at them if they looked so strange to us.

Yet, they are odd looking. They are nearly hairless, having only a tuft on the top of their heads, and they have only two legs!!

Looking to the Stars

For centuries people have looked to the stars. They have done so because it is thrilling to see a black sky sprinkled with millions of sparkling lights. They have done so to learn about the heavens. And they have done so to help them find their way to faraway ports and new lands.

One of the most exciting ways that people have looked to the stars is the way the slaves did in the United States before the Civil War. At that time many slaves tried to flee north to freedom. Runaway slaves were hunted. They had to hide during the day and do their traveling at night. The slaves needed the stars to show them the way to freedom. They needed the North Star most of all.

The North Star is above the North Pole of the earth. If you go toward the North Star, you go north. To the slaves, the North Star pointed the way to the free states and to Canada where slavery was illegal.

The play you are about to read is called *Freedom Star*. It is about two slaves who escape.

This play is a story of bravery and strong human feelings. In it you will see how the stars have helped some people to shape their futures.

Wade Hudson

Freedom Star

Cast of Characters:

Sarah Wilson—an eleven-year-old girl
Will—her eight-year-old brother
Mrs. Wilson—Sarah and Will's mother
Davis—a slave catcher
Mr. Jones—a stationmaster on the
                  underground railroad
Harriet Tubman
Three female slaves
Two male slaves

The play takes place during the 1850's
in Maryland and Pennsylvania.

Scene I

A one-room cabin on a plantation in Maryland.
SARAH WILSON *is standing in the center of the room,
staring at the floor. She is looking very sad. Her
brother* WILL *is sitting on the floor.* MRS. WILSON *is
standing near the door.*

Sarah: Do you know where they're going to take
    you, Mama?

Mrs. Wilson: I think it's Virginia.

Will: That's where Daddy is.

Mrs. Wilson: No, Will. They sold your father to a
    plantation in South Carolina.

Will (*running over to his mother and crying):* I don't
    want you to go, Mama! We don't have a daddy!
    And now we won't have a mama! (MRS. WILSON
    kneels in front of WILL. *She takes him in her arms.)*

Mrs. Wilson: We'll all be together again, Will—one
    day. A lot of people don't like slavery any more
    than we do. One day there won't be any more
    slavery. One day all people will be treated the
    same. Now stop crying. Okay?
    (WILL *dries his eyes.)*

Sarah: Let's run away, Mama. We can go up North.

Mrs. Wilson: With my new master coming at any
    minute to take me away? And even if he weren't,
    Sarah, running away is not that easy. It's a long
    way up North. And there are lots of slave catch-
    ers on the way. They'll catch you and bring you
    back. A lot of slaves have tried to run away.
    But very few make it. (*More to herself than to*
    SARAH *or* WILL) If Harriet Tubman had only come
    this way.

Sarah: Who's Harriet Tubman, Mama?

Mrs. Wilson: She's a brave black woman. She was once a slave herself. But she ran away. And since then she comes back every so often and helps other slaves escape. She has taken a lot of slaves up North to freedom.

Sarah: If she takes the chance, why can't we?

Mrs. Wilson: She knows how to stay away from the slave catchers. And she knows the way.

Sarah: She has a map?

Mrs. Wilson: No. I've heard she follows the North Star on clear nights. And when the sky's not clear, she goes by the moss on the north side of the trees. But it's not so easy.

Sarah (looking out the window of the cabin): Where's the North Star, Mama?

Mrs. Wilson: It's the one that points to the north.

Sarah: How can you find it? There're a lot of stars in the sky.

Mrs. Wilson (looking out the window): First you find the Big Dipper. Look. Now see the cup of the dipper? Pretend there's a line through the outside of the cup, away from the handle. Follow that line and you'll see...

Sarah: The North Star! Is it that bright one?

Mrs. Wilson: Yes, Sarah. It's the brightest star in the sky.

Will: How do you know all that about the North Star, Mama?

Mrs. Wilson: From your father.

Will: How did he know it?

Mrs. Wilson: He read it in books. When he was small like you, Will, he lived on a plantation in

Tennessee. The slave master there wasn't mean like Master Sam is. He used to give the slaves books to read. And that's where your daddy learned about the stars—from the books that old slave master used to give him. Your father was a smart man. I have to go now. I want you to look after each other. You hear? Now come say good-bye to me.

Will *(moving toward her):* Bye, Mama.

Sarah *(kissing and hugging her mother):* Bye, Mama. (MRS. WILSON *looks at* WILL *and* SARAH. *Suddenly she starts to cry. She turns quickly away from* SARAH *and* WILL *and runs out the door.)*

Sarah *(thinking for a while):* We're going to run away to the North. We'll leave tomorrow night.

There are too many people around here tonight. Tomorrow night will be different. Tomorrow we'll get some water and food and hide it. And tomorrow night, when everybody is asleep, we'll leave. (*She looks out the window.*) That North Star is going to show us the way to freedom.

Scene II

Late the next night SARAH *and* WILL *stop in the woods near a road.* SARAH *is carrying a canteen of water.* WILL *is carrying a bag of food.*

Sarah: Let's rest for a while. We're doing okay. We've made it into the woods without them seeing us.

(*They sit on the ground.* WILL *looks up at the sky.*)

Will: The North Star is sure a long ways away.

Sarah (*looking up at the sky*)*:* It sure looks beautiful.

Will: I wonder how far away it is?

Sarah: Miles and miles and miles.

Will: It's a lot farther than the moon, huh?

Sarah: Yes, a lot farther.

Will: When we get to the North, I'm going to school so I can learn all about the North Star and the Big Dipper and all the other stars.

Sarah: I'm going to school, too.

Will: Everybody goes to school in the North, huh?

Sarah: I guess so. Everybody who wants to go can go.

Will: Sarah, I can't wait till we get there.

(SARAH *gets to her feet.* WILL *rises also.*)

Sarah: Well, we still got a long way to go.

(*They walk back toward the woods.*)

Scene III

The following night. An old deserted house.
WILL *opens the door, and they walk in.*

Will: Looks like nobody lives here.

Sarah: We can sleep for a while. We'll be safe here.

Will: I wonder who lived here?

Sarah: It doesn't matter. At least we can get some sleep in a house. How much food do we have left?

Will *(looking into the bag):* Just a little.

Sarah: We should have brought more. We've still got a long way to go. Now let's get some sleep.
(They lie on the floor. SARAH *is almost asleep.* WILL *sits up.)*

Will: I wonder where Mama is.

Sarah: I do, too. After we get to the North, we'll think of a way to find her and Daddy and take them North, too. Now get some sleep.
*(*WILL *lies back on the floor. Both of them fall asleep. A few seconds later a white man opens the door and walks into the house. He is carrying a rifle, and a bag is slung across his shoulder. He is dressed in dirty clothes. The brim of his hat, pulled down over his eyes, makes him mean-looking. Hearing the door open,* SARAH *and* WILL *jump to their feet.)*

Davis: Well, well, well. What do we have here? A couple of runaways!

Will: Who're you?

Davis: Who am I? I'm a slave catcher. I bring runaways like you back to their rightful owners.
*(*SARAH *and* WILL *look at each other.)*

There's word going around that two young
slaves ran away from Sam Johnson's last night.
I don't suppose they could be you.

Sarah: We didn't run away.

Davis: Well then, where are your papers? If you're
not runaways, you must have papers that say
you are free.

(*Neither* WILL *nor* SARAH *answers* DAVIS.)

I'll get a lot of money for bringing you back.
Young slaves like you are worth a lot.

(*Suddenly* WILL *runs for the door, but* DAVIS *grabs
him before he can reach it.*)

I'll give you a good beating if you try that again.

(He pushes SARAH *and* WILL *against the wall of the cabin.)* I'm going to sit here in front of the door and get some sleep. Don't try running out. You'll never get past me. *(Talking more to himself than to* SARAH *or* WILL*)* I came up here to Maryland all the way from South Carolina to catch some runaways, and I didn't get any. Those runaways are getting smarter all the time. They've set up that underground railroad now. I bet you're on your way to that station in Pennsylvania. Too bad you got caught only ten miles from there.

*(*SARAH *and* WILL *look at each other.)*

Sarah: Mister, what's that station—a house?

Davis: What if it is? It won't do you any good. I'm taking you back to Sam Johnson's tomorrow morning. I can get at least a couple of hundred dollars for you. It won't be such a bad trip, after all. *(Pauses)* Now go to sleep. And remember, don't try to get past me.

*(*DAVIS *sits in front of the door and places his rifle across his knees.* SARAH *and* WILL *sit on the other side of the room watching him.* DAVIS *closes his eyes.)*

Scene IV

The next morning. DAVIS *gets up.* WILL *is asleep, but* SARAH *is awake.*

Davis: All right, you two. Get up.

*(*SARAH *nudges* WILL *and he gets up.)*

Sarah: We're hungry.

Davis: Too bad. Because there's no food.

Will: We got some food.

Davis: Where?

(SARAH *nudges* WILL, *indicating that he not answer.*)

(*Gruffly*) Where is it? (DAVIS *glances around the room and spots their sack in the corner. He reaches for it and begins to eat the last pieces of bread and meat that are in it.*)

Sarah (*protesting*): That's our food, mister. That's not yours.

Davis: It *was* your food. It's *mine* now. (DAVIS *eats the food.*)

(SARAH *puts her arm around* WILL'S *shoulder. They both watch* DAVIS.)

Let's go. We've got a long trip ahead. (*He picks up his sack and rifle. The three then leave the house.*)

Scene V

That afternoon. A lonely road. SARAH, WILL, *and* DAVIS *stop.*

Davis: We'll rest here. Sit down over there.
(SARAH *and* WILL *sit on the ground beside the road.* DAVIS *sits on the ground and rests against the tree. There is a rustling sound in the woods.*)

Sarah: That sounded like footsteps. Maybe there are some more runaways in the woods.

Davis: Get moving, you two. We're going to see.
(*As they start to move,* SARAH *falls.*)

Sarah: It's my leg, mister. I can't move.

Will: Sarah, Sarah, what happened?

Sarah: My leg. It's broken.

Davis: You two are making enough noise to scare away a ghost. I'm going to investigate. But don't try anything funny. I'll be right back. (DAVIS *moves into woods.*)

Sarah (*jumping up*): Come on. We haven't got a minute to lose.

Will: But what about your leg?

Sarah: Will, can't you see I'm just being a lot smarter than the slave catcher? There's nothing wrong with my leg. Let's go. (*They run off.*)

Scene VI

The following night SARAH *and* WILL *slump to the ground. They are exhausted.*

Will: We walked all last night. And tonight we're doing the same thing. We're lost. We can't find that station, Sarah.

Sarah: We'll make it. We can't give up.

Will: We don't have any food left. And we don't have any water.

Sarah: We'll make it. It can't be that far.

Will: But we haven't found the main road, yet!

Sarah: Why don't you stop complaining so much? We'll just have to keep on looking for the main road, that's all.

Will: I'm scared.

Sarah: I'm scared, too. *(Sarah gets up and looks around.)* Look, Will, there it is! *(They run off through the woods together.)*

Scene VII

A house. It is an underground railroad station. In the house there are three black women, two black men, and a white man, MR. JONES, *who owns the house. One of the women is* HARRIET TUBMAN.

Harriet Tubman *(to* MR. JONES*):* Well, Mr. Jones, we've almost completed another long journey. We don't have far to go, now.

Mr. Jones: Yes, Harriet. It's been a long journey. And dangerous, too. Don't you ever get scared?

Harriet Tubman: Can't afford to. My mind is bent on freedom for my people. As long as I got breath in my body, I'm going to do what I can to see that they get their freedom. *(Pauses)* I'm just doing what I think is right. And I think it's right for all people to be free.

Mr. Jones: I'll second that!

(Suddenly there is a noise at the door. HARRIET
TUBMAN *turns quickly and faces the door.)*

Mr. Jones: Quick! Go into that room.
*(*HARRIET TUBMAN *leads the slaves into another
room.* MR. JONES *then goes to the door. He opens
it.* SARAH *and* WILL *are at the door.)*

Mr. Jones: Hurry up! Come in—quickly.
*(*SARAH *and* WILL *come into the house.)*

Mr. Jones: Harriet! Come out here. We have
company!
*(*HARRIET TUBMAN *and the* SLAVES *come back into
the room.)*

Harriet Tubman *(walking over to* SARAH *and* WILL*)*:
Well, well. Who are you? And how did you
get here?

Sarah: We ran away.

Harriet Tubman: From where?

Sarah: From Maryland.

Harriet Tubman: Just you and the little boy?

Sarah: Yes, Ma'am. Is this the underground station?

Harriet Tubman: Yes, it is. You're safe now. You two
sure are brave.

Will: We just followed the North Star like Harriet
Tubman.
*(*HARRIET TUBMAN *looks at* MR. JONES*.)*

Mr. Jones: Son, this *is* Harriet Tubman.

Will: Harriet Tubman?

Mr. Jones: That's right.

Harriet Tubman: Mr. Jones, get them some food and
water. These children look half starved.

Sarah: I think there's a slave catcher following us,
Ma'am. He's been following us ever since we got
away from him.

Mr. Jones: That's probably Davis. *(Handing* WILL *and* SARAH *some bread and fruit)* He's that slave catcher from South Carolina. He was here two days ago looking for runaways.

Harriet Tubman: He caught you?

Sarah: Yes, Ma'am. And then we got away. But just a while back we saw him in the woods near here.

Harriet Tubman: Mr. Jones, we'd better be going. I want to get these folks to Canada as soon as possible. That slave catcher probably isn't that far behind. *(To the* SLAVES*)* Get ready so we can go. *(To* SARAH *and* WILL*)* You eat that on the way. We're ready to travel now.

Sarah: Yes, Ma'am *(Pauses)* Miss Harriet, what about our mama and daddy? They're still down there.

Harriet Tubman: You tell me all you can about them. Then we'll see what we can do to get them up here.

Will: May we help?

Sarah: Yes, Ma'am. We want to help, too.

Harriet Tubman: We'll find something for you to do. You found your way up from Maryland. We need brave people like you. We'll think of something. But for now, we have to travel. *(She places her hand tenderly upon* SARAH'S *head and smiles warmly at both* SARAH *and* WILL.*)*

Sky Words

People who first looked at the sky named the objects they saw for familiar things that looked like the objects. In the paragraphs below, you will learn some of the ways in which objects in the sky got their names.

The universe is made up of all the stars, planets, and galaxies in space. The word *universe* came from Latin words: *unus* (one) + *versus* (turned to) ⇒ *universe* (turned to one). Everything in space is turned into one great universe.

When the Greeks first saw comets, they thought the comets looked like long-haired women. So the Greeks named them *kometes*, which means "long hair." The Romans called the comets *stellae cometae*, or "hairy stars."

The *aurora borealis* is a display of streamers or arches of light seen in the northern sky. The word *aurora* means "dawn" in Latin. It comes from the name of the goddess, Aurora. *Borealis* means "northern," so *aurora borealis* means "northern dawn."

When the Greeks first saw a bright path of luminous stars across the sky, they called the path *galaxias*. They thought it looked like a path of milk. *Gala* is the Greek word for *milk*. Now we call a whole cluster of stars a *galaxy*. The Romans called this same bright path *via lactea,* or "road of milk." Can you think of our name for it?

THE MOON

Isaac Asimov

Scientists are learning more than ever about the moon. Astronauts have traveled to the moon. They have brought back information that helps us to understand the moon better.

Although our knowledge about the moon has grown, the moon itself has remained unchanged. The moon lights up the night. It makes the sky beautiful. It makes people stop, look, and wonder.

The Moon was formed billions of years ago. But no one is sure just how. Space was full of dust and rocks in those days, and these came together to form the Earth.

Perhaps when the Earth was first formed, a part of it broke loose and became the Moon.

Perhaps the dust and rocks came together in a whirling mass to form both a large Earth and a smaller Moon at the same time.

The Moon is about 2,200 miles (3,540 km) from side to side. This distance is called its diameter. The diameter of the Earth is about 8,000 miles (12,870 km) nearly four times wider than the Moon.

The Earth is larger and much heavier, too. So it pulls things toward itself. It has a stronger gravity, or gravitational pull. The Moon is caught in the Earth's gravitational pull. It moves around the Earth and can never get away. We say that the Moon is a satellite of the Earth.

You weigh what you do because the Earth's gravity pulls you. But the Moon's gravitational pull is

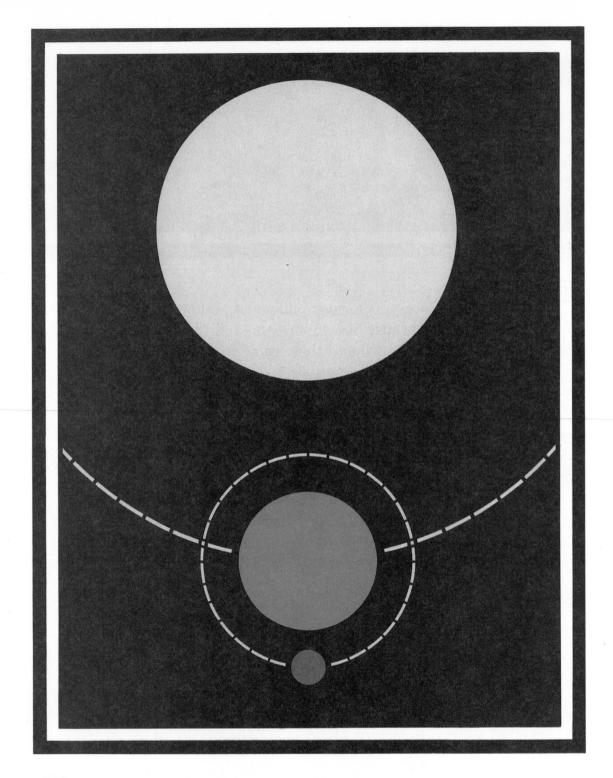

only one-sixth as strong as the Earth's pull. If you weigh 96 pounds (36 kg) on the Earth, you would weigh only 16 pounds (6 kg) on the Moon.

You could jump high and far on the Moon because you would be so light. You could lift large rocks that you couldn't even move here on Earth.

Air and water are held to the Earth by gravity. The Moon's gravity is too weak to hold air and water. So the Moon has no oceans, lakes, or rivers. It also has no air. It is an airless and very dry world.

The sounds we hear on Earth are carried by the air. There is no air on the Moon, so there is no sound. People who go to the Moon must talk to each other by radio.

Dust in the Earth's air scatters the sunlight. This makes Earth's daytime sky blue. The shadows are not completely dark. But on the Moon, where there is no air, the sky is always black. You would be able to see stars there even in the daytime. Sunny places on the Moon would be very, very bright. But the shadows would be almost black.

The air on Earth is always moving. The wind carries warmth from the hotter places to the colder ones. For that reason, it does not get too hot or too cold on most of the Earth.

The Moon has no air or wind to carry the Sun's heat. So it can get hot enough to boil water in places where the Sun is shining straight down. In the shadows, it can get very much colder than it gets at the South Pole on Earth.

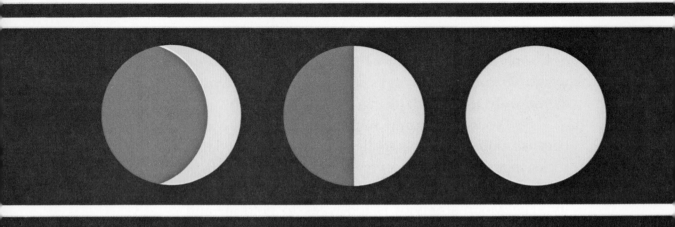

The surface of the Moon has mountains in many places. But there are some plains, or flat places, too. The larger plains are called *seas* because long ago people thought there was water in them. They know better now.

The Moon has thousands of *craters* on it. Craters are something like small plains with circular walls around them. Some craters are only a few feet wide. Others are dozens of miles across. Clavius, the largest crater on the Moon, is 146 miles (235 km) wide. The craters may have been made when rocks from space smashed into the Moon. Some craters have light streaks, called *rays*, around them. These rays may be material that splashed out of the crater when it was formed.

It is possible that there were once volcanoes on the Moon. A few may still be hot underneath. Sometimes people at telescopes see clouds inside craters. Gas may still be appearing. Volcanoes in the past may also have made the large cracks that are seen on the moon. These are called *rills*.

The Moon and the Earth are always moving. They move in different ways. One way they move is like a spinning top. This kind of movement is called *turning on the axis*. The Earth rotates, or turns on its axis, once every 24 hours. This time is called an Earth day.

The Moon takes longer to rotate once on its axis. Daytime on the Moon is two weeks long. Then there are two weeks of nighttime. Long days and long nights are one reason why it gets so hot on the Moon in its daytime and so cold in its nighttime.

The Earth and the Moon also move in another way. They go around the Sun together. The paths they follow are called *orbits*. It takes the Earth and the Moon a year to make a complete trip around the Sun. The Moon also travels around the Earth as it goes around the Sun.

The Moon is made of gray rock. It has no light of its own. It is like a mirror. It reflects, or bounces back, the light it gets from the Sun. Moonlight is sunlight that hits the Moon's surface and is reflected to us on Earth.

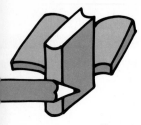

All Things Considered

Suppose you went to a friend's house to visit. You rang the bell, but no one answered. You looked through a window. No lights were on inside. The family car was not parked outside. You would probably decide that your friend was not at home.

Making a decision after checking the facts is called *drawing a conclusion*. You draw conclusions ever day. For example, you check the weather to decide if you need to wear a coat outside. You check the traffic to decide the safest route for riding your bike to school.

The best conclusions are based on all available information. In the selection "Galileo Galilei," Galileo believed that Aristotle's theories about the universe were wrong. However, people did not accept Galileo's conclusion at first. Galileo could not provide enough facts. Later, with the help of a telescope, Galileo was able to prove that his conclusion was correct.

Read each paragraph. Choose the conclusion that can be drawn from the paragraph. On your paper, write the conclusion. Then write the facts in the paragraph that led to the conclusion.

1. During the Revolutionary War, the British Navy sank several American ships. Other ships were captured by the British. Some American sailors left their jobs. Britain closed its ports to America. It became impossible for Americans to trade with other countries across the ocean.

Conclusions:
a. American shippers lost money during the war.
b. American shippers grew rich during the war.
c. American shippers were not affected by the war.

2. The price of gasoline affects almost everybody. Taxi-cab riders are especially concerned. The cost of gas affects the cost of a cab ride. Cabdrivers must charge enough money to pay for the gas they use and to earn a living.

Conclusions:
a. When gas prices go up, cab rides cost less.
b. When gas prices go up, cab rides cost more.
c. When gas prices go up, cab rides are free.

3. Desert people often wear white clothing. Sunlight bounces off white clothing. Black, on the other hand, absorbs light. For example, a black car in the sun will get hotter than a white car.

Conclusions:
a. Desert people wear white to stay warm.
b. Desert people wear white to drive cars.
c. Desert people wear white to stay cool.

4. The cat was thin and sad-looking. When Lucy bent to pat it, it shied away at first. She felt around its neck for a collar, but there was none. Most of the summer houses in the area were boarded up. Families had packed up and gone home for the winter. When she started to walk away, the cat followed her.

Conclusions:
a. The cat is unfriendly.
b. The cat has been abandoned.
c. The cat is out for a romp at the beach.

A TRIP TO MARS

Alma Whitney

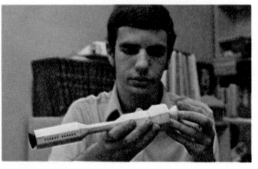

At the age of thirteen, Ned Potter, an aspiring scientist from New York, began his flight to Mars. It took him two years. Of course, Ned didn't really go to Mars. He made a slide show of what such a trip might be like. On the following pages you will see some of his slides. And you'll also see how Ned went about taking some of his slides. We think you will agree that they look like the real thing.

Icarus III orbits Mars.

371

An astronaut walks in space during the Icarus III flight.

Ned built his Icarus III out of paper. One model of the landing module is next to the craft.

To show Icarus III in flight, Ned hung it in front of black paper painted with white dots.

Ned used dolls dressed in space suits for closeup shots of the astronauts in flight.

Ned's orange living room rug became the surface of Mars.

On his paper model, Ned painted the details of the inside of the spacecraft.

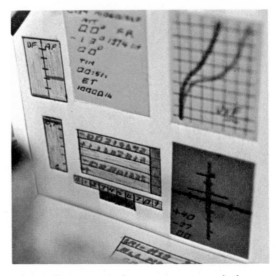

This close-up shows some of these details.

Ned photographed small dolls, the landing module, and the land rover on Mars.

In this slide, the astronauts are preparing to explore the surface of Mars in their land rover.

Icarus III approaches Mars.

The landing module descends toward Earth.

Using a bright lamp for the sun, Ned photographed Icarus III in one phase of its flight.

To get to Mars and back, Icarus III would follow a path around the sun. Here is Ned's shot of it.

Cotton clouds on a green rug provided the background for shots of the return flight.

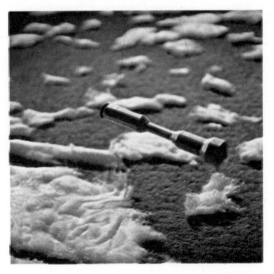

The spacecraft is returning to Earth in this slide, which appears near the end of Ned's show.

Ned attached the smaller model of his landing module to a toy parachute to show the re-entry.

He photographed the parachute upside down to capture the feeling of the parachute open and descending.

With his brother Will's help, Ned photographed a toy helicopter against a blue background.

Here is Ned's slide of the helicopter coming in to pick up the astronauts after they have landed in the ocean.

A parachute slows the landing module before splashdown.

the escape

Robert Heinlein

Many authors have imagined what forms of life might exist on other planets. One of these authors is Robert Heinlein. In his book, Star Beast, Mr. Heinlein describes a form of life from another planet that is living on earth.

The story takes place on earth far in the future, at a time when people fly around in harness flyers, air cars, and air buses. Space exploration is very advanced.

The star beast, whose name is Lummox, gets himself into a mess by deciding to take a walk.

Perhaps after you read this part of the book you would like to think up a star beast of your own and write about it.

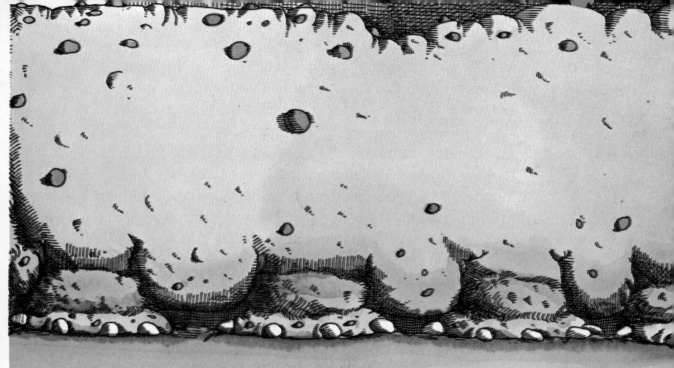

Lummox was bored and hungry. Being hungry was normal for Lummox. Creatures like him were always ready for a little snack, even after a full meal. Being bored was less usual. Lummox was bored because his chum and closest friend, John Thomas Stuart XI, had not been around all day.

Lummox lumbered around the backyard of the Stuart home, looking for anything—a grasshopper, a robin, anything at all that might be worth looking at. He watched a hill of ants for half an hour.

Growing tired of ants, Lummox moved away toward his own house. His number 7 foot came down on the ant hill and crushed it. But Lummox did not notice this.

Piled outside his shed were six bales of hay. Lummox pulled a small amount off one bale and chewed it. He did not take a second bite because he did not want John Stuart to notice he had taken any.

If John Stuart found out, he might refuse to scratch Lummox with the garden rake. Lummox was not supposed to touch food unless it was placed inside his shed.

Besides, Lummox did not want hay. He had had hay for supper last night. He would have it again tonight. And again tomorrow night. Lummox wanted something with more body and a more interesting flavor. He moved over to the low fence. This fence separated the several acres of backyard from Mrs. Stuart's garden. Lummox stuck his head over the fence and looked at Mrs. Stuart's roses. The fence marked the line that he must not cross. He had crossed it once, a few years earlier. And he had sampled the rose bushes. Mrs. Stuart had made such a fuss that Lummox hated to think about it even now.

But Lummox remembered some rose bushes that did not belong to Mrs. Stuart. He thought that if they didn't belong to Mrs. Stuart, they didn't belong to anyone. These bushes were in the garden of the Donahues, next door. Lummox had been thinking about a way to reach these bushes.

The Stuart place was surrounded by a ten-foot concrete wall. Lummox had never tried to climb over it. But he had nibbled at it in places. In the rear of the wall was a gap filled in with high timbers. Two of the timbers had come loose. Lummox lumbered over to the timbers. He smiled and carefully placed his head between the two big posts. He pushed gently. The timbers gave way, and Lummox was outside his yard.

Lummox paused and raised up like a caterpillar. His legs 1 and 3, 2 and 4, were off the ground. Lummox looked around. It was certainly nice to be outside. It had been a long time since John Thomas had taken him out, even for a short walk.

Suddenly an unfriendly character charged at Lummox. It yapped and barked at him. Lummox recognized the creature. It was an oversized dog that ran free in the neighborhood. Lummox liked dogs. But this one was another matter. This one thought that he was boss of the neighborhood. He bullied other dogs, terrified cats, and often challenged Lummox to come out and fight like a dog.

Nevertheless, Lummox smiled at the dog. Then he opened his mouth wide. In his baby-like voice he called the dog a very bad name. The dog gasped. He did not understand what Lummox had said. But he knew that he had been insulted. The dog began to bark louder than ever. He dashed around Lummox and tried to nip his legs.

Lummox remained reared up, watching the dog, but making no move. But then the dog cut close to where Lummox's first pair of legs would have been had they been on the ground. Lummox ducked his head, the way a frog strikes at a fly. His mouth opened, and he gobbled up the dog.

Not bad, Lummox decided as he chewed and swallowed. Not bad at all. And now to those ownerless rose bushes.

John Thomas Stuart XI got home shortly before dinner. He noticed as he landed that Lummox was not in sight. He assumed that his pet was in his shed.

John Thomas unstrapped his harness copter and went to hang it up in the hallway. His mother called, "John Thomas! Where have you been? Do you know what that beast has done?"

"What's the trouble?" John Thomas asked. Then he began to find some things out.

Lummox had gone for a stroll. (John Thomas hoped that Lummox had not gotten any iron or steel while he was out. Iron and steel made him grow so fast. He thought of the time Lummox had eaten a second-hand car.)

That was not what had happened this time. But Lummox had eaten some of Mrs. Donahue's prize roses. Mrs. Donahue had run after him with a broom. Lummox had not eaten Mrs. Donahue because he knew that people were not food.

But his feelings had been hurt. So he had lumbered away from there, pouting. He stopped pouting long enough to eat another neighbor's dog before he continued on his way.

Next Lummox had paid a visit to the vegetable garden of Mr. Ito, about a mile away. Mr. Ito did not know what it was that he found pulling up his cabbages and gulping them down. He had never seen Lummox before.

Mr. Ito got a gun that had been used long ago in a world war. He fired it at Lummox. The noise scared Mr. Ito. And the flash blinded him for a moment. When he opened his eyes, the thing had gone.

The gun had frightened Lummox almost out of his wits. Usually he used his legs in this order: 1, 4, 5, 8, 2, 3, 6, 7. This combination was good for speeds from a slow crawl to a fast trot.

But now he broke into a gallop. He moved legs 1 and 2 and 5 and 6 together. Then he shifted to legs 3 and 4 and 7 and 8. Using this combination, he raced toward the town.

When he got to the town, Lummox stepped onto a slidewalk. The walk ground to a stop. It had not been designed for six tons of concentrated load. Pedestrian traffic was thrown into confusion.

People screamed, children and dogs ran around, and safety officers tried to restore order. And poor Lummox, who had meant no harm, made a perfectly natural mistake.

He thought that the big windows of the department store looked like a place where he could get away from the mess. So Lummox walked through the windows and tried to hide in a model bedroom display. He was not very successful.

John Thomas was about to ask his mother a question when there was a thump on the roof. John Thomas looked up. "You expecting anyone, Mum?"

"It's probably the safety patrol. They said they . . ."

"The safety patrol! Oh, my!" John Thomas pushed a button to unlock the roof entrance.

Moments later, the elevator from the roof creaked to a stop. A safety sergeant and an assistant stepped out.

"Are you John T. Stuart?"

John gulped, "Yes, sir."

"Unless you want something to happen to that deep-space what-is-it that's your pet, you'd better snap to and come with us."

John Thomas kept quiet and went with the officers.

In the three minutes it took the patrol car to fly downtown, John Thomas tried to find out as much as he could.

"Is Lummox still in the department store?"

"Is that what you call it—Lummox? No, we got it out. It's under the West Arroyo viaduct...I hope."

"What do you mean, you hope?" John Thomas asked.

"Well, first we blocked off the streets. Then we got the thing out of the store with fire extinguishers. Nothing else seemed to bother it. Bullets just bounced off. Say, what's that beast's hide made of? Steel?"

John did not care to discuss this. He was still wondering if Lummox had eaten any iron. After he had eaten the second-hand car, Lummox's growth had taken an enormous spurt. He had grown from the size of a hippopotamus to his present size in just two weeks.

Since that time, John Thomas had tried to keep metal away from Lummox.

The safety officer went on. "We started after him, but he got away from us. He headed for the viaduct. Well, you'll see, right now. Here we are."

Six patrol cars were hovering over the end of the viaduct. Surrounding the area were many private air cars and an air bus or two. There were several hundred harness flyers as well. On the ground, a few regular safety officers were trying to hold the crowd back.

The safety chief's bright-red command car approached them. Chief Dreiser opened the door and leaned out. "Tell that Stuart boy to stick his head out."

John Thomas ran a window down and stuck his head out. "Here, sir."

"Lad, can you control that monster?"

"Certainly, sir."

"Land him, Sergeant. Let him try it."

"Yes, Chief." The sergeant started lowering the car. John Thomas could now see Lummox. He had hidden under the end of the bridge. John Thomas leaned out and called to him.

"Lum! Lummie boy! Come to papa."

The creature stirred, and the end of the viaduct stirred with him. About twelve feet of his front end emerged from under the bridge. Lummox looked around wildly.

"Here, Lum! Up here!"

Lummox caught sight of his friend and started to grin.

The sergeant opened a door and kicked out a rope
ladder. "Can you go down that, son?"

"Sure," said John Thomas. He shinnied down the
ladder until there was no more ladder. He was still six
feet above Lummox's head. He looked down. "Heads
up, baby. Take me down."

Lummox lifted another pair of legs from the
ground. He placed his broad skull under John Thomas.
John Thomas stepped onto it. Then Lummox lowered
him gently to the ground.

Lummox nuzzled his legs and made a sound like a
purr. "Bad Lummie!" said John Thomas. "You are a
mess, aren't you?"

Lummox looked embarrassed. He lowered his head
to the ground. "I didn't mean to do anything bad,"
he said in his high voice.

John Thomas turned to Lummox. "We're going
home," he said. "Make me a saddle."

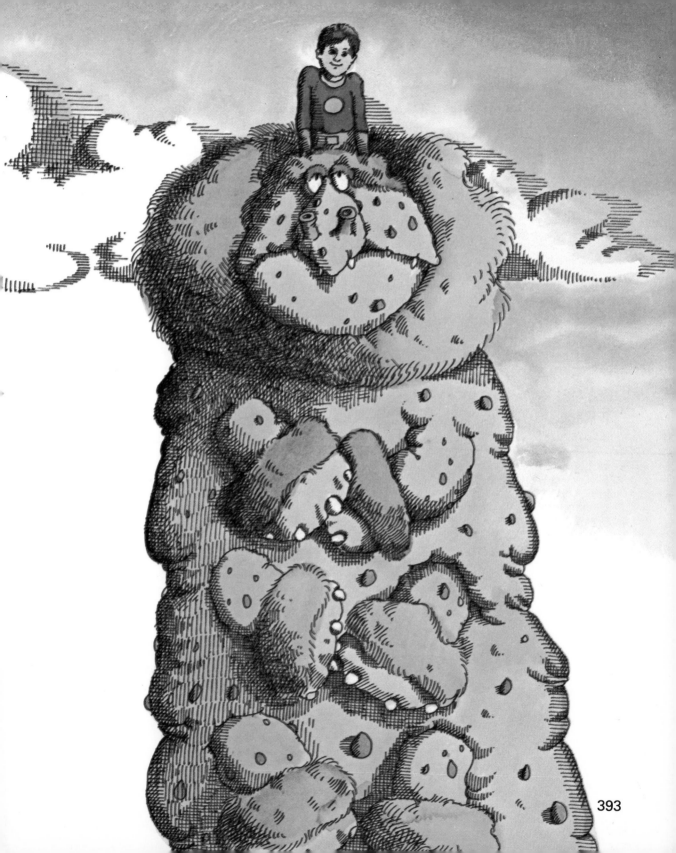

Lummox's midsection slumped down a couple of feet. He concentrated. Then his back shaped itself into a chair. John Thomas scrambled up.

Two patrol ground cars led the way. Two others brought up the rear. Chief Dreiser's tomato-red runabout hung over them at a safe distance.

The parade continued to the Stuart home in silence.

Chief Dreiser inspected the gap in the fence. John Thomas looked on, with Lummox hanging over their shoulders. John Thomas took a string and tied it across the opening.

"There! Now he can't get out again."

The safety chief pulled at his lip. "Are you all right in the head, son?"

"You don't understand, sir. The posts wouldn't stop him even if we repaired them. But the string will. Lummox!"

"Yes, Johnnie?"

"See that string?"

"Yes, Johnnie."

"You won't go out of the yard again, not ever, unless I take you."

"Yes, Johnnie."

"Promise? Cross your heart?"

"Cross my heart."

Dreiser chewed his thumb. "All right. I'll leave an officer with a portophone here tonight. Tomorrow we'll put some steel beams in place of that wood."

John started to say, "Oh, not steel," but he thought better of it. Dreiser said, "What's the matter?"

"Uh, nothing."

"You keep an eye on him, too," Dreiser said.

"He won't get out," John answered.

"You realize that you are both on probation."

John Thomas didn't answer. He hadn't realized it.

Dreiser went on in a kindly voice. "Try not to worry about it. You seem like a good boy. Now I've got to go and have a word with your mother. You had better stay here until the officer arrives."

John Thomas stayed while the safety chief went back to the house. Now was the time to give Lummox what-for. But he did not have the heart for it— not just then.

Language of the Future

New words are added to our language all the time. Whenever new inventions, styles, or ideas are created and named, our language expands. Several words in "A Trip to Mars" became part of our language only when people began to travel in space. *Astronaut, spacecraft, splashdown,* and *space suit* are examples. What other words can you think of that relate to space travel?

In the science-fiction story, "The Escape," the author made up several new words to name objects that might be part of a future world: *harness copter, slidewalk, air bus,* and *portophone*. Are parts of these words familiar? How would you describe each of these objects? How do you think each of these objects might be used?

You can make up your own words by combining words or word parts in new ways. For example, by combining *space* and *port*, you would create the word *spaceport*. In the world of the future, spacecraft may travel regularly between Earth's spaceports and spaceports above other planets.

Below are descriptions of possible objects of the future. Think of a name for each object.

- an instrument that sends smells and flavors over wires
- a machine that controls the weather
- a machine that will clean your room by itself

NIGHT

Stars over snow,
  And in the west a planet
Swinging below a star—
  Look for a lovely thing and
    you will find it,
It is not far—
  It never will be far.

       —Sara Teasdale

397

Words Under the Microscope

Science books may seem harder to read than other books. Many words in a science selection may be new to you. Sometimes, the new word and its definition are in the same sentence. Read this example from "The Moon."

It reflects, or bounces back, the light it gets from the sun.

To *reflect* means "to bounce back." The definition is given in the sentence.

Sometimes the definition is given in another sentence near the new word:

The Moon is about 2,200 miles from side to side. This distance is called its diameter.

The *diameter* is "the distance from side to side." The definition of *diameter* is given in the first sentence. The word *diameter* appears in the second sentence.

Often the definition for a new word is not directly stated. However, the words and sentences near the new word provide context clues to its meaning.

The Moon moves around the Earth and can never get away. We say that the Moon is a satellite of the Earth.

The definition of *satellite* is not directly stated. However, both sentences provide clues to the meaning. The first sentence says the Moon moves around the Earth; the second sentence says the Moon is a satellite. By looking at these clues, you can figure out the meaning of *satellite*: "an object that moves around another object."

Read each sentence or group of sentences. On your
paper, write the meaning of the underlined word
as it is used in the sentence. Check a dictionary to
make sure your definition is correct.

1. The scientist used her telescope to watch the
   nova, or exploding star.

2. Linda always dreamed of studying the stars.
   Finally, she became an astronomer.

3. Astronautics, the science of flight in space,
   is becoming very important as we explore more
   of the solar system.

4. Sometimes pieces of stone or metal travel through
   space. When they get close enough to Earth, they
   are pulled down by gravity. Usually these meteors
   burn up quickly in the Earth's atmosphere.

5. Some meteors burn up with an unusually large and
   bright flame. They are called fireballs.

6. The moon walkers saw dozens of craters. The small
   plains had circular walls around them. They seemed
   to have been formed by falling rocks.

7. Many of the craters had light streaks, called rays,
   around them.

8. Volcanoes may have made the large cracks that
   are seen on the Moon. These cracks are called rills.

9. People used to think the large plains on the Moon
   had water in them. They called them seas.

10. The top of the building was shaped like a dome.
    Inside, people watched as lights, resembling the
    stars and planets, moved across the inside of the
    dome. Janet loved visiting the planetarium.

WONDERS

People have always gazed at the sky with wonder. Long ago, people explained the mysteries of the universe by making up stories. Later, new discoveries in science allowed people to test old ideas and gather new information. Although we have learned much about the stars, the moon, and the planets, many questions remain unanswered.

Thinking About "Wonders"

1. How would it have been helpful for people in Galileo's time to know the facts about supernovas?
2. People in Galileo's time called the telescope a "magic glass." Why?
3. What was Maria Mitchell's contribution to science?
4. What are some of Yeddo Ski-Kredo's fears about UFO's that might be shared by people today?
5. Most of the information in "The Moon" is factual. What information in the selection are scientists still trying to prove?
6. As we gain more information about the universe, how do you think your life may change?
7. At the end of "Freedom Star," Sarah and Will are on their way to Canada with Harriet Tubman. Write a paragraph telling about how their lives changed when they got to Canada.

OUTLETS

We all need outlets—for expressing ideas and feelings, for having fun, for dreaming about the future. There are many, many outlets from which you can choose. Play a sport. Paint a picture. Dream a dream. All you have to do is find the outlets that are right for you.

Some of the people you will meet in "Outlets" are real. Others are imaginary, but they may seem like you or someone you know. All have found special outlets for expressing themselves. Two young musicians express themselves by playing musical instruments. A man expresses himself by making musical instruments for others. A group of children decorate a classroom with scenes from their everyday lives. A young woman captures the spirit of a famous American President in her sculpture.

As you read, think about the outlets these people chose for expressing themselves. Try to figure out what leads people to choose certain outlets.

Music

Can you dance?
I love to dance!
Music is my happy chance.
  Music playing
  In the street
  Gets into
  My hands and feet.

Can you sing?
I love to sing!
Music, like a bird in Spring,
  With a gold
  And silver note
  Gets into
  My heart and throat.

Can you play?
I'd love to play!
Practice music every day—
  Then you'll give
  The world a chance
  To dance and sing
  To sing and dance.

—Eleanor Farjeon

Mariko Plays the Koto

Merrill O'Brien

Every Saturday, Mariko, who is ten years old, takes a lesson in how to play the koto, the Japanese harp. Mariko is Japanese, but she does not live in Japan. She lives in New York with her parents.

Mariko has been studying the koto since she was six years old. Her teacher is a Master of Koto who learned to play the instrument in her native Japan.

The koto is a beautiful wooden instrument about six feet long and ten inches wide. It is curved slightly upward like a Japanese bridge.

Mariko plucks the thirteen strings with pieces of ivory called *tsume*. They are fitted to the tips of the three middle fingers of her right hand with leather bands. Her left hand presses the strings to make the sound higher or lower.

Before she plays her koto, Mariko must tune it. Under each string is an ivory or plastic piece shaped like an upside-down "Y" and called a *ji*. Mariko moves the *ji* under each string to bring it to the proper pitch.

The strings used to be made only of many strands of tightly twisted white silk. Now they are also made of nylon, which lasts much longer.

Mariko sits on the floor to practice the koto, the traditional way it is played in Japan. But sometimes in recitals she sits on a chair, and small stands support each end of her koto.

Kotos are expensive musical instruments. A good one costs as much as a fine piano in the United States.

Japanese people have been playing the koto for more than a thousand years. No one knows who invented it or just when it was first made. There are similar instruments in China and Korea.

For many centuries it was played only by members of the Imperial Court of Japan and by Buddhist priests. Then the government began encouraging people to play the koto as a means of earning a living.

Many Masters of the Koto have been blind. For this reason, koto players were taught to play by ear, and there was little need for written music. The method of writing musical scores for the koto that is used today was developed in this century.

This is a section of the Japanese musical notation for "Sea in the Spring." It was written especially for the koto; each of the Japanese characters is a number indicating one of the instrument's thirteen strings. The music is read from top to bottom.

The most distinguished kotoist of modern times was a blind person, Michio Miyagi, who was born in 1894 and died in 1956. He was a great composer as well as an excellent player of the koto. He composed thousands of musical scores for the koto, including more than 600 based on children's songs. His most famous work is "Haru no Umi," which means "Sea in the Spring."

Today many people in Japan play the koto. But to be awarded the title of "Master of Koto Music," one must be able to pass difficult written and performance tests.

When a koto player becomes a Master, he or she is then given a professional name.

Mariko hopes someday to be a koto Master and to have a professional name.

A LITTLE CULTURE

Dina Anastasio

Far away, in the town of Anywhere, a large old schoolhouse stood in the shade of a huge maple tree.

Every morning at eight o'clock, old Mr. Sleeves, the fifth-grade teacher, rang the school bell, and children of various ages walked through the door. They moaned and groaned and wished they were in bed instead of in that cold, dreary building.

And every morning, as the fifth graders said their hellos and talked, Mr. Sleeves called for quiet.

On one cold morning, when all the children were seated, Mr. Sleeves stood in front of them in his heavy dark coat.

"I don't like this room!" he said.

"Yes, sir," the children agreed, for they didn't like the room either. It was drafty and dreary, and very, very plain.

"What this room needs is a little art!" said Mr. Sleeves.

"Yes, sir," the children said, for a little art would certainly brighten up the place.

"Now," continued Mr. Sleeves, "I have here a catalog. In it are pictures—or should I say pictures of pictures. They are pictures of some of the greatest paintings in the world. I have chosen five. They will be here tomorrow to provide a little art and culture for this dreary place!"

"Yes, sir," said the children, for art and culture are nice things to have.

That afternoon, when school was out, the children went their separate ways. Andrew went to help his father in the bakery. Maria took out her bicycle and wasn't seen until suppertime. Gerald went to his room with twenty-six comic books. And Suzanne, having fought with her brother for an hour and a half, was put to bed without supper.

The next day, when the children arrived at the schoolhouse, the prints were on the walls. Mr. Sleeves, in his heavy dark coat, was walking about making sure that all the pictures were perfectly straight.

He waited for his class to be seated. Then he walked to the front of the room and asked, "Well?"

No one said anything. They were all looking at the pictures. Mr. Sleeves waited. Still no one spoke.

"Well?" Mr. Sleeves said again.

From the back of the room came a small, timid sound.

"Well," whispered Eugene, the bravest in the class, "they are very nice pictures. And I can tell that the artists are very talented. But I just don't like them—sir."

The room was silent for a long time as Mr. Sleeves and the other children stared in wonder at Eugene. They couldn't quite believe their ears.

Eugene looked at his feet and moved around in his chair a bit. Then he looked at Mr. Sleeves.

"Well?" said Eugene.

Mr. Sleeves cleared his throat and said, "May I ask why you don't like them?"

"I don't like them," answered Eugene, "because I don't understand them. And I don't understand them because I have never known people like the ones in those pictures. They are people from long ago, and they don't mean anything to me."

"Yes, sir," said the children. They all agreed with Eugene. But until now, no one had dared to say so.

Mr. Sleeves walked back and forth in front of the children. Every few feet he stopped, faced the children, and shook his head back and forth, back and forth.

Finally he stopped. "Without the pictures," he said, "this room is boring. With the pictures, it is not! So, unless you have a better way of brightening up this room, the pictures will stay! Anyway, they provide a little culture, which is something you can all use!"

"Not *my* culture!" whispered Eugene. But Mr. Sleeves didn't hear him, which was a very good thing for Eugene.

That afternoon, when school was out, the children met beneath the maple tree. They all agreed that, although the paintings were very fine, they just didn't like them. They put their heads together and tried to think of another way of brightening up the room. Gerald went inside and borrowed Mr. Sleeves's catalog. By four o'clock, the children knew just what they were going to do. They contributed as much money as they could, and they set off for the village to buy materials. Then they went home and began to work.

Mr. Sleeves's paintings remained on the walls for two weeks, while spring came to Anywhere. One morning, when the maple tree was full and green, Mr. Sleeves arrived at the school. The children were already seated at their desks. This had never happened before, and Mr. Sleeves was extremely surprised. But he was even more surprised when he looked around his schoolroom. His paintings were gone, and in their place were four walls of the most interesting drawings and photographs he had ever seen. There were pictures of the maple tree in winter and the maple tree in spring. There were boys and girls on bicycles and boys and girls in a fifth-grade classroom. There were pictures of dogs playing, babies crying, and grandmothers smiling. And there were also some prints of famous paintings, ordered from Mr. Sleeves's catalog. These paintings showed people from other times and places living, working, and having fun. The children understood the paintings and liked them very much.

Mr. Sleeves stood very still. Then he turned to the children and smiled.

"This is what you like?" he asked.

"Yes, sir," said the children.

"Eugene?" said Mr. Sleeves, looking toward the back of the room.

Eugene stood up.

"This is *our* culture," he said. "This is what we know and understand. This, to us, is art!" And then he sat down.

Mr. Sleeves smiled. Then, muttering something about the room being too warm, he took off his coat and said, "Get to work!"

The children sighed and thought of their warm beds. But when they looked around at their beautiful schoolroom, they decided that they'd rather be there than anywhere else.

DRAWING FUNNY PICTURES

Jack Markow

These faces don't even have noses or ears, but they still look like faces. And they show feelings. Why? Because the eyes and the mouths look like they are in motion. The eyes and the mouth are the most expressive parts of a face. Sometimes, eyebrows and hair can also show feelings. For example, hair standing on end shows someone is very afraid.

Draw some faces that show how you feel at different times.

I know
the answer.

I didn't do
my homework.

I dropped
my book on my toe.

Now put a funny head on top of a body. Add legs and arms. You have a funny person! Here are some ideas that may help you draw your own funny people.

By using circles, you can make a person fat. And by using straight lines, you can make a person thin. By putting a small head on a long body, you can make a person look tall. If you put a big head on a little body, you can make a person look short.

You can make your funny people move.

This man is funny, but he's stiff.

Throw him into the air. Make lines under him to show a shadow. He moves, but he still looks stiff.

Now he's *really* moving! This is shown by his shadow and by the lines above his shadow. And his arms and legs are bent.

You can make a man run by drawing his body straight and showing only his legs moving.

It is better to draw his body leaning forward with his arms bent. The lines behind him show that he's moving fast.

You can draw to show speed and action.
But lines can have other uses.

Straight lines can show speed.

Puffs and lines show a car moving fast. Lines near wheels help to show a speeding car.

A corkscrew line tells you that this man has fallen.

A curly line shows that this man is feeling dizzy. Little straight lines show how much a bump on the head hurts.

Wavy lines can show that something is cooking.

VINNIE REAM:
Sculptor of Lincoln

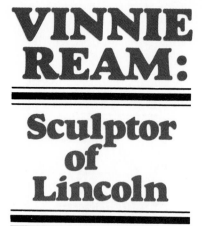

Elisabeth P. Myers

"Look, folks!" the driver said. "There's President Lincoln!"

The Robert Ream family had just arrived in Washington from Missouri that morning in 1862. They looked in the direction the driver had pointed. They saw a tall man in a stovepipe hat and a black shawl walking along the cobblestone street.

"What a sad face!" said fourteen-year-old Vinnie Ream.

The driver nodded. "Sadder than ever lately, too, Miss, since his son Willie died. Just eleven, Willie was."

"President Lincoln would be a wonderful subject for sculpture," said Vinnie. "Someday I'll do a head of him!"

Vinnie's parents did not laugh at her. Though young, their daughter was already a talented artist. Missouri Representative James Rollins had seen some of her work. He had said she could someday be famous if she worked hard enough.

Vinnie had hoped to go to art school in Washington. But money was scarce in Washington that wartime spring, so she looked for work instead. She got a job as a post office clerk and was lucky enough to have Saturdays and Sundays free.

She spent her spare time exploring the city, sketch pad in hand. One day she was in the Capitol Rotunda (a large, round room under the dome) studying the statues shown there. Suddenly someone said, "Vinnie Ream, isn't it?"

420

Vinnie looked around. "Representative Rollins! How nice to see you!" She held out her sketchbook. "See, I'm still working at being an artist!"

Rollins took the book. He leafed through the pages and stopped on seeing her drawing of a figure on horseback.

"The statue of Andrew Jackson that's in Lafayette Square!" he said. "You've caught the spirit of it exactly!" He paused. Then he said, "Vinnie, how would you like to meet the sculptor?"

Vinnie clapped her hands. "Could I?"

"Nothing easier. Clark Mills works near here. Let's go to see him now."

Mills was preparing clay when his visitors arrived. He wiped his hands on a wet towel and greeted them.

"My young friend here wants to be a sculptor like you," Rollins said.

Vinnie blushed, but Mills smiled at her. He picked up a lump of clay.

"Catch!" he said.

Vinnie was surprised, but she caught it. She turned the clay gently in her hands, liking the feel of it.

"Do a portrait of me," Mills suggested.

Vinnie didn't hesitate. She took one long look at him. Then she sat down and set to work. In a short time, she had modeled a head. It was rough, but it looked like Mills.

"Not bad," he said. "Now try a subject you know better."

Vinnie was excited now. She took another lump of clay and began to mold it. She was so busy that she did not notice that Rollins had left the room. Nor did she notice that Mills had returned to his own work.

Several hours passed. Vinnie's fingers grew tired, but still she kept on. Mills often looked up from his task to watch her, but he said nothing until she gave the clay a final stroke and sat back to look at it.

"That certainly is a fine head," Mills said then.

The tone of his voice made Vinnie's heart pound. "Thank you," she said softly.

Mills handed her a towel. "Next time you come, bring a smock," he suggested.

And Vinnie did return—just as often as she could.

On November 8, 1864, Lincoln was elected to a second term as president. Vinnie wondered how he could stand the problems he had to face each day. Every time she saw him, he looked sadder and more bowed-down than the time before.

Her desire to mold a head of this "man of sorrows" grew until at last she sought Representative Rollins again.

"Do you think Mr. Lincoln would let me sculpt him while he's working at his desk?" she asked. "I'd be so quiet he wouldn't know I was there!"

"If I get a chance, I'll ask him," Rollins said. "But don't get your hopes too high."

At first, Lincoln refused. "There are already too many likenesses of this homely face," he said.

But when Rollins told Lincoln more about Vinnie, Lincoln became interested. The tale of Vinnie's first visit to Clark Mills made him grin.

"She has courage!" he said. "I think I'll let her sculpt me after all!"

Vinnie spent a half-hour with Abraham Lincoln twice each week for five months. True to her promise, she never spoke except to answer him. Vinnie studied President Lincoln's many moods. In her diary, she wrote about two moods she remembered especially. In one, Lincoln was sitting in "a chair at his desk, his head bowed upon his chest...or at the window, from which he had often watched his son Willie playing. Sometimes great tears rolled down his cheeks."

Vinnie's visits with the President ended suddenly. She worked in the White House as usual Friday, April 14, 1865. But she never saw Lincoln alive again. The same night he was shot. And he died the next morning.

Soon after his death, people began to ask for a life-size statue of the dead President. They wanted a statue placed in the Capitol Rotunda. Congress asked sculptors to apply for the job. A committee was sent to view the head Vinnie had done. They returned to the Capitol to report, "It's Lincoln to the life!"

427

On July 28, 1866, the contract to do a life-size statue was awarded to Vinnie Ream.

She worked for nearly three years on a plaster model. When it was done, she traveled to Carrara, Italy. There she chose the marble for the final statue.

She had told Congress she would complete her task by January, 1871. And she kept her word.

The unveiling took place on January 25. President Grant gave a short speech. So did the Speaker of the House of Representatives, James G. Blaine. Finally the moment came. The covering of the statue was lifted, and a silence fell upon the great hall. It lasted several minutes before someone broke the spell by clapping. Then the room was filled with applause.

Vinnie held her head high through the applause. But her eyes were full of tears. When she was called upon to say a few words, she could only whisper, "Thank you. Thank you all."

Then the Speaker of the House of Representatives said, "It is for us to thank you. You have made the President live again. No one can look upon this statue and not feel as if he were in the actual presence of Abraham Lincoln."

The greatest triumph of Vinnie Ream was her statue of Abraham Lincoln which stands in the Rotunda of the Capitol Building, Washington, D. C.

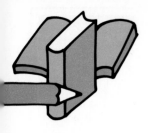

At a Glance

You have probably seen a movie preview. It shows brief scenes from a movie to be shown at a later time. A preview helps you decide if you want to watch the entire film later.

You can preview books as well as movies. For example, you might find many articles with information for a report. You do not have time to read all the articles carefully. So instead, you preview each article to see if it will be helpful to you. If you decide the article might be useful, then you read the article more carefully.

There are two steps in previewing an article. First, look at the title of the article. Notice any subheadings that come under the main heading, or title. Look at any pictures and their captions.

Second, skim the article. Glance at the paragraphs. Read only the most important words. Usually, these key words will give you the main idea of the paragraph.

Checking headings and pictures and skimming articles are helpful ways to select material for a report. Once the material has been selected, you must read each article slowly and carefully.

ACTIVITY A The first part of a long article appears on the next page. Take the first step in previewing: Look only at the title, the subheadings, the picture, and its caption. Then answer the questions.

THE HISTORY OF MUSIC

Music in Ancient Egypt

Music has existed for thousands of years. A rock dating from 800 B.C. has a song engraved on it. This engraving is evidence that an early system of musical notes had been developed even at that time.

Ancient Egyptians had instruments of all basic types. The people banged sticks together and jingled metal rods. They sang in the temple of the gods.

Music in Ancient Greece

Music played an important part in Greek society. Two great thinkers, Plato and Aristotle, believed that music directly affected the souls and actions of people. Greeks used music with dance and theater.

Like the Egyptians, the Greeks also sang songs to praise their gods. Choruses of voices worshiped the gods through their singing.

A Greek musician plays the harp.

1. What is the subject of the entire article?
2. What two countries does this part of the article discuss?
3. Name an instrument played by the Greeks.

ACTIVITY B   Now skim the article. Read only the key words in each paragraph. Then answer the questions.

1. How long has music existed?
2. What kind of instruments did ancient Egyptians use?
3. How did ancient Greeks use music for entertainment?
4. What part did music play in ancient Greek religion?

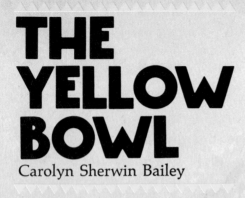

THE YELLOW BOWL

Carolyn Sherwin Bailey

From where she stood, at the top of the sky-ladder, the Hopi girl, Nampeyo, could see all of the First Mesa, her home. Her whole world lay before her: the Painted Desert of Arizona, the far glimmer of blue rivers, the distant line of snow-topped mountains.

There at the top of the natural steps that made the sky-ladder in the rocks, Nampeyo saw the Medicine Man at work on his sand painting. He bent before the Hopi shrine, a huge pile of rocks. Out of this grew flowering shrubs and wild flowers. He was making a sacred picture on a flat space in front of the shrine.

Nampeyo liked the old man. He had given her the Katchina doll which she now took out of a deep pocket in her skirt. But the Medicine Man was old-fashioned, the boys and girls thought. They respected him. But they did not listen to him.

She held the small figure of the Katchina up to the sunlight. It was no ordinary doll. It was carved of soft cottonwood, the holy wood of her people. The feathered head-dress, flat painted feet, embroidered skirt, and masklike face represented a Rain Dancer's costume. When she was a child, the Medicine Man had led the Rain Dancers in a ceremony and given the Katchina to Nampeyo. All the little ones of the village were given these dolls. And the boys and girls prized them. Now Nampeyo, being thirteen, must give up dolls. She was sorry about that.

When Nampeyo came home, her mother was grinding the last of the winter's corn on the great stone in the center of their one large room. It was a pleasant room, hung with gay blankets, the family's clothing, and the ceremonial masks. Low couches covered with more soft blankets lined the walls. Nampeyo started to hang the Katchina on a hook in the adobe wall beside her mother's old doll. There it would remain.

But something stopped Nampeyo. She seated the Katchina, stiff and staring, on the white wool of her bed blanket.

Her mother smiled. "Wait awhile before you put it away. Your grandmother used to tell me that Katchinas were the spirits of living people who had their homes in the mountains. In the summer they came secretly to the valleys. They brought gifts of sweet melons and corn from their farms. And your grandmother told me, also, that a Katchina doll has a message for those who can hear. Let it remain there on your bed, daughter. I don't think a Katchina likes to hang from a hook."

Nampeyo had a busy day. She helped with the corn grinding, swept the floor, made the bread, and weeded the new garden. After supper, she sat a moment on the edge of her bed beside the Katchina. The Katchina's eyes were bright.

Nampeyo was alone. Her father and brothers were down in the valley where they lived until the fields were plowed and planted. Her mother had gone to teach a weaving design to a neighbor.

The things in the room seemed alive to the girl. The eyes of the Katchina seemed to move, then rest on a dark corner. Echoing among the cliffs came the notes of a drum. Its deep tones beat through the night, closer and closer. Nampeyo ran out of the house trembling. She almost fell upon the Medicine Man, who was walking home.

"The Katchina is alive!" Nampeyo cried. "It is looking toward something in the room that I cannot see." She held the old man's hand as they entered the dim room.

"The Katchina wants us to follow her eyes," said the Medicine Man. "Come let us see what she looks at."

The Medicine Man led Nampeyo to an old pile of pottery tools. He lifted them in turn, blowing off the dust. There were spoons made from dried gourds, colored pebbles for polishing, and paint brushes made of soap weed. There were some old round molds, the stones left from an ancient firing kiln, and pointed stone tools for drawing designs on the surface of soft clay.

"For generations, your people have made good pottery," he said. "They molded and decorated it slowly, in peace and well-being. Your family has kept these tools because they were precious. Even these gourd spoons were blessed by the Hopi priests. Look at your long fingers, Nampeyo. When you were a very small child, you used to dig up our colored clays and shape little bowls for your Katchina. Who knows what a doll remembers?"

"I like the feeling of clay. Perhaps I could mold a yellow bowl in beauty now?"

The old man nodded his head. "So it shall be," he agreed. "When you have finished your home duties, bring the Katchina up the rock steps to the shrine. There we will collect and sift our colored clay, yellow, red, and white. We will build a kiln and look about us at the sky, the earth, the birds, and the animals for our designs. You shall be a potter, Nampeyo. Would you like that, my girl?"

"Oh, so much!"

She held his hand in thanks and watched him as he started to climb up, up, to his house. Then she went inside and lay down beside the Katchina. She held the doll close, and was soon fast asleep.

All spring, all summer, Nampeyo spent her free time with the Medicine Man. The other young people wondered at her interest in the old priest and his strange work. Sand painting had gone out of fashion in the First Mesa. The pottery on sale at the trading post was quickly turned on a wheel and painted in patterns that meant nothing. But Nampeyo and her friend kept at their work.

The clay that they dug out of nearby pits had to be finely sifted. They built a stone kiln near the shrine. And they gathered corn stalks when harvest time came, for drying and feeding the fire. The paints had to be mixed; black was taken from the bee-plant and stored in clay jars. An orange-red paint was made from iron deposits in the earth. Their kiln had a grate on which the pottery rested as it was slowly fired. As it hardened, the pottery would turn yellow, orange, or brown, according to the skill of the potter. While Nampeyo and the Medicine Man made ready for modeling their bowl, they talked. The Medicine Man explained each step of the art.

"Roll the clay into smooth, long coils," he told her. "The overlapping of these coils will build the bowl smooth and high for the painting. Shape it from the inside out and then smooth it with your tool. That sharp stone is for drawing the design. Choose an old picture. Straight lines and curves may be combined to show the rain filling the earth with running water. A cross will be a star. A half circle draws the moon.

Fill in your lines with paint, earth black or red. We shall dry the bowl in the sun a little and then fire it. Ah, my child, you take to the art as if the Katchinas themselves had taught you."

"Will anyone like our work?" she asked her old friend as another spring came to the First Mesa.

"Wait and see," he told her. "Today we shall take our work down to the trading post. Your pottery will be different from the cheap ware. Never, in my long life, have such beautiful bowls as yours been displayed."

That spring day, a train left some curious travelers at the First Mesa. They swarmed the trading post and crowded about the old man. He wore the ancient blanket and headdress of his ancestors. Beside him was Nampeyo, her eyes shining with pride. About the two were set the pieces of pottery for which their people had long been famed.

A man separated himself from the others. He lifted a yellow bowl Nampeyo had made. "Who made this?" he asked the Medicine Man. "It must return with me to the museum. It is a perfect example of the lost art of Hopi pottery design."

"Who but our Nampeyo, sir," he replied. "She is now a young woman. And she plans to give her life to the art of her ancestors."

"The Medicine Man taught me," Nampeyo quickly said.

As he looked at Nampeyo's bowl, the man said, "This will be our museum's most beautiful piece."

The Katchina listened, forgotten in Nampeyo's pocket. Nampeyo was the star of the occasion. The Medicine Man was the hero.

Spring faded into summer. Winter came to Nampeyo's home, with long days of shaping more clay, modeling and painting more colored bowls. Another year came. And Nampeyo was at the trading post with even more beautiful examples of her work. There were bold black designs of birds, tadpoles, leaves, and flowers. And there were hummingbirds, ears of corn, and butterflies on orange, yellow, and cream pottery.

As long as he could, the Medicine Man taught her and explained the meaning of her work to visitors to the First Mesa. But then Nampeyo was alone with her art. And when she was older, she became blind. But her fingers had worked the art so long that she did not need her eyes. She still offered ancient Hopi pottery to those who cared to learn from it.

Nampeyo was a real person. She spent her life bringing back the art of Hopi pottery making. Today her work is shown in museums and carried on by her pupils. From it we may learn about the meaning art had in the lives of an ancient people of our land. As we study the designs on Nampeyo's bowls, we find that useful things may be beautiful. And that beauty may last longer than people and machines.

KATCHINA DOLLS

American Indians of the southwestern United States believed Katchinas were good spirits who brought rain for crops and scolded anyone who misbehaved. They said Katchinas once lived on earth, but had moved away, leaving their masks behind.

In this painting, the dancer wears the mask of a warrior Katchina.

This is a warrior Katchina dancer from the Hopi tribe.

Here is a Mud Head Clown with an eagle Katchina riding on its back.

by R. Poceye

Museum of the American Indian, Heye Foundation

This is the story of Peter Parker— a boy who learned about jazz.

When he was still quite small, Peter Parker had strong musical feelings. When his father sang, Peter moaned. When his mother sang, Peter howled.

By the time he was five, Peter had his own toy trumpet.

At six, he was given a phonograph that was as small and sturdy as he.

And at seven, a transistor radio was added. It filled a bit more of Peter's huge hunger for music.

Suddenly one day, Peter put a bold sign outside the door of his room: MUSIC IS BEING MADE—DO NOT ENTER.

The door was then closed.

From that day on, the sign appeared and remained in place from four to six every afternoon. From behind the door, Peter's parents could hear a trumpet playing or the phonograph playing Prokofiev or the radio playing Rossini.

Often all three played at once. And the loudest by far was the trumpet.

Soon Peter had a real trumpet and a real teacher, whose feelings about music were as strong as Peter's. Peter's parents began to hear musical scales coming from his room. First, simple scales that soared slowly and floated back down again, sometimes stumbling on the way.

Then more and more difficult scales that climbed quickly and fell with dizzying speed.

From exercises, Peter went on to play real tunes—tunes that sounded like a small stream in a great hurry or a deep and peaceful river or a lightning storm or nothing Peter's parents could imagine at all.

Peter told them that these last, strange sounds were called modern music.

They nodded. But they were not quite sure they understood.

Soon Peter and his teacher began to play together. Gradually it became difficult to tell Peter apart from his teacher.

By the time he was fourteen, Peter was an excellent and proud trumpet player. There was hardly any music printed that he couldn't read.

One summer afternoon, although the sign was on Peter's door and he was undisturbed, he could not concentrate. Somewhere, in some other house nearby, a small jazz band was playing.

Leading all the other instruments was a tenor saxophone player. He sounded more daring and more full of surprises than any musician Peter had ever heard. Peter was curious—and restless.

Peter took his trumpet, left his room, followed the sound, and discovered three young men in the garage of a house on the next block. Seeing his trumpet, the young musicians asked Peter to join them.

Peter looked and looked again. But nowhere could he see any printed music.

He tried to join in their music. But some-

thing was terribly wrong.

Peter could not find a place for himself. Every time he tried, the music sputtered to a stop. He just didn't fit.

"Look, kid," the tenor sax man told him, "you know your way around that horn all right. But you don't know jazz. When you do, come back again. We'll be around."

Peter sadly went home. But he had been excited by the music he had heard in the garage.

So he began to listen to jazz records, especially records which featured trumpet players. Soon he was having fun trying to play some of his classical pieces in jazztime.

Peter also began to hear that all jazz trumpet players had their own ways of playing.

It was almost like people talking—with growls and chuckles and roars and whispers and shouts and sudden in-between notes.

Finally Peter Parker felt ready.

He ran to the garage in the house on the next block.

But when he started to play with the other young musicians, there was still something terribly wrong.

He just didn't fit. Whatever he tried to play with them, the result was the same. Peter's horn stuck out as if he were all alone. He could not find a place for himself.

The other young musicians seemed to be having a conversation. But when he started to blow, it was as if he were using another language than theirs.

He looked at his trumpet, but nothing was wrong with it.

He looked at the other players. They were shaking their heads.

"Look, friend," the tenor sax man told him, "you know how to play jazz on the trumpet, but you don't know how to play with people. When you do, come back again. We'll be around."

Peter sadly went home. He thought and thought. He finally realized that on all the records he had heard, he had been listening only to the trumpet player, not to what the other musicians were doing. So Peter began to listen to his records in a new way.

He learned about the blending with other instruments. He learned about improvising countermelodies, tunes that fitted in with the solos other people were playing.

Up to then, Peter had been playing along with his records, on top of the music. But now he tried to get inside the music, until he felt as if he were part of the conversation.

He began to improvise with recordings of all kinds of music.

He leaped into symphonies and out again.

He poked his trumpet into string quartets, and he chatted with oboes, with violins and harps and even a bassoon, and with all kinds of jazz bands.

Now once again Peter felt ready, and returned to the garage of the house on the next block.

This time, when he started to play with the other young jazz musicians, he fitted in perfectly.

But after a while the other musicians stopped, and they looked at him sadly.

Peter felt chilled. "Look, kid," the tenor saxophone player said, "you know everything except what to say in the music. You and that trumpet make a fine machine. But jazz isn't a machine. Jazz is how you feel. What do you feel? When you know, come back again. We'll be around."

Peter sadly went home. At first he was puzzled. But little by little he began to be angry. He rushed to his room, tore the sign off his door, grabbed his trumpet, and began to play.

The first notes were full of rage—raw and ugly.

But for some strange reason playing them made Peter feel good. He looked at the trumpet, and he thought, "These are my notes. This music is me." As the hours went by, the angry notes turned into triumphant notes, then into happy ones—all kinds of notes filling the room. "And all these notes are mine!" Peter said. "These notes are how I feel."

And that day and on the days that followed, something began to happen inside Peter. He was becoming more and more restless, and he didn't quite know why. There were times when he felt so good that he couldn't hold all his joy. There were other times when he felt all alone. And sometimes he was afraid, afraid of how angry he could be at his parents, at his teachers, at his friends, and even at himself. But whatever he felt came out in his music. It was as if his trumpet had become part of him.

Finally Peter felt really ready, and he went back to the garage on the next block.

And this time, when he started to play with the other jazz musicians, he knew right away that he belonged. They played together for a long time, full of the pleasure and surprises of making music.

Out of breath, Peter put his trumpet aside. He found it hard to stop smiling. "Say," he said to the tenor saxophonist, "where does it end? I mean, what more do I have to know?"

Then the tenor saxophonist grinned at him. "You just have to keep on being yourself. That's what jazz is. You. And that's why jazz is always changing. You dig? Come on, let's blow."

When Peter Parker returned home, he made a new sign and put it on his door.

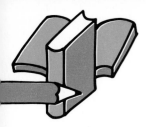

What's the Idea?

A paragraph is a group of sentences that talk about one subject. Usually, the paragraph makes one important point. This point is called the *main idea*.

Sometimes the main idea of a paragraph is stated in one sentence. The sentence might be at the beginning, middle, or end of the paragraph. Read the paragraph below.

> Artists may paint in different forms. Mural paintings are done on large wall surfaces. Panel paintings are small pictures painted on wooden boards. Screen paintings are done on paper and silk.

In that paragraph, the main idea is stated in the first sentence: *Artists may paint in different forms.* Now read this paragraph.

> Some artists use oil paints when they work. Others use water colors. Still other artists draw with ink. Artists may choose their own materials.

In that paragraph, the main idea is stated in the last sentence: *Artists may choose their own materials.*

Often, the main idea of a paragraph is not stated in one sentence. The main idea may be contained in two or more sentences. Read the paragraph below.

> An opera is a kind of story. It is told entirely through song. The men and women in the story sing everything to each other. No words are spoken. Operas have been written in several different languages.

In that paragraph, the main idea is shared by two sentences. The main idea is: *An opera is a story told entirely through song.*

Read each paragraph. Write the main idea.

1. Musical instruments are played in different ways. Some instruments, such as drums, are struck. You blow through some instruments, such as trumpets. Sometimes you stroke strings, such as on guitars.

2. The piano was not invented by one individual. It was developed over many years. Ancient people plucked harp strings with their fingers. Later, in the Middle Ages, people struck dulcimer strings with a hammer. Eventually, a piano was made. It had a keyboard to control the hammers that struck the strings.

3. Actors are only some of the people needed to present a play. The director tells the actors where to move onstage. Other workers make the scenery and the costumes. People backstage operate the lights and the curtains. It takes many people to produce a play.

4. William Shakespeare wrote three types of plays. His humorous plays are called *comedies*. He also wrote *histories* that tell about kings and queens. The plays that are very serious are called *tragedies*.

5. Dancers do many exercises. These exercises keep them in shape. They stretch their bodies and do knee bends. They jump and whirl in the air.

6. Ancient people made jewelry from pieces of wood, bone, or iron. Later, they began to use gold and silver for jewelry. Today, expensive jewelry is still made from gold as well as precious stones, or gems.

Listen to the Angels Laughing

Thomaline Aguallo

Antonia is always happy in her grandmother's house. Grandmother has a lion's-paw table and a bathtub that squats on fat white feet, and there is a stained-glass angel on her front door. Grandmother's piano is a great big person visiting on a Sunday afternoon. It sits in the parlor with a wide yellow smile, and it is wearing a Spanish silk shawl.

Grandmother's porch is a palace of flowers, a jungle of color for Antonia's eyes. Antonia lies in a Mexican hammock and fluffs the fur of the marmalade cat. Antonia is nine.

In Grandmother's house it is sunny and warm. It smells of cinnamon and apples and hot herb tea. It smells of chocolate and chili and tortillas wrapped warm and waiting in a snow-white cloth. It smells of the peppermint plant growing outside the kitchen-door.

Grandmother is in the kitchen when Antonia comes in. She is wearing her ruby earrings and a straw sun hat. A big apron covers her dress of bright orange and yellow poppies. Grandmother's hands are white with flour, and she is singing, singing, singing Spanish songs. Antonia doesn't always under-stand the words, but her grandmother always sings the songs. They make Antonia feel good inside.

Grandmother's hair is thick and braided, and her lap is soft and warm. Grandmother wraps her arms around Antonia, as they sit together in the rocking chair in the bright sun of the kitchen.

Grandmother has a box full of jewelry: filigree earrings, turquoise beads, and an amber necklace that catches the light. Grandmother has a black-veiled hat trimmed with velvet roses and a taffeta coat that is the color of the evening sky.

But best of all, Antonia loves the fragile old music box that Grandfather bought in Portugal. "You must open it very gently," Grandmother tells Antonia, "and then the music will come — like the summer rain."

When Antonia stays at Grandmother's house, she sleeps in Grandmother's own soft bed. Sometimes the dark feels too big, too quiet—and Antonia feels very small. It is then that Grandmother brings in the music box. *"Escucha los angeles riendo, mi niña,"* Grandmother says. [Listen to the angels laughing, my little one.] Antonia opens the box and hears the music. Grandmother kisses her and smooths her long dark hair. Antonia is peaceful now. She can fall asleep.

In the summer, Antonia helps her grandmother in the garden. She weeds and waters. She picks peas and lettuce and carrots and piles them in her grandmother's wicker basket. She eats fresh corn right off the stalks and tomatoes that hang like Christmas balls on tall green vines.

In the wintertime, the wind comes. It blows the branches of the pepper tree against the windows of Grandmother's house. Sometimes in the evening, Grandmother sews, and Antonia straightens up the sewing box—folding the fabric, wrapping the balls of ribbon, untangling the lace, winding the thread.

Antonia says, "Please tell me a story."

"I have told you all the stories I will ever know," says Grandmother, her fingers flashing like silver in the evening light. But she tells Antonia about when she was a little girl growing up in Texas.

Somehow the days at Grandmother's house always end the same way: Antonia and Grandmother sitting at the kitchen table, playing checkers with lemon drops on the red-checkered cloth. They drink hot foamy chocolate out of thick white mugs. They eat hot tortillas with butter and jam oozing at the corners. They laugh together, and Grandmother sings a Spanish song.

Then one spring day, the drapes are drawn, and Grandmother's house is dark and quiet. Grandmother is sick, and no one sings any more in Grandmother's house. Antonia comes to visit as usual, but her mother is with her now. The house smells of medicine and of someone else's perfume.

The air feels heavy to Antonia, as if she were wearing someone else's winter coat. Antonia knows her mother is worried. Though her mouth smiles for Antonia, her eyes are old and sad. Sometimes she speaks crossly to Antonia and looks at her as though she takes up too much space in Grandmother's house.

Antonia is told to sit on the brocade couch. She is given a coloring book and a box of crayons, all sharp and pointy the way she likes them. But it is lonely to color without Grandmother sitting near, telling her how well she uses colors, how nicely she keeps inside the lines.

"I want to see my grandmother," Antonia says, pulling at the sleeve of her Aunt Mercedes' dress.

"*Ay, que niña!*" [What a child!] Aunt Mercedes scolds. "Your grandmother needs a lot of rest. She must have quiet now."

"But I want to help my grandmother!" Antonia says. "Mama, can Grandmother see that the orange trees are blooming?"

"Oh, Antonia," says her mother. "Please be still. If you want to help your grandmother, just sit down on the couch. Be quiet as a mouse. That's all you can do."

But Antonia knows they are wrong. She knows she can do more.

Antonia pictures her grandmother lying in a room where it is always night. "What does Grandmother think about?" she wonders. "Does she know when the sun is shining? Does she know the strawberries are flowering in the berry patch by the side of the house?" Antonia remembers how it feels to be in the dark, when it seems that you are all alone.

So one day, when there is no one to notice her or to tell her to stop, Antonia goes up the stairs to her grandmother's room. In her arms she carries something wrapped up like a baby. Grandmother is lying quietly on her big soft bed. The room is shadowy and hot. The only light comes from a candle in a small red glass.

As softly as she can, Antonia tiptoes to Grandmother's window. She draws back the curtain and pulls up the shade. She opens the window. She lets in the light and the smell of wet grass and sweet peas and ripening strawberries.

Antonia sits on her grandmother's bed. "Grandmother," Antonia says. "Listen, Grandmother." She unwraps her grandmother's music box. She opens it with fingers made of feathers. The music box sings like summer rain.

"Oh, Grandmother," Antonia says. *"Yo te amo, abuelita."* [I love you, little grandmother.]

Grandmother's eyes are open and smiling. *"Yo te amo tambien, mijita,"* Grandmother says. [I love you also, little daughter.]

Antonia holds her grandmother's hand. She sings a bit of a Spanish song. They listen to the angels laughing. They both feel good inside.

When I Learned to Whistle

I remember the day when I learned to whistle.
It was in spring and new sounds were all around.
I was five or six and my front teeth were missing,
But I blew until my cheeks stuck out.

I remember walking up and down the block,
Trying to impress those that heard me
With the tunes and sounds that came from my mouth,
For I sounded much better than the birds in the trees.

I remember being hurt, for nobody seemed to care,
And then I met an old man who stopped and smiled.
He too blew until his cheeks stuck out.
He sounded just like me, for his front teeth were missing.

—Gordon Lea
Age 11

Antonio Stradivari

Irene Bennett Needham

After his lunch, the old man rested in the hot Mexican sun. He thought of the music he would play that night. He stretched his hands in the warmth of the sun. He thought of his beloved violin. He smiled to himself. He remembered buying it in 1931 from a stranger who needed money. He had paid him $2.50. He also remembered that in 1931, during the time of depression, no one had had much. How cross Maria had been! He had spent some of the precious grocery money on a violin!

Suddenly the quiet was broken by the sound of running feet.

"Señor! Señor Sanchez," the boy said as he reached the man's side. "For you. A telegram!"

Slowly the man opened it. He began to read. First he smiled, then he laughed.

The boy's eyes were round. "What is it?"

"From the American who liked my violin so when he saw it at Christmas." He laughed again. The whole village had been amused by the stranger's tremendous interest. The stranger had looked inside the violin as if he were looking for gold. "He says my violin was made by Señor Antonio Stradivari. And somebody will buy it for $100,000."

Señor Sanchez was not the first person to learn that his violin was a treasure. He is just one of the most recent. His violin was recognized in 1970. Stories like this one could be told about many people in different parts of the world. Stradivari's violins have turned up in Italian barns, English attics, and American warehouses. Some have been carefully protected.

Others have been harmed by carelessness.

Stradivari's earliest known violin is dated 1666. And he died in 1737. Sometime between these two dates, Stradivari made the instrument that was found in Mexico.

Almost nothing is known of Stradivari's early life and family. But we do know that he was born in 1644. He was probably born in one of the small villages around Cremona, Italy. As a boy of twelve or thirteen, he began to learn violin making with Nicolo Amati. Amati was famous all over Europe for his fine violins. However, it was not until after Amati's death in 1684 that Stradivari began making his own violins in any number. Until then, no doubt, he worked with the other apprentices. They made parts, varnished them, and

helped with all the other jobs in the big workshop.

Stradivari became skilled at his craft. Over the years, he made slight improvements in his violins. Stradivari never made poor violins. But he made some that were much better than all the others.

Fortunately, Stradivari's great talent was noticed. Top prices were paid for his instruments from the time he began to sell them. When Stradivari lived, many rich people had their own orchestras. It was also usual for them to have a set of the best instruments they could afford. Most of them sent to Cremona for string instruments. And many of them asked for Stradivari's. As early as 1682, a banker had Stradivari make a set of string instruments for King James II of England. Other sets of Stradivari instruments were owned by Italian and Spanish noble families.

Today few stringed instruments can match the quality of the Cremona instruments. Amati and Stradivari made instruments that are better than any made since. Some people say that the varnish, the exact recipe for which has been lost, is what made them so special. But no one really knows.

Many of the world's best violinists have chosen Stradivari's violins. But few individuals now can afford to collect them. Some of the most beautiful are held in museum collections. There they can be seen by everyone or lent to famous artists for concerts and recordings. It has been estimated that Stradivari could have made as many as 1,100 instruments, including cellos, violas, and guitars. Of these, only about 600 have been definitely identified. So it is not impossible that a Stradivari instrument might be found in your town.

Sam Clemens of Hannibal

Margery C. Rutherford

Characters

Narrator
Sam Clemens, age ten
Tom Blankenship, age eleven
Laura Hawkins, age ten
Mr. Lange, steamboat captain
Mr. James, ship's mate
Two Voices (offstage)

Production Notes

Setting: *1845, Hannibal, Missouri. No scenery is necessary.*

Playing Time: *15 minutes*

Costumes:* **Sam, Tom, *and* **Narrator** *wear jeans, straw hats, and checkered shirts.* **Laura** *wears long dress.* **Mr. Lange** *and* **Mr. James** *may wear uniforms or nautical caps.*

Properties: *cardboard knife, piece of wood, apple, key, piece of blue glass, pilot's wheel on stand, feed sacks*

Sound Effects: *offstage steamboat whistle, as indicated in the script*

(**Narrator** *enters and stands left.*)

Narrator: You may have met Tom Sawyer, Becky Thatcher, and Huckleberry Finn in books written by Mark Twain. But did you know that Mark Twain wasn't the writer's real name? It was his pen name—the name he used when he wrote his books. His real name was Samuel Langhorne Clemens, and the way he chose his pen name should interest you. Sam Clemens was born in 1835 and was raised in Hannibal, Missouri, a little town on the Mississippi River. Some of the stories he wrote took place in a town very much like Hannibal. It is said that he patterned his character Tom Sawyer after himself.

(**Sam** *enters right and walks slowly to center.*)

(**Narrator** *indicates* **Sam.**) That's Sam when he was ten years old. People say that other characters in his books were copied from boys and girls he knew in his childhood.

(**Tom Blankenship** *enters right and walks to center. He is whittling on a piece of wood.* **Sam** *is frowning and looking thoughtful.*)

(**Narrator** *indicates* **Tom.**) Do you recognize this young man? This is Tom Blankenship, whom you may know as Tom Sawyer's good friend, Huckleberry Finn. Becky Thatcher was copied after Sam's friend Laura Hawkins, who lived near the Clemenses' home.

(**Laura** *enters right, eating an apple. She
walks up right.*)

These were happy days for Sam, Tom, and
Laura, and these were the days Mark Twain
wrote about.

(**Narrator** *exits.*)

Sam: I've been thinking, Tom. I'm going to run away. And when they find out, they'll be sorry. I'll go away, far away, and they'll never know where I am.

Tom: Will you become a pirate, maybe?

Sam: Probably.

Tom: When I run away, that's what I'm going to be.

Laura *(crossing to center):* Who's running away?

Sam: Hello, Laura.

Laura: Are you going to run away, Sam?

Sam: Maybe I will. Maybe I won't.

Laura: Is he, Tom?

Tom: He's thinking about it.

Laura: Oh, Sam, why would you do a silly thing like that?

Sam: Lots of reasons.

Laura: What reasons?

Sam: Well, you know that I'm always getting into trouble and getting whippings. Remember that fence I was supposed to whitewash?

Laura: I know you never finished it.

Sam: I guess I didn't. And you remember how I ate the watermelon when I wasn't supposed to because it wasn't ripe?

Laura: Yes, and you got sick, too.

Sam: And then, this morning, I put a frog in the sugar bowl.

Laura: What happened?

Tom: Is your mother scared of frogs?

Sam: No, she's not scared. But you know how she won't even kill flies 'cause she doesn't want to hurt them.

Laura: Yes. I remember the day she scolded the
cats for catching mice.

Sam: Well, she thought that putting a frog in the
sugar bowl was cruel. But I wish you could
have seen that old frog covered with sugar
and jumping all over the kitchen. (**Sam, Tom,** *and*
Laura *laugh.)* It was funny—till I got a
whipping. So, I'm running away.

Laura: Sam, will you ever come back?

Sam: Never. I won't ever come back. And maybe they'll hear about me and how rich I am, 'cause I'll be richer than anybody. And they'll be sorry.

Tom: When are you going to leave?

Sam: Right now. Tonight. Tonight after everyone's asleep, I'll sneak out of the house and I'll get on the next steamboat. I know what I'll do! I'll be a river pilot! And every time I go down the Mississippi, past old Hannibal, I'll wave to you. And you can come down to the landing to see me if you want to.

Laura: I'm going to miss you, Sam.

Tom: Here, Sam, you can take my knife with you. *(He hands Sam his knife.)* Maybe it'll come in handy sometime. And I have a piece of blue bottle glass to look through. Here, take it. *(He gives Sam a small piece of blue glass.)*

Laura: And here's a key, Sam. It won't unlock anything, but you can have it to keep. *(She hands him the key.)* And here—here's the rest of my apple. *(She gives Sam the apple.)*

Sam: Thanks. Maybe I'll write to you, and maybe I'll see you again. Well, goodbye. I—I guess I'll miss you.

Laura: Goodbye, Sam.

Tom: Goodbye.

> *(Sam exits left.)*

Laura: Tom, do you think we'll ever see him again?

Tom: Oh, sure. He'll be back. Maybe. *(Tom and Laura exit right. Narrator enters and stands at left.)*

Narrator: And so, that very night after the house was quiet and everyone else was asleep, Sam gathered together the gifts Tom and Laura had given him. And he added to them a firecracker, a piece of chalk, two marbles, and the tooth he had lost the week before. Then he crept out the window, grabbed a branch of the apple tree, and climbed down the trunk as he had done many times before.

(**Mr. Lange** *enters right with steamboat pilot's wheel on a stand. He places it center and steers.* **Mr. James** *brings in some feed sacks, puts them down, and then stands with his back toward the sacks.*)

Off Sam ran to the boat landing, where a river steamboat was docked. When no one was watching, Sam edged his way up the gangplank and hid safely in a pile of feed sacks on the lower deck.

(**Sam** *enters and hides behind sacks.*)

And then the steamboat started to move, and Sam listened to the wonderful sounds of the river.

(*Sound of steamboat whistle is heard from offstage.*)

1st Voice (*offstage*): Mark twain!

2nd Voice (*offstage in distance*): Mark twain!

Narrator: The men were measuring the depth of the water, and Sam wanted to watch. But he poked his head out from behind a feed sack just at the wrong time.

(**Sam** *pokes his head up, just as* **Mr. James** *turns.*)

The ship's mate, Mr. James, caught Sam and brought him up to the captain, Mr. Lange, who was at the wheel. (**Narrator** *exits.*)

(**Mr. James** *takes* **Sam** *by the arm and leads him to* **Mr. Lange.**)

1st Voice *(offstage):* Quarter less twain!
2nd Voice *(offstage in distance):* Quarter less twain!
Mr. James: We have company, Mr. Lange. Says his name's Sam Clemens.

Mr. Lange: A stowaway! Well, now, what would a lad like you be doing aboard the Mary Lee?

Sam: I want to be a river pilot, sir.

Mr. Lange: I'll bet you ran away from home.

(**Sam** *nods.*)

Playing hooky from school most likely.

Sam: Oh, no, sir, but I guess I've done my share of that, too.

Mr. James: You don't like school?

Sam: No. Seems like I get whippings there all the time. And besides, school takes too much time out of my day.

Mr. Lange: Don't you like any subjects?

Sam: No, sir, I don't. But if I had to choose, I guess I'd say spelling. We have spelling bees every Friday at Mr. Cross's school on the square. I'm pretty good in them. Won a medal in spelling once. Almost won first prize, but I missed a word.

Mr. James: What word did you go down on?

Sam: Triumph. But I can spell it now. T-R-I-U-M-P-H.

Mr. Lange: Good for you!

1st Voice *(offstage):* Mark twain!

2nd Voice *(offstage in distance):* Mark twain!

Sam: I like that.

Mr. James: What do you like?

Sam: When the men call out "Mark twain."

Mr. James: Do you know what it means?

Sam: Oh, yes, sir. It means we are in safe water. The man who is calling out has a pole, and it has black and white stripes around it to show

how deep the water is so we won't run aground.

Mr. Lange: Absolutely right! Sounds as if you've been around the river awhile.

Sam: I have. All my life I've lived right in Hannibal, Missouri.

Mr. Lange: Do you have many friends in Hannibal?

Sam: Oh, yes, sir.

Mr. Lange: Who's your best friend?

Sam: I have lots of friends. Tom Blankenship's just about my best friend. Tom doesn't have a ma, just a pa, and his pa doesn't care much what Tom does. He never goes to Sunday school, and he never has to take a bath—not ever. His pa just doesn't care anything about baths —or shoes either. And you know something else? Tom never has to go to school!

Mr. James: Well, boy, now that you've run away, you'll never have to go to school either—or take baths.

Sam: No, I'll bet I won't—ever.

Mr. Lange: What do you boys do back there in Hannibal?

Sam: I guess we have the most fun rolling rocks down Holliday's hill. We roll big ones down, and they crash at the bottom. And we like to go to the cave just outside of town. Once we got lost in it while we were exploring, and we couldn't find the way back for a long, long time. Lots of people have gotten lost in there. Starved and died, too, before they could get out.

1st Voice *(offstage):* Half less twain!

2nd Voice *(offstage in distance):* Half less twain!

Mr. Lange: Have any pets at home, Sam?

Sam: We have ten cats, maybe eleven. The red one ran away last Tuesday, and he hasn't come back yet. So I didn't count him. Sure am worried about that red one.

Mr. James: I imagine he'll be back soon as he gets hungry enough. Animals usually do.

Sam: Not this one, I don't think.

Mr. James: Why not?

Sam: Well—well, I fed him some pain killer. He didn't seem to mind at first. Then he started acting kind of funny. So I guess maybe I shouldn't have fed it to him.

Mr. James: No, I guess maybe you shouldn't have.

Mr. Lange: You boys go swimming much?

Sam: Mostly every day. Once I swam all the way across the Mississippi and all the way back without stopping! Got a cramp in my leg on the way back and had to swim the rest of the way with my arms only.

Mr. James: What did your ma and pa say? I'll bet they were mad.

Sam: They never found out. And I hope they never do. I'm already in enough trouble.

Mr. Lange: I won't tell. Will you, Mr. James?

Mr. James: Never. I won't tell anyone.

Sam: As long as you've sworn not to tell, there's something else I don't want them to know.

Mr. James: What's that?

Sam: The other day at school I turned loose my pinchbug *(laughing)*, and you should have seen those kids!

Mr. Lange: And what did the schoolmaster do?

Sam: Switched me. But that didn't hurt much.

Mr. Lange: *(laughing):* It sounds to me as if you have a pretty good time there at home.

Sam: Oh, yes—I mean—well, no, not exactly. I don't like it that much.

Mr. Lange: Sam, if you're aiming to be a river pilot, there's something I'd better tell you.

Sam: What's that?

Mr. Lange: River pilots have to finish school. They have to know about the stars, how to read maps, and how to plot a course. They have to write carefully and keep logs, and they read a lot.

Sam: They do?

Mr. Lange: You bet they do. You know the old saying, Sam, a person can only grow as tall as he lets himself? You know what that means?

Sam: Yes, sir. That means I have to grow up some.

Mr. Lange: You're right, Sam. Grow in tallness, but also grow in learning. A fellow can't learn too much these days. So my advice to you is to go right back to Hannibal and finish up your schooling. Then when the time's ripe, you just come looking for Henry Lange, and we'll see about finding you a spot on the Mississippi.

Sam: Thank you anyway, Mr. Lange, but I really think I'd rather stay here.

Mr. Lange: Bet your ma is scared stiff 'cause you're gone. And I'll bet your pa is out looking for you right now. What's your pa do?

Sam: Pa's a lawyer back home.

Mr. Lange: Well, you're a nice boy, and it seems your ma and pa have taken a lot of time to raise you right. I'm sure they love you, Sam.

Sam: I—I guess they do.

Mr. Lange: You should think about how sad and lonely they're going to be without you.

Sam: I guess—maybe—I'd better get on the next boat for Hannibal.

Mr. Lange: Good idea, Sam. Someday you'll make a dandy river pilot. Just you wait and see.

Mr. James: We just passed west shore sandbar, sir. Shall I take the wheel now?

Mr. Lange: Yes, Mr. James.

(**Mr. James** *takes the wheel.*)

And I'll go down and see if I can scare up three cups of hot chocolate. How does that sound?

Mr. James: Sounds good to me.

Mr. Lange: You hungry, Sam?

Sam: Yes, sir. My friend Laura Hawkins gave me part of her apple, and that's all I've had to eat since supper.

Mr. Lange: Then maybe I can find a sandwich, too. Would you like to come with me or stay up here and help Mr. James?

Sam: I'd rather stay here, sir.

Mr. Lange: Now you know, that's exactly what I figured you'd like to do! I'll be right back.
   (**Mr. Lange** *exits.*)

Mr. James: If you're going to be a river pilot, Sam Clemens, you may as well start learning now. Want a try at the wheel?

Sam: Yes, sir! (**Sam** *goes over to wheel.*)

1st Voice *(offstage):* Mark twain!

2nd Voice *(offstage in distance):* Mark twain!

   (Steamboat whistle sounds offstage. **Narrator** *enters left.)*

Narrator: And Sam Clemens did grow up to become a river pilot. But that's not why we remember him. Sam Clemens grew up to be Mark Twain, one of America's most outstanding writers and humorists. And Sam Clemens, the boy from Hannibal, Missouri, took his pen name from the call of the men on the steamboats as they marked the depth of the water with the words *mark twain.*

1st Voice *(offstage):* Mark twain.

2nd Voice *(offstage in distance):* Mark twain!

   (curtain)

NEW YEAR JOURNAL

In his book **The Innocents Abroad,** Mark Twain remembers "the journal I opened with the New Year once when I was a boy." This is that journal.

MONDAY. Got up, washed, went to bed.
TUESDAY. Got up, washed, went to bed.
WEDNESDAY. Got up, washed, went to bed.
THURSDAY. Got up, washed, went to bed.
FRIDAY. Got up, washed, went to bed.
NEXT FRIDAY. Got up, washed, went to bed.
FRIDAY FORTNIGHT. Got up, washed, went to bed.
FOLLOWING MONTH. Got up, washed, went to bed.

"I stopped then," he adds, "discouraged. Startling events appeared to be too rare in my career to make a diary necessary. I still think with pride, however, that even at that early age, I washed when I got up."

Which Trunk Is The Right Trunk?

In "Sam Clemens of Hannibal," the author says:

Sam climbed down the <u>trunk</u> of a tree.

What is a *trunk*? A large box? A long snout? The stem of a tree? If you looked the word up in a dictionary, you would see that all three answers are correct. The word *trunk* has more than one meaning.

How can you tell which meaning the author is using? Look at the other words in the sentence. They will give you clues.

Which meaning of *trunk* is being used in each of these sentences:

I packed my clothes in the <u>trunk</u>.

The elephant lifted its <u>trunk.</u>

In the sentences below, the underlined words may have more than one meaning. Match each underlined word with its correct meaning in the sentence. Remember, the other words in the sentence will give you clues.

1. The elephants <u>trumpet</u> to each other across the jungle.
2. The musician played a <u>trumpet.</u>

    a. a musical instrument   b. make a blaring noise

3. Peter knew he had found the <u>right</u> answer.
4. He turned <u>right</u> at the corner.

    a. correct   b. toward the east

5. The ball began to <u>roll</u> down the hill.
6. He spread butter on the <u>roll.</u>

    a. a small piece of bread   b. move

Sometimes

Sometimes I make up songs
to the rhythm of the swing swinging,
and the creak of the chair creaking.

They just come to me.
I don't know how, and
I don't know why.

I make up songs, and I
sing them to myself, and
to the wind.

—Eleanor Schick

For Many Reasons

In the story "Sam Clemens of Hannibal," Sam ran away from home for many reasons. He was always getting into trouble. He didn't like school, either. He also wanted to find adventure as a river pilot.

Sam eventually decided to return home. By reading carefully, you can discover his reasons. Sam missed his friends in Hannibal. He missed swimming every day and playing with his cats. Sam also didn't want to hurt his parents. He knew he had to return to "grow tall," or grow up. He needed to finish his education, too.

You must read carefully to discover why characters act as they do. Sometimes, the reasons are obvious. Other times, you need to think hard to discover the reasons.

ACTIVITY A   Read the story. Then read the list of possible reasons why Tina studied hard for her test. On your paper, write the reasons that were stated or hinted at in the story.

Tina opened her spelling book and read the words again. Her big spelling test was the next day.

"If only I could get a perfect score," Tina thought.

Tina wanted a perfect score badly. Her Uncle Albert had promised her a gift if she scored 100%. Then there was Karen Thomas. Karen always teased Tina about her spelling mistakes. Getting 100% would really show her!

Tina thought how proud she would be to get 100%. Her parents would be happy, too. Then Tina realized the most important reason for studying hard. If she worked hard at her studies, she would become a better speller.

"Tina," the teacher said later, "I have something for you." Tina saw 100% on her paper. She grinned from ear to ear.

Possible Reasons Why Tina Studied Hard for the Test

1. A perfect score would make her feel proud.
2. She wanted a present from her teacher.
3. She wanted Karen Thomas to stop teasing her.
4. A perfect score would make her parents happy.
5. She wanted the gift from Uncle Albert.
6. She wanted to go to a different school.
7. She would become a better speller.
8. She had no other school work that night.
9. She was doing very poorly in spelling class.
10. She wanted to win the spelling bee afterward.
11. She wanted to be the best speller in the class.

ACTIVITY B   Read the story. On your paper, write the answer to each question.

Stan and Bill were brothers. When they grew older, Stan moved to the country. Bill stayed in the city. Stan liked the quiet sounds of the country. People did not rush to do things. Stan enjoyed fishing in the lake behind his house.

Bill rarely left the city. He loved to visit the museums and stores. He attended many plays. The large library provided many books for him to read.

1. Write three reasons why Stan lived in the country.
2. Write three reasons why Bill lived in the city.

OUTLETS

Do you play a musical instrument? Paint pictures? Play a sport? Dream of what you might do or be someday? All these are outlets through which we express ourselves. They are the special ways we share our thoughts and feelings. Our outlets may give pleasure to both ourselves and others. They may also change as we explore new ways to express ourselves.

Thinking About "Outlets"

1. Why did the students think Mr. Sleeves' paintings were not good choices for their classroom?
2. What helped Vinnie Ream capture the spirit of Abraham Lincoln in her sculpture?
3. How did the music box help Antonia and her grandmother express their feelings for each other?
4. In what ways did Peter's music change as he took each step in his "Journey into Jazz"?
5. Think about Mariko and Nampeyo. How is each girl's way of expressing herself influenced by her background?
6. What are some of your outlets for expressing yourself? Why did you choose them?
7. Mark Twain makes fun of journals in his "New Year Journal." Think about what you know of his boyhood from the play, "Sam Clemens of Hannibal." Write a journal for three imaginary days of Mark Twain's boyhood.

EXPLORATIONS

The American West has a long and rich history. At one time, American Indians were the only people who lived there. Then, in the 1700's, people traveled north from Mexico to settle along the Pacific coast in what is now California. Still later, thousands of pioneers traveled long distances to start new lives in the West. Some moved to find richer farm lands, better climates, or gold. Others traveled simply for the excitement of exploring new territory. In those days, a journey to the West was an adventure that could last for many, many months.

In "Explorations," you will share some of the excitement of the westward movement. First, you will read an essay that tells facts about wagon-train life. Then you will share the adventures of a pioneer family. You will read a biography of an artist who captured the spirit of the old West in his paintings. You will also read parts of a letter from a courageous young girl who describes her difficult journey to California.

As you read, compare your world with the world of the pioneers. Think about how traveling across the country has changed since the days of the pioneers.

WHEELS

Wheels over the mountains
Wheels over the plains—
Covered-wagon wheels
In the winds and the rains

Marked the path
Of the pioneers
Across our land
In the early years.

Straight through the wilderness
Westward bound
The wagons moved on,
Breaking new ground.

And now, far above
That ancient trail
Carved by the wheels
The jet planes sail.

From the eastern shore
To the west they flow
And they skim in half a day
All the continent below.

And where are their wheels?
Tucked inside,
With nothing to do
But ride and ride.

Across those miles
That were hard and slow
For the covered wagons
Of long ago.
                    —Claudia Lewis

Prairie Schooners

Glen Rounds

The Westward Movement is a well-known and important event in American history. Many, many movies and books have told of the long journeys taken by so many people. Most pioneers traveling West joined long wagon trains headed in that direction. As a group, the pioneers — or emigrants, as they were sometimes called — were able to help one another survive the hardships of the difficult journey. They were able to share their hopes, dreams, and sorrows during the long months of moving.

But were the wagon trains really like those seen in the movies? Were all wagons the same? What did the emigrants take with them on their journeys? What were their day-to-day experiences and problems?

This nonfiction selection gives factual information about the wagon trains. You may find it more fascinating than the make-believe stories you have read in books or seen in movies.

The wagon trains carrying the emigrants and their goods were of many kinds and sizes. There were lightly built outfits from the flat farming states. There were huge high-sided Conestogas built for hauling freight in the eastern mountains. There was even an occasional two-wheeled cart or top buggy to be seen among them. Some were drawn by strings of six or eight pairs of horses or oxen. Others were hitched to a single team of two.

The size and condition of a wagon outfit depended on what was thought suitable. It also depended on what the emigrant could afford: a big wagon, a middle-sized wagon, a small wagon, or a two-wheeled cart. All had canvas wagon covers stretched over wooden bows to protect their loads.

The wagons pitched and swayed across the wide plains with their white canvas tops ballooning and whipping in the wind. Seen from a distance, they looked like small ships. From their appearance, they came, naturally enough, to be called *prairie schooners*.

The emigrants faced many of the same problems as sailors preparing small ships for a long voyage into unknown seas. Their wagons were carefully supplied and packed for the long trip. From the Missouri River westward to Oregon, the settlers faced a trip of up to one hundred and fifty days. It was a trip that would take them across an unknown land.

The first five hundred miles was a sea of rolling plains. The trail rose steadily to the foot of the Rocky Mountains, where it was crossed by sluggish, dangerous rivers. Beyond these rivers were more weeks of travel over high mountain passes, through deep canyons, and across wide deserts.

For the entire trip, a wagon train would have to be as self-contained as a fleet of wooden sailing ships at sea. The train would pass a few forts and trading posts run for fur trappers. But there would be no place for the travelers to put in for repairs or to buy supplies or equipment.

Space in the wagons was precious. The emigrants had to find room for their clothing and household goods. They also had to pack enough supplies for the entire trip, which might be longer than planned due to accidents, bad weather, and a hundred other possibilities. These provisions had to share the limited space with supplies for a farm: ploughs, shovels, axes, seed grain, and other items.

Nor was that all. The months of jolting travel over the rough trail would damage even the strongest wagons and equipment. Axles would break. Iron tires would work loose from wheels shrunk by long spells of dry weather. Wooden spokes would splinter and have to be replaced by others made on the spot. Chains and ox yokes would break or be lost. Then always, there would be sore-footed oxen and horses needing new iron shoes to save them from permanent injury.

So even more would be added to the constantly growing loads. Tools for rough blacksmithing,

carpentry, and wagon building were needed. Nails, rivets, rods, and scrap iron for making horseshoes, ox shoes, or wagon hardware must be fit in. Water barrels, lashed to the outsides of the wagons, were a necessity that must not be overlooked. Everything had to be provided. Even small items, such as horseshoe nails, could save the day in certain circumstances.

Not every wagon carried the full list of these items, of course. But careful leaders made sure, before setting out, that somewhere in the train these necessary things could be found when needed.

Getting a wagon train lined up and ready to start the first day's travel was not the simple matter one might think. The emigrants would have been up and stirring their cookfires at the first light. They would all have the best intentions of making an early start. But almost as soon as breakfast was over, things would begin to go wrong.

Someone was almost sure to discover that one ox—if not more than one—had wandered off. Hitching would have to be delayed until the creature was found and brought back. A half-trained animal might break loose and run, scattering people and upsetting cook-pots and grub boxes until it was finally cornered. An ox, finding itself being yoked to an ox that was a complete stranger, might set up a disturbance of its own—tangling chains and threatening to overturn the wagon.

Yokes and other gear were misplaced or some important part was found to be missing. All through the camp, cattle bawled and people shouted and waved their arms. Meanwhile, children and barking dogs were underfoot everywhere.

Any of the experienced freighters passing on the nearby Santa Fe Trail could have straightened out the confusion in short order. But among any group of emigrants, there were usually only a few people who really understood livestock and complicated gear. These few were constantly being called from their own outfits to take charge of one emergency or another for the less-experienced.

So what with one thing and another, it was usually well into the day before the teams were finally hitched. They at last began pulling the wagons into line. Even then, the delays were not yet over. At the last minute, some family was sure to have lost a dog or had a child wander away.

But sooner or later, everybody would at last be ready. The wagons would roughly point in the direction of the Oregon Trail. But the picture of the white-hatted wagon boss standing in his stirrups crying "Wagons, Ho!" was seldom, if ever, seen in real life. More often, the lead driver waited until everybody down the line seemed to be ready. Then he whacked the nearest ox with his whip and hollered, "Git!" or something like it. After waiting a proper time, the next driver did the same—and so it went down the line until every wagon was moving.

Once under way, such a wagon train made a handsome sight. The long line of white-topped prairie schooners stretched out for a mile or two across the plain. They rocked slowly over the rough ground. On either side of the trail were small bunches of loose stock—oxen, cows, horses, mules, and even sheep. These were herded by older boys and girls or by adults working their way to the new country.

From the starting place to the first night's camp was only a few miles. But almost before the emigrants were off the old campground, they began to sample the delays that would plague them for the next few months.

The first trouble usually came to the herders of the loose stock. Perhaps a headstrong old cow did not like the looks of the trail ahead. It might suddenly curl its tail and run back toward the herds it could still hear bawling on the old campground. By the time it had been headed off and brought back, a dozen others might be lumbering off in many different directions.

While the herders ran here and there dealing with these emergencies, the teamsters were having their own problems. Most of the wagons were drawn by two to four pairs of oxen. A teamster walked to the left and a little behind the lead team. The teamster's job was to guide the team to the right or to the left by shouts of "Gee!" and "Haw!" accompanied by whacks from a bullwhip. The loudness and authority of the command was important, but there was still room for considerable misunderstanding. Many of these folk were inexperienced teamsters and got into trouble even with well-trained animals. But many of the teams were simply unreliable. So almost at once, the orderly line of wagons began to show longer and longer gaps.

Confused drivers shouted "Haw!" when they meant "Gee!" They turned the wheels the wrong way while going down a slope. They tangled their teams in their chains and even upset their wagons. A command given too soon or too late or too loud or not loud enough could mean the difference between a wagon staying on firm ground or slipping into a gulley.

Suddenly, a team might be floundering helplessly, and a wagon would be stuck in a boggy spot. The driver would have to wade waist deep into the stinking mire and unhitch the team. The wagon outfits behind would have to unhitch and help. After the unfortunate greenhorn had attached chains to the rear of the bogged-down wagon, neighbors would hitch their wagons to the chains and pull the unfortunate one back to firm ground. As often as not, the oxen were still trapped. Then there was more wading to attach ropes to their horns so they could be pulled out one at a time.

Somewhere else along the line, a clumsily-tied water barrel would be jolted loose. This meant another delay while the barrel was hoisted back and someone was found to show how it should be tied properly to the wagon.

These and dozens of similar mishaps dogged all but the most careful emigrants on the first leg of the trip. However, since they were still a long distance from treacherous country, only a few wagons stayed behind to help the unfortunates in trouble. The rest went on. So hour by hour, the line of wagons lengthened as stragglers fell farther and farther behind.

Under these circumstances, it is not surprising that the first night's camp was often very disorganized. The first arrivals, after picking a site, unhitched the teams. Some of the people took the teams to water before herding them out to graze. Meanwhile, others began the unfamiliar job of getting out the grub boxes and starting fires. The children carried water or looked for firewood.

Supper was quickly eaten. There were constant interruptions, for the stock had not yet learned the habits of the road. Thus, there were frequent alarms as the creatures scattered in this direction and that.

All the while, the wagons that had been delayed on the trail straggled onto the campground in two's and three's, adding to the confusion. People trying to make camp in the dark drove their wagons over ox yokes and other gear. They stumbled into the tent ropes and picket lines of earlier arrivals. Cattle blundered over cookpots and grub boxes which were resting beside dead fires.

The loads of many of the latecomers were jumbled by the day's jolting. Some latecomers searched hopelessly inside the dark wagons for lost grub boxes. Others tried to arrange bedding while the crying of their hungry and tired children shortened their already ragged tempers. It would be long past midnight before the last wagon was in place, the last team turned out to graze, and the last pair of muddy boots scraped and set to dry.

It is small wonder that many families changed their minds about making the trip and turned back after the second or third day.

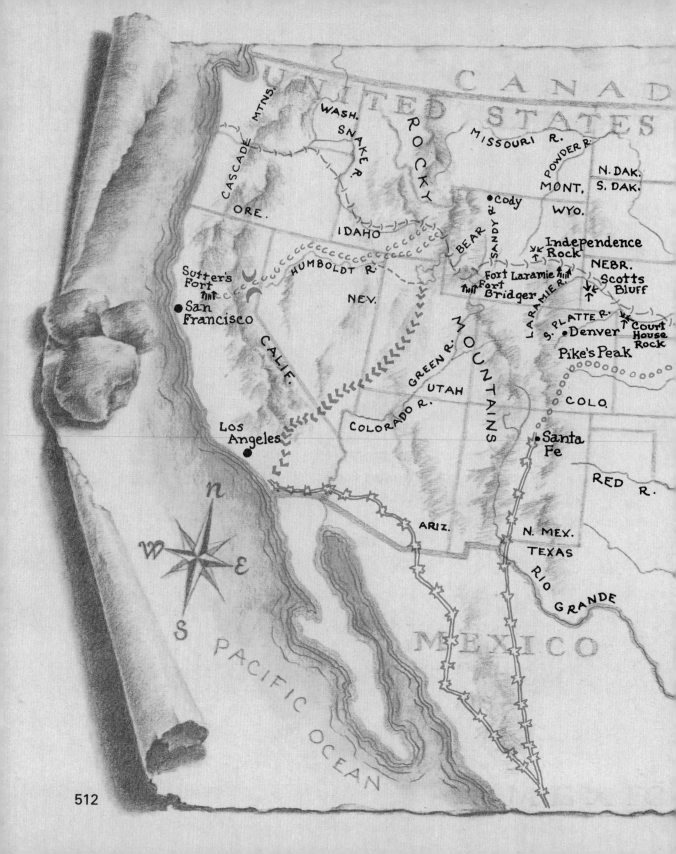

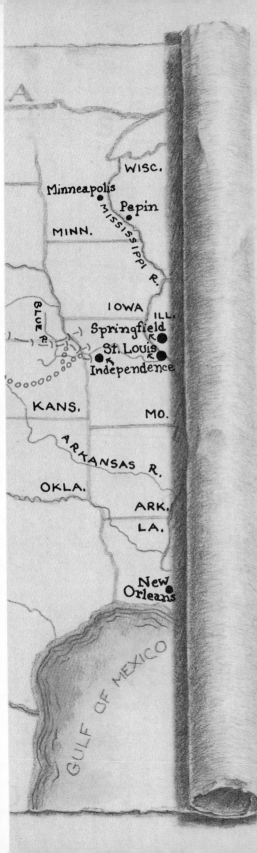

Westward Ho!

This map shows some of the routes used by settlers of the American West. As early as 1769, Spanish settlers traveled northward from Mexico to what is now California on *El Camino Real,* "the royal road." Later, in the 1800's, the Oregon Trail became the most widely used route to the West. As you read the selections in "Explorations," use this map to find the routes people used and the places they went.

Legend:

⋇ Landmark   ● City

ᚾᚾ Fort   • Town

✕ Donner Pass

– – – – – Hastings Cut-off

< < < < < < < Old Spanish Trail

•ooooooooo Santa Fe Trail

⊢⊣⊢⊣⊢ El Camino Real

–⟨–⟨–⟨ Oregon Trail

ccccccccc California Trail

Scale 0   100   200   300   400 miles

A Pioneer Family

Laura Ingalls Wilder

Little House on the Prairie *is one of Laura Ingalls Wilder's best-loved books. It is the story of a family —mother, father, and three daughters—traveling west from Wisconsin.*

This book and the other books in the Little House *series give you an idea of what life was like at the time when the western frontier was opening up. The books are fictional accounts, but they are based on the author's own experiences as a child traveling with her family.*

Here are the first two chapters of Little House on the Prairie. *As you read, you will realize how different your world is from the world of the pioneers. You will realize how different were the things they did and said. But you will also realize how similar are the emotions and feelings of people then and today.*

Part One
Going West

A long time ago, when all the grandfathers and grandmothers of today were little boys and little girls or very small babies, or perhaps not even born, Pa and Ma and Mary and Laura and Baby Carrie left their little house in the Big Woods of Wisconsin. They drove away and left it lonely and empty in the clearing among the big trees, and they never saw that little house again.

They were going to the Indian country.

Pa said there were too many people in the Big Woods now. Quite often Laura heard the ringing thud of an ax which was not Pa's ax, or the echo of a shot that did not come from his gun. The path that went by the little house had become a road. Almost every day, Laura and Mary stopped their playing and stared in surprise at a wagon slowly creaking by on that road.

Wild animals would not stay in a country where there were so many people. Pa did not like to stay, either. He liked a country where the wild animals lived without being afraid. He liked to see the little fawns and their mothers looking at him from the shadowy woods, and the fat, lazy bears eating berries in the wild-berry patches.

In the long winter evenings, he talked to Ma about the Western country. In the West the land was level, and there were no trees. The grass grew thick and high. There, the wild animals wandered and fed as though they were in a pasture that stretched much farther than a man could see, and there were no settlers. Only Indians lived there.

One day in the very last of the winter, Pa said to Ma, "Seeing you don't object, I've decided to go see the West. I've had an offer for this place, and we can sell it now for as much as we're ever likely to get, enough to give us a start in a new country."

"Oh, Charles, must we go now?" Ma said. The weather was so cold and the snug house was so comfortable.

"If we are going this year, we must go now," said Pa. "We can't get across the Mississippi after the ice breaks."

So Pa sold the little house. He sold the cow and calf. He made hickory bows and fastened them upright to the wagon box. Ma helped him stretch white canvas over them.

In the thin dark before morning, Ma gently shook Mary and Laura till they got up. In firelight and candlelight, she washed and combed them and dressed them warmly. Over their long red-flannel underwear she put wool petticoats and wool dresses and long wool stockings. She put their coats on them, and their rabbit-skin hoods and their red yarn mittens.

Everything from the little house was in the wagon, except the beds and tables and chairs. They did not need to take these, because Pa could always make new ones.

There was thin snow on the ground. The air was still and cold and dark. The bare trees stood up against the frosty stars. But in the east the sky was pale and through the gray woods came lanterns with wagons and horses, bringing Grandpa and Grandma and aunts and uncles and cousins.

Mary and Laura clung tightly to their rag dolls and did not say anything. The cousins stood around and looked at them. Grandma and all the aunts hugged and kissed them, and hugged and kissed them again, saying good-by.

Pa hung his gun to the wagon bows inside the canvas top where he could reach it quickly from the seat. He hung his bullet-pouch and powder-horn beneath it. He laid the fiddle-box carefully between pillows, where jolting would not hurt the fiddle.

The uncles helped him hitch the horses to the wagon. All the cousins were told to kiss Mary and Laura, so they did. Pa picked up Mary and then Laura, and set them on the bed in the back of the wagon. He helped Ma climb up the wagon seat, and Grandma reached up and gave her Baby Carrie. Pa swung up and sat beside Ma, and Jack, the brindle bulldog, went under the wagon.

So they all went away from the little log house. The shutters were over the windows, so the little house could not see them go. It stayed there inside the log fence, behind the two big oak trees that in the summertime had made green roofs for Mary and Laura to play under. And that was the last of the little house.

Pa promised that when they came to the West, Laura should see a papoose.

"What is a papoose?" she asked him, and he said, "A papoose is a little, brown, Indian baby."

They drove a long way through the snowy woods, till they came to the town of Pepin. Mary and Laura had seen it once before, but it looked different now. The door of the store and the doors of all the houses were shut; the stumps were covered with snow; and no little children were playing outdoors. Big cords of wood stood among the stumps. Only two or three men in boots and fur caps and bright plaid coats were to be seen.

Ma and Laura and Mary ate bread and molasses in the wagon, and the horses ate corn from nosebags, while inside the store Pa traded his furs for things they would need on the journey. They could not stay long in the town, because they must cross the lake that day.

The enormous lake stretched flat and smooth and white all the way to the edge of the gray sky. Wagon tracks went away across it, so far that you could not see where they went; they ended in nothing at all.

Pa drove the wagon out onto the ice, following those wagon tracks. The horses' hoofs clop-clopped with a dull sound; the wagon wheels went crunching. The town grew smaller and smaller behind, till even the tall store was only a dot. All around the wagon there was nothing but empty and silent space. Laura didn't like it. But Pa was on the wagon seat and Jack was under the wagon; she knew that nothing could hurt her while Pa and Jack were there.

At last, the wagon was pulling up a slope of earth again, and again there were trees. There was a little log house, too, among the trees. So Laura felt better.

Nobody lived in the little house; it was a place to camp in. It was a tiny house, and strange, with a big fireplace and rough bunks against all the walls. But it was warm when Pa had built a fire in the fireplace. That night Mary and Laura and Baby Carrie slept with Ma in a bed made on the floor before the fire, while Pa slept outside in the wagon, to guard it and the horses.

In the night, a strange noise wakened Laura. It sounded like a shot, but it was sharper and longer than a shot. Again and again she heard it. Mary and Carrie were asleep, but Laura couldn't sleep until Ma's voice came softly through the dark.

"Go to sleep, Laura," Ma said. "It's only the ice cracking."

Next morning Pa said, "It's lucky we crossed yesterday, Caroline. Wouldn't wonder if the ice broke up today. We made a late crossing, and we're lucky it didn't start breaking up while we were out in the middle of it."

"I thought about that yesterday, Charles," Ma replied, gently.

Laura hadn't thought about it before, but now she thought what would have happened if the ice had cracked under the wagon wheels and they had all gone down into the cold water in the middle of that vast lake.

"You're frightening somebody, Charles," Ma said, and Pa caught Laura up in his safe, big hug.

"We're across the Mississippi!" he said, hugging her joyously. "How do you like that, little half-pint of sweet cider half drunk up? Do you like going out west where Indians live?"

Laura said she liked it, and she asked if they were in the Indian country now. But they were not; they were in Minnesota.

It was a long, long way to Indian territory. Almost every day, the horses traveled as far as they could; almost every night, Pa and Ma made camp in a new place. Sometimes they had to stay several days in one camp because a creek was in flood and they couldn't cross it till the water went down. They crossed too many creeks to count. They saw strange woods and hills, and stranger country with no trees. They drove across rivers on long wooden bridges, and they came to one wide yellow river that had no bridge.

That was the Missouri River. Pa drove onto a raft, and they all sat still in the wagon while the raft went swaying away from the safe land and slowly crossed all that rolling muddy-yellow water.

After more days, they came to hills again. In a valley, the wagon stuck fast in deep black mud. Rain poured down and thunder crashed and lightning flared. There was no place to make camp and build a fire. Everything was damp and chill and miserable in the wagon, but they had to stay in it and eat cold bits of food.

Next day, Pa found a place on a hillside where they could camp. The rain had stopped, but they had to wait a week before the creek went down and the mud dried so that Pa could dig the wagon wheels out of it and go on.

One day, while they were waiting, a tall, lean man came out of the woods, riding a black pony. He and Pa talked awhile, then they went off into the woods together, and when they came back, both of them were riding black ponies. Pa had traded the tired brown horses for those ponies.

They were beautiful little horses, and Pa said they were not really ponies; they were western mustangs. "They're strong as mules and gentle as kittens," Pa said. They had large, soft, gentle eyes, and long manes and tails, and slender legs and feet much smaller and quicker than the feet of horses in the Big Woods.

When Laura asked what their names were, Pa said that she and Mary could name them. So Mary named one, Pet, and Laura named the other, Patty. When the creek's roar was not so loud and the road was drier, Pa dug the wagon out of the mud. He hitched Pet and Patty to it, and they all went on together.

They had come in the covered wagon all the long way from the Big Woods of Wisconsin, across Minnesota and Iowa and Missouri. All that long way, Jack had trotted under the wagon. Now they set out to go across Kansas.

Kansas was an endless flat land covered with tall grass blowing in the wind. Day after day, they traveled in Kansas, and saw nothing but the rippling grass and the enormous sky. In a perfect circle the sky curved down to the level land, and the wagon was in the circle's exact middle.

All day long Pet and Patty went forward, trotting and walking and trotting again, but they couldn't get out of the middle of that circle. When the sun went down, the circle was still around them, and the edge of the sky was pink. Then slowly, the land became black. The wind made a lonely sound in the grass. The campfire was small and lost in so much space. But large stars hung from the sky, glittering so near that Laura felt she could almost touch them.

Next day, the land was the same; the sky was the same; the circle did not change. Laura and Mary were tired of them all. There was nothing new to do, and nothing new to look at. The bed was made in the back of the wagon and neatly covered with a gray blanket; Laura and Mary sat on it. The canvas sides of the wagon-top were rolled up and tied, so the prairie wind blew in. It whipped Laura's straight brown hair and Mary's golden curls every-which-way, and the strong light screwed up their eyelids.

Sometimes a big jack rabbit bounded in big bounds away over the blowing grass. Jack paid no attention. Poor Jack was tired, too, and his paws were sore from traveling so far. The wagon kept on jolting; the canvas top snapped in the wind. Two faint wheel tracks kept going away behind the wagon, always the same.

Pa's back was hunched. The reins were loose in his hands; the wind blew his long brown beard. Ma sat straight and quiet, her hands folded in her lap. Baby Carrie slept in a nest among the soft bundles.

"Ah-wow!" Mary yawned; and Laura said, "Ma, can't we get out and run behind the wagon? My legs are so tired."

"No, Laura," Ma said.

"Aren't we going to camp pretty soon?" Laura asked. It seemed such a long time since noon, when they had eaten their lunch sitting on the clean grass in the shade of the wagon.

Pa answered, "Not yet. It's too early to camp now."

"I want to camp, now! I'm so tired," Laura said.

Then Ma said, "Laura." That was all, but it meant that Laura must not complain. So she did not complain any more out loud, but she was still naughty, inside. She sat and thought complaints to herself.

Her legs ached, and the wind wouldn't stop blowing her hair. The grass waved, and the wagon jolted, and nothing else happened for a long time.

"We're coming to a creek or a river," Pa said. "Girls, can you see those trees ahead?"

Laura stood up and held to one of the wagon bows. Far ahead she saw a low dark smudge. "That's trees," Pa said. "You can tell by the shape of the shadows. In this country, trees mean water. That's where we'll camp tonight."

Part Two
❧❧❧❧❧❧❧ Crossing the Creek ❧❧❧❧❧❧❧

Pet and Patty began to trot briskly, as if they were glad, too. Laura held tight to the wagon bow and stood up in the jolting wagon. Beyond Pa's shoulder and far across the waves of green grass, she could see the trees, and they were not like any trees she had seen before. They were no taller than bushes.

"Whoa!" said Pa, suddenly. "Now which way?" he muttered to himself.

The road divided here, and you could not tell which was the more-traveled way. Both of them were faint wheel tracks in the grass. One went toward the west; the other sloped downward a little, toward the south. Both soon vanished in the tall, blowing grass.

"Better go downhill, I guess," Pa decided. "The creek's down in the bottoms. Must be this is the way to the ford." He turned Pet and Patty toward the south.

The road went down and up, and down and up again, over gently curving land. The trees were nearer now, but they were no taller. Then Laura gasped and clutched the wagon bow, for almost under Pet's and Patty's noses, there was no more blowing grass; there was no land at all. She looked beyond the edge of the land and across the tops of trees.

The road turned there. For a little way, it went along the cliff's top, then it went sharply downward. Pa put on the brakes; Pet and Patty braced themselves backward and almost sat down. The wagon wheels slid onward, little by little lowering the wagon farther down the steep slope into the ground. Jagged cliffs of bare red earth rose up on both sides of the wagon. Grass waved along their tops, but nothing grew on their seamed, straight-up-and-down sides. They were hot, and heat came from them against Laura's face. The wind was still blowing overhead, but it did not blow down into this deep crack in the ground. The stillness seemed strange and empty.

Then once more, the wagon was level. The narrow crack down which it had come opened into the bottom lands. Here grew the tall trees whose tops Laura had seen from the prairie above. Shady groves were scattered on the rolling meadows; and in the groves, deer were lying down, hardly to be seen among the shadows. The deer turned their heads toward the wagon, and curious fawns stood up to see it more clearly.

Laura was surprised because she did not see the creek. But the bottom lands were wide. Down here, below the prairie, there were gentle hills and open sunny places. The air was still and hot. Under the wagon wheels, the ground was soft. In the sunny open spaces, the grass grew thin, and deer had cropped it short.

For a while, the high, bare cliffs of red earth stood up behind the wagon. But they were almost hidden behind hills and trees when Pet and Patty stopped to drink from the creek.

The rushing sound of the water filled the still air. All along the creek banks, the trees hung over it and made it dark with shadows. In the middle, it ran swiftly, sparkling silver and blue.

"This creek's pretty high," Pa said. "But I guess we can make it all right. You can see this is a ford, by the old wheel ruts. What do you say, Caroline?"

"Whatever you say, Charles," Ma answered.

Pet and Patty lifted their wet noses. They pricked their ears forward, looking at the creek; then they pricked them backward to hear what Pa would say. They sighed and laid their soft noses together to whisper to each other. A little way upstream, Jack was lapping the water with his red tongue.

"I'll tie down the wagon-cover," Pa said. He climbed down from the seat, unrolled the canvas sides, and tied them firmly to the wagon box. Then he pulled the rope at the back, so that the canvas puckered together in the middle, leaving only a tiny round hole, too small to see through.

Mary huddled down on the bed. She did not like fords; she was afraid of the rushing water. But Laura was excited; she liked the splashing. Pa climbed to the seat, saying, "They may have to swim, out there in the middle. But we'll make it all right, Caroline."

Laura thought of Jack and said, "I wish Jack could ride in the wagon, Pa."

Pa did not answer. He gathered the reins tightly in his hands. Ma said, "Jack can swim, Laura. He will be all right."

The wagon went forward softly in mud. Water began to splash against the wheels. The splashing grew louder. The wagon shook as the noisy water struck at it. Then all at once, the wagon lifted and balanced and swayed. It was a lovely feeling.

The noise stopped, and Ma said, sharply, "Lie down, girls!"

Quick as a flash, Mary and Laura dropped flat on the bed. When Ma spoke like that, they did as they were told. Ma's arm pulled a smothering blanket over them, heads and all.

"Be still, just as you are. Don't move!" she said.

Mary did not move; she was trembling and still. But Laura could not help wriggling a little bit. She did so want to see what was happening. She could feel the wagon swaying and turning; the splashing was noisy again, and again it died away. Then Pa's voice frightened Laura. It said, "Take them, Caroline!"

The wagon lurched; there was a sudden heavy splash beside it. Laura sat straight up and clawed the blanket from her head.

Pa was gone. Ma sat alone, holding tight to the reins with both hands. Mary hid her face in the blanket again, but Laura rose up farther. She couldn't see the creek bank. She couldn't see anything in front of the wagon but water rushing at it. And in the water, three heads; Pet's head and Patty's head and Pa's small, wet head. Pa's fist in the water was holding tight to Pet's bridle.

Laura could faintly hear Pa's voice through the rushing of the water. It sounded calm and cheerful, but she couldn't hear what he said. He was talking to the horses. Ma's face was white and scared.

"Lie down, Laura," Ma said.

Laura lay down. She felt cold and sick. Her eyes were shut tight, but she could still see the terrible water and Pa's brown beard drowning in it.

For a long, long time, the wagon swayed and swung, and Mary cried without making a sound, and Laura's stomach felt sicker and sicker. Then the front wheels struck and grated, and Pa shouted. The whole wagon jerked and jolted and tipped backward, but the wheels were turning on the ground. Laura was up again, holding to the seat; she saw Pet's and Patty's scrambling wet backs climbing a steep bank, and Pa running beside them, shouting, "Hi, Patty! Hi, Pet! Get up! Get up! Whoopsy-daisy! Good girls!"

At the top of the bank they stood still, panting and dripping. And the wagon stood still, safely out of that creek.

Pa stood panting and dripping, too, and Ma said, "Oh, Charles!"

"There, there, Caroline," said Pa. "We're all safe, thanks to a good tight wagon box well-fastened to the running-gear. I never saw a creek rise so fast in my life. Pet and Patty are good swimmers, but I guess they wouldn't have made it if I hadn't helped them."

If Pa had not known what to do, or if Ma had been too frightened to drive, or if Laura and Mary had been naughty and bothered her, then they would all have been lost. The river would have rolled them over and over and carried them away and drowned them, and nobody would ever have known what became of them. For weeks, perhaps, no other person would come along that road.

"Well," said Pa, "all's well that ends well"; and Ma said, "Charles, you're wet to the skin."

Before Pa could answer, Laura cried, "Oh, where's Jack?"

They had forgotten Jack. They had left him on the other side of that dreadful water, and now they could not see him anywhere. He must have tried to swim after them, but they could not see him struggling in the water now.

Laura swallowed hard, to keep from crying. She knew it was shameful to cry, but there was crying inside her. All the long way from Wisconsin, poor Jack had followed them so patiently and faithfully, and now they had left him to drown. He was so tired, and they might have taken him into the wagon. He had stood on the bank and seen the wagon going away from him, as if they didn't care for him at all. And he would never know how much they wanted him.

Pa said he wouldn't have done such a thing to Jack, not for a million dollars. If he'd known how that creek would rise when they were in midstream, he would never have let Jack try to swim it. "But that can't be helped now," he said.

He went far up and down the creek bank, looking for Jack, calling him and whistling for him.

It was no use. Jack was gone.

At last there was nothing to do but to go on. Pet and Patty were rested. Pa's clothes had dried on him while he searched for Jack. He took the reins again, and drove uphill, out of the river bottoms.

Laura looked back all the way. She knew she wouldn't see Jack again, but she wanted to. She didn't see anything but low curves of land coming between the wagon and the creek; and beyond the creek, those strange cliffs of red earth rose up again.

Then other bluffs just like them stood up in front of the wagon. Faint wheel tracks went into a crack between those earthen walls. Pet and Patty climbed till the crack became a small grassy valley. And the valley widened out to the High Prairie once more.

No road, not even the faintest trace of wheels or of a rider's passing, could be seen anywhere. That prairie looked as if no human eye had ever seen it before. Only the tall wild grass covered the endless empty land and a great empty sky arched over it. Far away, the sun's edge touched the rim of the earth. The sun was enormous, and it was throbbing and pulsing with light. All around the sky's edge ran a pale pink glow, and above the pink was yellow, and above that blue. Above the blue, the sky was no color at all. Purple shadows were gathering over the land, and the wind was mourning.

Pa stopped the mustangs. He and Ma got out of the wagon to make camp, and Mary and Laura climbed down to the ground, too.

The family made camp that night on the prairie. Luckily, Jack had managed to cross the creek, and he eventually caught up to them.

The remaining chapters in Little House on the Prairie *tell what happened when the family settled in their new home in Kansas. Later, the family left Kansas to move still farther west. The story of their westward journey is continued in the rest of the* Little House *series.*

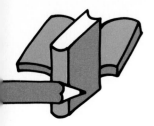

Follow the Trail

Pictures and drawings are often used to give information. Sometimes, a picture or a drawing can tell you as much as — if not, more than — several paragraphs of writing. A picture or a drawing may also be easier to understand. One important kind of picture or drawing that gives information is a map.

A *map* is a drawing that represents an area. It will show you where places are located. It will also show you the distances between places. A map uses special symbols to give information. It is important for you to understand what these symbols mean.

The *key* on a map explains the symbols used on that map. These symbols may represent cities or towns and historic sites. They may also represent highways, trails, rivers, and mountains.

The *scale* is a line, or bar, divided into sections. It explains how distances are represented on the map. For example, one inch (2.54 centimeters) on a map may represent one hundred miles (160 kilometers).

The map in "Explorations" is entitled "Westward Ho!" It follows the selection "Prairie Schooners." This map shows the western part of North America as it was around the year 1830. Turn to the map and find the key. The key explains the symbols for a landmark, a fort, a city, and a town. It also explains the symbols for seven different trails and passes. Find these symbols on the map. Use this map to complete the activities on the next page.

ACTIVITY A   Study the map, "Westward Ho!" Use the key to help you answer each question. Write your answers on your paper.

1. In what state is Fort Laramie located?
2. Through which states does the Oregon Trail pass?
3. Name three landmarks shown on the map.
4. Which river passes by Denver, Colorado?
5. Which trail runs between Santa Fe, New Mexico and Independence, Missouri?
6. Which river runs through New Mexico?
7. Which states share borders with Mexico?
8. In which state is Court House Rock?
9. Which two trails are joined by Hastings' Cut-Off?
10. In which state is Pikes Peak?

ACTIVITY B   The map "Westward Ho!" is mainly an historical map that shows the routes, important landmarks, and forts used by settlers going West. Therefore, it does not have a precisely accurate scale of distances as a modern road map would. But we can find the approximate distances between two places on the map by using the mileage scale at the bottom of the key.

Suppose that you are a settler going west with a wagon train. Use the scale in the key, the map, and a ruler to determine the approximate distance in miles between the places listed below. Write the answers on your paper.

What is the approximate distance in miles between:

1. Scott's Bluff, Nebraska, and Fort Laramie, Wyoming?
2. Minneapolis, Minnesota, and Springfield, Illinois?
3. The east border and the west border of the state of Nevada at its widest point?
4. Cody, Wyoming, and San Francisco, California?

Sweet Betsy from Pike

There are many versions of this popular folk song. It is a song that was sung by the "Forty-Niners" as they traveled to California by covered wagon during the Gold Rush in 1849.

A Song of the Gold Rush

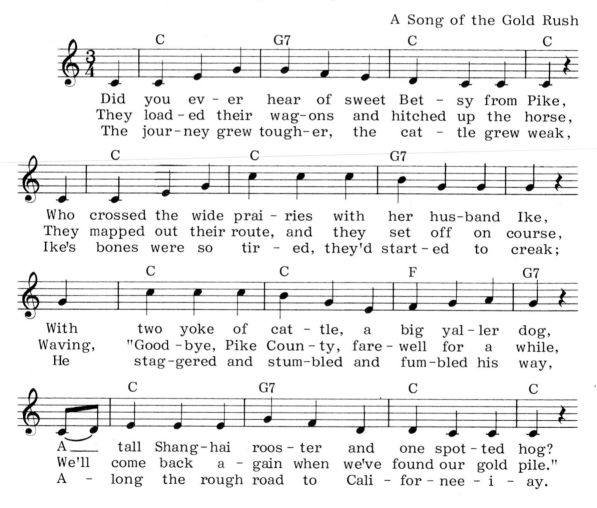

Did you ev - er hear of sweet Bet - sy from Pike,
They load - ed their wag-ons and hitched up the horse,
The jour-ney grew tough-er, the cat - tle grew weak,

Who crossed the wide prai - ries with her hus-band Ike,
They mapped out their route, and they set off on course,
Ike's bones were so tir - ed, they'd start-ed to creak;

With two yoke of cat - tle, a big yal - ler dog,
Waving, "Good -bye, Pike Coun - ty, fare - well for a while,
He stag-gered and stum-bled and fum-bled his way,

A___ tall Shang-hai roos - ter and one spot - ted hog?
We'll come back a - gain when we've found our gold pile."
A - long the rough road to Cali - for - nee - i - ay.

538

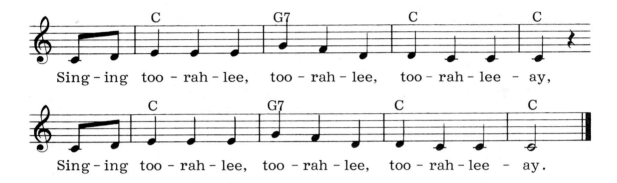

Sing-ing too-rah-lee, too-rah-lee, too-rah-lee - ay,

Sing-ing too-rah-lee, too-rah-lee, too-rah-lee - ay.

They reached the hot desert, but Betsy pushed on,
Though the wagon broke down, and the food was near gone.
Said Ike, "Dear Pike County, we'll come back to you."
Said Betsy, "You'll go by yourself, if you do!"
    Singing too-rah-lee, too-rah-lee, too-rah-lee-ay,
    Singing too-rah-lee, too-rah-lee, too-rah-lee-ay.

They camped on the prairie for weeks upon weeks,
They swam the wide rivers, and crossed the tall peaks.
Poor Ike got discouraged, and Betsy got mad.
The dog drooped his tail and looked wondrously sad.
    Singing too-rah-lee, too-rah-lee, too-rah-lee-ay,
    Singing too-rah-lee, too-rah-lee, too-rah-lee-ay.

Weak and thirsty, poor Betsy crawled up to a stream,
And there found the answer to her fondest dream.
Instead of plain water that ran clear and cold,
The stream overflowed with big nuggets of gold.
    Singing too-rah-lee, too-rah-lee, too-rah-lee-ay,
    Singing too-rah-lee, too-rah-lee, too-rah-lee-ay.

539

Babe at the Circus

Dell J. McCormick

It took the pioneers many months to cross the western frontier. Nowadays, people cover the same distance in a few hours. Would you believe that this distance was once covered on foot in less than a day?

According to the tall tale, "Babe at the Circus," Paul Bunyan's Blue Ox, Babe, did just that. Some of the characters in this tale are folk heroes. They are patterned after the rugged lumberjacks who worked in logging camps many years ago.

After working hard all day, the lumberjacks would build huge fires and eat enormous suppers. Then they would sit back and take turns telling tall tales. These tales told of larger-than-life people and animals that accomplished feats which were impossible for the ordinary person.

Paul Bunyan was the biggest and strongest of the logging giants created by the tellers of tall tales. Together, Paul Bunyan and his giant Blue Ox carved out the West.

One day, a stranger appeared in camp. He said he was from Barnum and Bailey's circus and wanted to hire Babe the Blue Ox for a season. Paul thought he might just as well let Babe go for a while, as the logging business was kind of dull at the time. Besides, his feed was costing plenty. Johnnie Inkslinger tried to figure it out, but he ran out of figures along about the middle of July and gave it up.

Babe had a touch of hay fever that year, and Paul thought maybe a change of scenery would do him good. Every time Babe sneezed, he blew down almost a whole section of standing timber.

One day, he sneezed near the kitchen and blew a whole bin of flour out over the camp. It was raining at the time, and everyone in camp got stuck in the flour paste. Work was delayed for four days.

Paul hated to see Babe go, but he told the stranger that it was a deal, anyway. Then he sent Brimstone Bill along as Babe's keeper.

The circus was playing in Denver at the time, so Babe and the two men set off early the next morning. Everything went along fine, until they ran into some marshy country and Babe's hoofs started sinking into the soft ground. The circus man fell into one of Babe's footprints, and it was ten days before they could rescue him with a rope ladder.

Brimstone Bill told him that was nothing compared to the time a whole family fell into a big footprint of Babe's out in North Dakota. That time, it was eighteen years before the son finally worked his way out and told about the accident.

When the Babe got to Denver, the circus people thought they had just about the best attraction in the country, for nobody had ever seen such a huge ox. According to Brimstone Bill—who ought to know—Babe was at that time forty-two axe handles and a plug of chewing tobacco between the eyes. When he flicked a fly off his hind quarters, the swish of his great tail started a wind that blew hats off people two miles away.

Bill said he was a little underweight that year though; for when he arrived at the circus, he weighed just a little under one hundred and fourteen tons. They soon fattened him up, however; and Barnum himself came out from New York to see how the great Babe looked.

Barnum took one look and went back to his private car, saying, "There isn't any such animal! There couldn't be. It's just something my press agent made up."

He took the first train back to New York, and from that time on, he never believed a single advertisement, even if he wrote it himself.

In the meantime, Babe was enjoying himself hugely and liked the circus better every day. He made friends with everybody and ate popcorn balls and peanuts.

The elephants got underfoot at first, and it was difficult for him to keep from trampling on them. He could outpull any ten elephants; and if a circus wagon became stuck in the mud, it was always Babe they called on to

pull it out. His great fame went before him from city to city, and each day the crowds grew larger and larger.

The circus people built a special tent for him. It was so large it covered six city blocks and required a hundred and thirty workers to put it up each time the circus moved. Twenty workers kept him provided with great bales of hay. He ate so fast it took five people with pike poles to pick the baling wire out of his teeth. Every third day, a wagonload of turnips was brought in for dessert.

The local fire department furnished him with water in return for free tickets. But on very hot days, the fire fighters were so busy keeping two hose carts going day and night that they didn't have time to stop and see the show.

Babe loved being the center of attraction and grew fat and sleek. He licked his glossy coat until it shone, and he wanted his horns polished at least once a day. Polishing his horns was quite a job, for only the best steeplejacks would tackle such a dangerous task.

Every day, Babe would sit on a large platform in the center of his tent while great mobs of people would crowd in to see him. He sold photographs of himself for twenty-five cents apiece and smiled at the pretty girls and showed his fine white teeth. Every once in a while, he would slowly turn his head sideways so the people in front could see his fine profile. He was also very proud of his glossy tail and brushed it regularly every morning and night.

Every day, he became more touchy and complained that the food was poor and that his straw bed was bumpy. If even so much as a lump the size of a popcorn ball was found in his bed, he refused to sleep until the entire bed was changed.

Babe refused to be in the circus parade unless he led it. If it were raining the least little bit, he refused to go out and claimed he caught colds very easily. One day, the little boy who took care of his hoofs failed to show up, and Babe sat in his tent all day and sulked and would not see anybody. It was a different Babe from the good-natured ox that had roamed the woods with Paul and his crew. Brimstone Bill began to wish they were both back in camp again.

One day, the circus was playing near Minneapolis, Minnesota, and Babe was leading the parade as usual. He was strutting down the main street in step to the music of the band when he met his first automobile. Here was something he had never seen before. Neither had many of the people in the crowd, for the auto had just come into use. This auto was the first one in that part of the country.

Babe did not like the fact that the auto was getting more attention than he was. He decided to look it over. He knew it wasn't a wagon because no horses were pulling it. Yet it moved along by itself and made strange noises.

The parade stopped as Babe carefully sniffed the strange wagon. He backed away and squinted at it with one eye. He wondered whether it would be worthwhile to squash this puny thing with his great hoof.

Suddenly, the auto backfired! Babe was caught off guard. It scared the great Ox half to death. With a wild roar of fear, he leaped over a two-story building and started for open country.

Brimstone Bill had just enough time to take a firm grip on the halter rope and swing up on his back, as Babe ran snorting and leaping through the fields north of the town. The great Babe thought only of putting as much distance as possible between himself and the new animal that made noises like a sawmill and spitfire. He was fat and overweight, but he ran madly on. Whole townships were cleared in a single stride.

Brimstone Bill saw that Babe was headed west, so he let the Ox go his way. At the rate they were going, it wouldn't be long until they would be back in Paul's camp. Babe's feet were

547

hitting the ground about once every quarter of a mile. He never stopped once to eat or rest. On and on he ran, through forests and over mountains.

Bill said afterwards that it was the fastest cross-country trip ever made. The crack Northern Pacific passenger train had left two days before, but Babe passed it before it got to Butte, Montana. The telephone poles flashed by so fast they looked like a picket fence. Bill tried to wave at some people standing along a country road, but they were thirty miles behind before he could take his hand off the halter.

They ran into a head wind toward the end of the trip, and it took Babe over two hours to cross the state of Idaho. But he made up for it in the Big Bend country, and Bill was pretty well shaken up by the time they got to Paul's camp.

Everybody was glad to see them back. Bill said he enjoyed the trip, except for a stretch in Montana where the blackbirds were so thick they kept getting in his hair. Somebody asked him if the Rocky Mountains and the Cascades had bothered him any. Bill shook his head.

"Now that you mention it, I don't think I noticed any mountains—but the trail was a little bumpy in a couple of places!"

Together again, Paul and Babe continued to perform astonishing feats. Other tales tell how they traveled across the country creating mountains, lakes, and rivers along the way. You can read more adventures of Paul, Babe, Brimstone Bill, and other folk heroes in the book Tall Timber Tales, *from which this tale was adapted.*

Different Voices

Literature is everything that you read. Most people like a variety of literature. You might get tired of reading the same kind of literature all the time. Fortunately, there are many kinds for you to enjoy.

Literature is divided into two major categories: fiction and nonfiction. *Fiction* is writing that tells about make-believe characters and events. *Nonfiction* is writing that tells about true characters, events, and facts.

These kinds of literature are included in the category, fiction:

A *novel* is a book that tells a long story. Usually, the story is divided into chapters. The selection "A Pioneer Family" is really two chapters from a novel. The novel is based on events in the author's life, but the characters and specific events were created, or made up, by the author.

A *short story* also tells a story, but this story is much shorter than the story in a novel. Usually, a short story is about as long as a chapter in a novel. The characters and events are made up by the author.

A *tall tale* is a humorous, different kind of story. The people and animals in a tall tale are larger-than-life characters who do impossible things. "Babe at the Circus" is a tall tale.

A *fable* is a story that teaches a lesson or has a moral. Often, the characters in a fable are animals who speak. You may have read some of Aesop's fables.

A *play* is a story performed by actors. What the actors say and do tells the play's story.

A *poem* is writing done in a special form. Often, this form is a verse, or stanza. Sometimes, the last words in the lines of a poem will rhyme. Poems may describe things or tell a story. "Wheels" is a lyric poem that describes something. "Sweet Betsy from Pike" is a song, but it is also a narrative poem that tells a story.

These kinds of literature are included in the category, nonfiction:

An *essay* is writing that reports on a subject. "Prairie Schooners" reports on wagon trains. The descriptions by the author are based on factual information.

A *biography* is the true story of a person's life. But it is written by another person. An *autobiography* is also a true story of a person's life. But it is written by the person whose life it is.

A *letter* is a document written to another person. It may tell the writer's feelings and experiences. "My Dear Cousin" is a letter.

Read each description below. On your paper, write the name of the kind of literature that is described.

1. A very long story about a make-believe family
2. A descriptive report on American-Indian tribes
3. Verses that describe a beautiful spring day
4. The life of Martin Luther King, Jr., written by a friend
5. A story of a mouse who teaches a lesson to a lion
6. A detective story performed on a stage by actors
7. A humorous story about a man who can cross a large mountain with one step

552

Alfred Jacob Miller, Painter of the Old West

Judith Lechner

Have you ever dreamed that a stranger would one day walk through your front door and offer you the most exciting adventure of your life? Just such an unlikely thing happened to an artist named Alfred Jacob Miller one spring morning back in 1837.

Miller was twenty-six years old. He was a talented painter, who had studied in many of the art capitals of Europe—Paris, Rome, Florence, and Venice. He was trying to earn his living as an artist, but it was as difficult then as it sometimes is now. He wanted to paint landscapes (pictures that show views of natural scenery or the countryside). His landscapes were beautiful, but few people wanted to buy them.

People preferred to spend their money on portraits. In those days, there were no cameras to take photographs of family members. Instead, people hired artists to make oil paintings of their loved ones. If you go to a museum today, you may see some of these portraits. They usually show a mother and a father seated in a finely furnished parlor with their children grouped around them.

Miller came from Baltimore, Maryland, a city of art and culture. But in Baltimore, there were already too many portrait painters. So he decided to move to New Orleans, Louisiana, where there were fewer painters. In New Orleans, many rich Southerners and Westerners might want him to paint their portraits.

When he got to New Orleans, Miller rented a studio where he could live, work, and display his paintings to the public. On a spring morning in 1837, he was painting at his easel as usual. A handsome, well-dressed gentleman entered, nodded to Miller, and started to inspect the paintings hanging on the walls of the studio. Miller quietly continued painting. He was used to people coming into the studio to look at his work.

The stranger said nothing. Then he stopped and stood for a long time in front of a landscape of Baltimore. Miller was especially proud of that painting. The visitor seemed fascinated by the picture. Finally, he walked over to the artist.

"I like the way you painted that view," he snapped in a precise, clipped voice. Then he turned abruptly and left.

Several days later, the stranger appeared at the studio again. This time he was more friendly. It was a custom of the time to introduce oneself with a calling card. Proudly, the stranger handed his card to Miller. It read, "Captain W. D. Stewart, British Army."

Captain Stewart looked sternly at the young, city-bred artist. "I am a retired army officer," he said. "I have spent the last four summers and a winter in the Rocky Mountains. I have seen sights that few people have seen. I have seen the beauty of the Rocky Mountains and the West, the ways of life of the American Indian tribes, the mountaineers who trap the beaver to make fashionable beaver hats. I am making another trip to the Rocky Mountains soon. I want a fine artist to come along and paint pictures for me of the sights of the West. I want a record of my journey to take home to my family castle in Scotland. Will you come with me?"

Miller was thrilled. He was being offered quite an adventure. The West was then mostly unknown, though a few fur trappers lived there. Fur-trading companies traveled there to get their goods, but Miller would go where few Eastern artists had ever been. He would be one of the first to record this little-known world in drawings and paintings. He would be like a modern-day photographer going along on a space mission to take pictures of the moon.

Would he go? Miller couldn't wait. He was ready to leave that moment.

Before long, Miller and Stewart left New Orleans. Their first stop was St. Louis, Missouri. In 1837, St. Louis was a western frontier town. It had long been a center for the fur trade. Trappers in their buckskin costumes and American Indians in their tribal dress walked the streets. Miller stared in wonder.

Wagon trains belonging to the fur-trading companies were stocking up with supplies for their long journeys westward. They carried goods and money to be paid to trappers and American Indians for furs. Each train had soldiers to guard it.

The wagon train that Miller and Stewart joined was headed for Fort Laramie—800 miles (1,300 kilometers) away on the Oregon Trail. It would be a difficult and dangerous journey, so Miller knew this would be an exciting time in his life. When the party set out in May, he decided to keep a diary of the trip. Parts of this diary exist today and tell of the rough life on the trail.

Miller was a "soft" Easterner who had never experienced the discomforts of a wagon train. In order to toughen him up a bit, Captain Stewart insisted that Miller catch his own horse every morning. Catching a horse wasn't an easy job. Each morning, the horses were untied and allowed to graze for an hour or two. Then, when the party wanted to move on, each person had to find and catch a horse. Some of the horses would have wandered far away. Poor Miller's efforts to catch his horse must have been funny to the rough, tough soldiers.

Miller knew he was lucky to be the first artist to sketch wagon-train life. He spent most of each day drawing. He was free to join in any activity—a buffalo hunt, a visit to a Shoshoni tribal camp—just as long as he brought back sketches. He worked constantly.

The sketches Miller drew are exciting to see. They were made on the spot. They show people shooting

buffalo and roping wild horses. There is even a picture of a horse and rider slipping into the quicksand near a river. There are also everyday scenes: pictures of mountaineers setting traps for beavers in streams, pictures of the nightly roundup of horses at camp, and pictures that were based on stories heard around the campfire.

Some of Miller's best work shows the dramatic scenery he saw. He was impressed by the majestic Rocky Mountains and the clear, undisturbed lakes and rivers.

He was the first artist to picture western landmarks, such as Scott's Bluff in what has become the state of Nebraska. He painted the original Fort Laramie in Wyoming and showed the Cheyenne and Sioux tribespeople gathered there to trade. He captured scenes that would disappear all too quickly, and thus, he saved them for future generations to see.

How does an artist capture an exciting event as it is happening? A camera is quick and accurate. Can the artist do as good a job? Yes, if he or she has an excellent memory and great skill at sketching. Miller had both these qualities. He made on-the-spot sketches with black or dark brown ink. First, he brushed a thin wash of ink over the white drawing paper. The wash gave the drawing a tinted background. When the background dried, he drew with a pen on top of it. He always tried to include as many details as possible.

When he didn't have time to finish, Miller wrote a note on the sketch so he could later include details that had been left out. For example, one sketch of a buffalo herd has two notes on it. One says "more distance," meaning that the herd had to seem farther away. The other says "more dust," meaning that more dust had to be added to the area in which the buffalo were running.

Miller did not consider his sketches final pictures. He usually redid them back at camp each afternoon. Then, he would add more details and color the scene with watercolors. After the trip was over, Miller copied some of these pictures again using oils.

At that time, oil paintings were what most art collectors wanted to buy. They were considered more valuable and "finished" than ink sketches or watercolors. Today, however, we prize all Miller's work. We admire the sketches and watercolors, as well as the oils, for being so accurate and full of life.

Trappers, Walters Art Gallery, Baltimore

Stewart had planned something special to top off Miller's trip. Every year for the past thirteen years, a celebration had been held at the Green River in Wyoming. Stewart had attended two of these celebrations on his earlier trips West. That July, several hundred mountaineers would meet with three thousand American Indian tribespeople at the annual event.

Scene at Rendezvous, Walters Art Gallery, Baltimore

Both groups brought beaver, buffalo, mountain sheep, deer, and antelope skins, which they had gathered during the winter's trapping and hunting. They sold these furs to traders who took them back East. After the trading was done, everyone stayed for a whole month of celebration. For days, everyone feasted, enjoyed horse races, and joined in tribal ball games and dancing. Miller sketched it all. He was the only artist ever to record this exciting spectacle.

Captain Stewart, even though he was an aristocrat, was very much at home at this rowdy celebration. He loved the rough and tumble of the "Wild West." He was accepted as an equal by the American Indians and by the mountain trappers, for they all admired his courage and toughness. To honor Captain Stewart, the Shoshoni tribe staged a grand parade of two thousand warriors in tribal dress, riding their finest horses.

Miller painted watercolors of this colorful pageant. He also did portraits of the dignified and impressive Shoshoni chiefs and sketched a tribal council.

His portraits of the mountaineers are fine works, too. He showed the strong minded and physically tough people who trapped beaver during freezing winters in the Rockies. He painted portraits of such famous mountaineers as Jim Bridger, Joseph Walker, Thomas Fitzpatrick, and Kit Carson. He pictured the easygoing friendship of trappers and tribespeople. He showed them speaking sign language to each other and smoking pipes together by the campfire.

When the Green River celebration was over, Miller and Stewart started home. They arrived back in St. Louis in mid-October of 1837. Miller's baggage bulged with the two hundred sketches and watercolors he had made. He knew these works would be his fortune, for he now realized that he was one of the most talented and well-trained artists to have visited the American West. He had painted scenes seldom before seen by Easterners and was convinced that art collectors would jump at the chance to buy his work.

First, he had to put together a set of pictures for his employer, Captain Stewart. Later, he made copies of both the watercolors and the oils to sell on his own.

When Miller exhibited his work in New York and Baltimore, one critic felt that he had "prettied up" nature unnecessarily. Some people today might agree, but most of the people in Miller's day liked his grand style of painting nature. They loved the vivid colors and the play of sunlight on prairie grass and mountains. They liked Miller's way of making the viewer feel the strong emotions that are inspired by magnificent scenery.

In 1840, after his first success in America, Miller went to Scotland. Stewart had asked him to come. The captain was now Sir William Drummon Stewart and had inherited his family's castle and estates.

Miller stayed at the castle for more than a year. The nobility of England and Scotland flocked there to admire his work. A beautifully bound portfolio of his watercolors and sketches was always on view in the drawing room.

Both Stewart and Miller were envied and admired. They had lived through many exciting adventures. They had braved dangers and seen unusual sights. The stories they told must have fascinated their listeners. Many asked for and bought copies of the watercolors and oils Miller had made. His work was sent to London and attracted crowds there, too.

In the spring of 1842, five years after the start of his great adventure, Miller returned to Baltimore. He was happy that he could live again in his native city with his family and friends nearby.

Alfred Jacob Miller left a valuable record of the Old West. His paintings provide insight into a special period in American history. They are displayed in many museums and historical societies around the country: the Peale Museum in Baltimore; the New York Historical Society in New York City; the Joslyn Art Museum in Omaha, Nebraska; and the Whitney Gallery of Western Art in Cody, Wyoming; to name a few. You will also find the paintings reproduced in books that can be found in the art section of many libraries.

The paintings of Alfred Jacob Miller are well worth looking at, for they are the next best thing to having traveled the Oregon Trail yourself.

The Devil's Gate, Walters Art Gallery, Baltimore

La canción del camino

Aunque voy por tierra extraña
solitario y peregrino,
no voy solo, me acompaña
mi canción en el camino.

Y si la noche está negra,
sus negruras ilumino;
canto, y mi canción alegra
la obscuridad del camino.

La fatiga no me importa
porque el báculo divino
de la canción, hace corta
la distancia del camino.

¡Ay, triste y desventurado
quien va solo y peregrino,
y no marcha acompañado
por la canción del camino!

–Francisco Icaza, poet

Although Francisco Icaza (1863-1925) spent most of his life in Spain as a representative of the Mexican government, he has been praised as one of Mexico's finest poets.

The Song by the Way

A solitary pilgrim I,
Through foreign lands I stray;
Yet am I not alone—my song
Goes with me all the way.

And if the night around be black,
I make it bright as day;
I sing, and then the song lights up
The darkness of the way.

I do not sigh for weariness
However far I stray;
The heavenly staff of song makes brief
The distance of the way.

Ah, sad indeed that pilgrim's lot
Who goes alone all day,
Nor has, for comrade of his march,
A song along the way!

–Translation by Alice Stone Blackwell

My Dear Cousin

a letter by
Virginia Reed

Introduction

adapted from the recollections of
Lucia Shepardson de Wolf

Some years ago, I knew a delightful lady of seventy, Mrs. Virginia Reed Murphy. I knew her well. There was warm friendship between us. I can see her yet—not very tall, slender, very neat. But somehow there was a shadow in her clear, blue-grey eyes. After I had become well acquainted with her, I learned why. She had been a member of a group of pioneers who were stranded for five months in the Sierra Nevada Mountains. The memory of that dreadful winter had never fully left her.

Virginia Reed was twelve years old when her family started from Illinois to California, for Mrs. Reed's health. Virginia was the oldest of the four children. Martha (Patty) was eight; James was six; and little Thomas was four. A number of neighbors joined in the trip. As they made their slow way across the endless miles, other covered wagons were added to the company. It became quite a long wagon train.

The start was made in the spring. But when the mountains were reached in the autumn, trouble loomed ahead. At Bridger's Fort (now in southwest Wyoming), the company divided. Eighty people, including the Reeds, took a shortcut that was said to shorten the trip. From then on, trouble never left the travelers.

Winter came, and there were many hardships. Finally, the group was snowed in at Donner Lake, by what was later known as one of the heaviest snowfalls on record. For several months, the travelers were stranded. They suffered both extreme cold and hunger. Some of them starved.

Virginia and her family survived the terrible experience and reached California. Gradually, they regained their strength. Then one morning, Virginia sat down to write a letter to her cousin, Mary, in Illinois. It was the first letter she had ever attempted, because she had never before been away from those she loved. She did not pause until she was finished.

Once, her father looked over her shoulder to see what she was doing. He smiled as he corrected a few misspelled words—but only a few. He decided that the natural flow of the writing would be spoiled if he interfered.

In the parts of the letter you will read, the misspellings and other writing errors have been corrected. Here, however, is one of those parts as Virginia wrote it:

Ma spred down a bufalo robe and we all laid down on it and spred something over us and Ma sit up by the fire and it snowed one foot on top of the bed so we got up in the morning and the snow was so deep we could not go over the mountains and we had to go back to some cabins built by emigrants 3 years ago, and build more cabins and stay thare all Winter till 20 Feb, without Pa.

May the 16, 1847

My dear cousin,

I take this opportunity to write to you to let you know that we are all well at present, and I hope this letter may find you all well. My dear cousin, I am going to write to you all about our troubles in getting to California.

We had good luck until we lost our best yoke of oxen; and when we came to Bridger's Fort, we lost another yoke. We sold some of our provisions and bought a yoke of cows and a yoke of oxen. The people at Bridger's Fort persuaded us to take Hastings' Cut-Off. They said it saved 300 miles. We went that way and had to go through a long drive of forty miles, as they said, without water or grass. Hastings said it was forty miles, but I think it was eighty miles.

We traveled day and night; and at noon the next day, Papa went on to see if he could find water. He had not been gone long before some of the oxen gave out, and we had to leave the wagons and take the oxen to water.

(Several men took the cattle to find water, which was more than ten miles away. Mr. Reed returned to the group with as much water as he could carry.)

Papa got to us about daylight the next morning. We waited, thinking the men would come back with the cattle. We waited till night. Then we thought we would start and walk to Mr. Donners' wagons that night, a ten-mile distance. We took what little water we had and some bread and started. Papa carried Thomas, and all the rest of us walked.

We got to Donners, and they were all asleep. So we lay down on the ground. We spread one shawl down. We lay down on it and spread another over us. Then we put the dogs on top—Tyler, Barney, Trader, Tracker, and little Cash. It was the coldest night you ever saw. The wind blew very hard, and if it had not been for the dogs, we would have frozen.

(Most of the cattle had strayed away or been stolen before they were watered. The food and supplies were almost gone. The Reeds sold almost all they possessed, including their extra clothing. Then Mr. Reed again left to go for more food and supplies.)

It was raining then in the valleys and snowing in the mountains. We went on our way for three or four days till we came to the big mountains. The snow there was about three feet deep. There were some wagons there. The people said they had attempted to cross the mountains and could not. Well, we thought we would try it. So we started, and they started again with their wagons.

The snow was then way up to the mule's side. The farther we went up, the deeper the snow got. The wagons could not go, so the people un-hitched their oxen and walked with us. They were carrying a child apiece and driving the oxen in snow up to their waists.

We went on that way for two miles. The mules kept falling down in the snow headfirst, and the guide said he could not find the road. We stopped and let two men go on to hunt for the road. They found the road to the top of the mountains and said they thought we could get over if it did not snow any more.

Well, the women were all so tired from carrying their children that they could not go on that night. So we made a fire and got something to eat. Ma spread down a buffalo robe, and we all lay down on it and spread something over us. Ma sat up by the fire. It snowed one foot on top of the bed. When we got up in the morning, the snow was so deep we could not go over the mountains. We had to go back to some cabins built by emigrants three years ago. We had to build more cabins and stay there all winter, till the 20th of February, without Pa.

We had not the first thing to eat. We seldom thought of bread, for we had not had any since October. The cattle were so weak, they could hardly get up after they lay down.

(A small group started out for food but had to turn back because of another snowstorm. Then Virginia, her mother, and two other people decided to try to cross the mountains and bring back food and supplies.)

We went and were out five days in the mountains. Eliza gave out and had to go back. We went on a day longer. We had to stop for a day and make snowshoes. Then we went on awhile and could not find the road. So we had to turn back.

I could go on very well while I thought we were getting ahead. But as soon as we had to turn back, I could hardly get along. We got back to the cabins at night. I froze one of my feet very badly. That same night there was the worst storm we had that winter. If we had not come back that night, we would never have gotten back. We had nothing to eat then but hides. Oh Mary, I would cry and wish I had what you all wasted!

Oh, my dear cousin, you don't know what trouble is yet. Many a time, we were cooking the last thing and did not know where the next would come from. But for us, there was always some way provided. There were fifteen in our cabin, and half of us had to lie in bed all the time. Ten starved to death while we were there, and we were hardly able to walk.

It would snow and cover the cabins all over for two or three days at a time. To make a fire, we would have to cut pieces of log from the inside walls of the cabin. I could hardly eat the hides.

(A party from Sutter's Fort on the other side of the mountains finally came to rescue the stranded travelers. However, some people, including two of the Reed children, were too hungry and tired to make the trip. After several of the rescuers promised to return for the children, Virginia, her mother, and one brother agreed to go ahead with the group.)

In snow up to our knees, we went over great, high mountains as straight as stair steps. Little James walked the whole way over all the mountains with snow up to his waist. He said every step he took meant he was getting nearer to Pa and something to eat.

When we had traveled for five days, we met Pa and thirteen men going to the cabins. Oh Mary, you do not know how glad we were to see him! We had not seen him for five months. We thought we would never see him again.

(*Mr. Reed went on to the cabins to rescue his two children and the other people who had stayed behind. Although his party was also trapped by a snowstorm and went without food for several days, it finally reached Sutter's Fort, and the Reed family was reunited.*)

Mary, I have not written you half of the trouble we have had, but I have written enough to let you know that you do not know what trouble is. We have left everything, but I don't care. We have gotten through with our lives. But don't let this letter dishearten anybody.

My dear cousin, we are all very well pleased with California, particularly with the climate. Be it ever so hot a day, there are always cool nights. It is a beautiful country; it is mostly valleys. It ought to be beautiful country to pay us for our trouble getting here.

It is the greatest place for cattle and horses you ever saw. It would just suit Charley, for he could ride down 300 horses a day. And he could learn to be a *vaquero,* that is, one who lassos horses.

We are all very fleshy. Ma weighs 10040 (one hundred forty) pounds and is gaining. I weigh 81. Tell Henriet that if she wants to get married to come to California. Eliza is going to marry a man by the name of Armeho.

Mary, take this letter to Uncle Gresham and give my love to all my friends. Mama sends her very best love to you all.

To dear cousins,
Virginia Elizabeth B. Reed

Wheel Ruts

Old wheel ruts deep still mark the trace
Where the prairie schooners passed this place.
A name marked faint on a crumbling stone,
In the desert dust a whitened bone,
Bleached bone in the desert dust
And iron wheel-rim red with rust.
The form forgotten but still we find
The living image of the mind.
In cloud shapes in the wind-swept sky
The long processions still roll by,
Still drifting high above Pike's Peak
Across the blue and white tops streak.

—James Daugherty

Tabitha Brown

Evelyn Sibley Lampman

Tabitha Brown was more than sixty years old when, in 1846, she traveled west with her children and grandchildren. Grandma Brown was crippled, and she needed a cane to walk. No one thought she would survive the trip from Missouri to Oregon. But Grandma Brown was a true pioneer. Not only did she survive the trip, but she also went on to start a new life for herself in the West. She helped run a boarding school in Oregon for both white and American-Indian children.

The homes of the early settlers of the West were spread out. It was impossible to find a central place for a school to which they could send their children daily. Still, education was important to the settlers. Grandma Brown's boarding school was an answer to their problem. Children could live at the school instead of traveling long distances back and forth to classes every day.

At first, classes at Grandma Brown's school met in a church. During this time, some of the pupils lived in Grandma Brown's cabin. Finally, a new school was built in which the children could both live and go to classes. The new school officially opened on Independence Day.

On Sundays, Grandma always woke her pupils by singing. She stood on the floor of the cabin at the foot of the ladder which led to the tiny loft. Her voice floated up through the opening. It was still full and clear.

This morning, Grandma was singing "Yankee Doodle." Theresa was instantly awake. She realized that this was Independence Day. She reached out to shake little Mattie. Mattie slept on the straw pallet next to Theresa. Mattie was four, and it was up to Theresa to see that someone was taking care of her.

Mattie was already awake.

"It's white-dress day!" she squealed. "White-dress day!"

"Yes, but it's too soon to put on the new dresses," Theresa told her. "We'll wear our old clothes until the chores are done."

All the girls hurried to get dressed. Jane, Rachael, and Theresa dressed themselves. Then they helped the younger girls. There had been no need for a second call this morning. Independence Day was the biggest celebration in all the year. It was far more exciting than Thanksgiving or anyone's birthday.

When they came down the ladder, the table was set for breakfast. In the center was a bowl of wild flowers. Above the blooms was a thin stick of wood. A small American flag had been nailed to the wood.

"Grandma made it," announced Jane proudly, "out of scraps left over from our white dresses."

"What is it?" Mattie pushed close to the edge of the table. She peered curiously at the centerpiece.

"It's a flag—our flag!" Jane told her in surprise. "Don't you know what a flag is?"

Mattie and the other smaller children shook their heads. They were frank to admit that they had never seen such a thing. Rachael said nothing. Theresa guessed, from the puzzled look on her face, that she had never seen one either.

Grandma lifted the red, white, and blue flag from the bowl. She spread the cloth flat so they could see it more closely.

"This is the emblem of our country, the United States of America," she explained. "Every country has its own emblem, or flag. The flag stands for all the people of that country. Once we belonged to another country, called England. We had another flag. But we wanted to be on our own. We had to fight for our freedom. Today, Independence Day, celebrates when we made up our minds that we were going to do so. Whenever you see this flag, you must be very respectful. It's your flag — yours and mine."

"It's not my flag," said Rachael in a soft, stubborn voice. "I'm Indian, not American."

"Nonsense!" Grandma's eyes snapped angrily. "Indians are Americans, too. Your people were here before the *Mayflower* landed, Rachael. You're the first Americans; and if anybody tries to tell you something different, you just send them to me."

"All right, Grandma." Rachael smiled. When she looked at the little flag, her eyes grew proud.

"Where'd you get the red and blue cloth, Grandma?" asked Theresa. Even small scraps of material were scarce in Oregon Territory.

"I dyed it. The blue's from crushed leaves of wild flowers and the red's from currants. We mustn't leave it out in the rain or the colors will fade. But I guess there's no danger of that happening today."

Certainly the weather left nothing to be desired. The sky was cloudless. It grew warmer as the sun climbed higher. But everyone knew that by three o'clock, a wind would cool things off.

The settlers had looked forward to the opening of the new boarding school. Since the school was to open on Independence Day, most of them had taken time off from their chores. By mid-morning, wagons were beginning to dot the meadow. Under the trees, people were gathering with huge baskets filled with lunch. A small crowd of young people waited in front of the closed door of the new building. Promptly at eleven o'clock, Mr. Clark, the head of the school, would open the door. Then he would invite everyone to view the completed school.

Inside Grandma Brown's cabin, the excited girls were getting into their new white dresses. "I declare, if you don't look like a field of flowers," beamed Grandma proudly. She went from one to another. She adjusted gathers, smoothed shoulders, and fluffed up sleeves. At last, Grandma decided they were ready for public viewing.

"Go straight to the boarding school," she ordered, opening the door. "Stand on the porch in the order the singing master taught you. And when it's time, don't forget to sing out. There's nothing worse than not being able to hear the words of a song."

The girls in their white dresses were joined by the white-shirted boys. They crossed the yard toward the new building. People saw them coming. Conversation broke off as everyone turned to smile at the pupils. Theresa noticed a girl in a patched gray dress. The girl pulled at the arm of the bearded man beside her.

"Pa, will I have a white dress when I start school?" Her high-pitched voice rose above the mumbled admiration of the crowd.

"Not likely, Emaline." The man shook his head. "But when I get back from the gold diggings, I'll buy you all the dresses you can wear."

Jane, who was walking ahead, stopped. "You mustn't count on a white dress right away. There wasn't any material left," said Jane. She softened the blow by adding, "But you never can tell when Grandma Brown may come up with another. She can do anything she sets her mind to."

The crowd of young people blocking the entrance to the new boarding school fell back. They formed an aisle as the students arrived.

Theresa followed Jane down the aisle. For the first time, she began to be nervous. She was thinking about the song the pupils were going to sing. She hoped she wouldn't make a mistake.

Theresa heard little of the opening ceremonies. She was too busy trying to pick out the faces of her family in the crowd. By now, everyone had left the lunch baskets. They had gathered around the porch.

Mr. Clark made a long speech. Then he introduced Grandma. She would act as housemother to the residents of the new boarding school. Theresa realized they had come to the most important part of the program. The pupils were going to sing. Then the doors would be opened to the public. The faces of the crowd had been friendly. Now they were serious. Her hands grew moist. She knew that when she opened her mouth, nothing would come out. If it did, it would be as rough as the voice of a crow.

Grandma wasn't expected to make a speech. She only bowed. Then the singing master stepped forward. He cleared his throat and gave the pupils a pitch. He, too, must have been a little nervous; for after giving the pitch, he turned back to the audience and announced the selection before giving the singers the pitch a second time. His face grew very red. Some of the people in the audience recognized his mistake. They snickered. In her anger at their rudeness, Theresa forgot her own fright. She sang all the verses and chorus of "Flowers, Wildflower Flowers" perfectly. She wanted to make the singing master proud.

After this, Mr. Clark opened the doors. He invited everyone to inspect the new building. People surged forward. Theresa slipped through the crowd and joined the members of her family who were waiting for her.

It was the most wonderful Fourth of July that Theresa could remember.

✫ ✫ ✫

Throughout her life, Grandma Brown believed in the importance of education. She always tried to help people. That Fourth of July was special for many of the new settlers and their children. Grandma Brown's hard work and her love of children helped make the new school possible.

Tabitha Brown was a remarkable person in other ways, too. To find out more about her pioneer adventures and her new life in Oregon, read Wheels West, by Evelyn Sibley Lampman.

What and Why?

Suppose you found a large pile of garbage in the street. You asked many people why it was there. Each one replied, "I don't know. I tossed on only one little piece." Soon, you would realized what caused the garbage pile.

A *cause* is the reason something happens. An *effect* is the result. The cause of the garbage pile was the fact that many people littered. The *effect*, or result, was that large pile of garbage.

In "My Dear Cousin," the travelers are caught in a snowstorm. Their wagons cannot pass through the deep snow and must be left behind. The cause is the snowstorm. The effect, or result, is the loss of the wagons.

Often, a cause occurs much sooner than its effect. In "My Dear Cousin," the family sold some of its provisions. Later, the money from the sale was used to buy cows and oxen. The purchase of the cows and oxen resulted from the sale of the provisions. If the family had not sold the provisions earlier, it would not have had the money to buy the animals.

Read each paragraph. On your paper, write a complete sentence to answer the question that follows the paragraph.

Before 1971, people had to be twenty-one years old to vote in most states in the United States. Then, a new law was passed by Congress. It lowered the voting age nationwide to eighteen. Now, people who are eighteen or older can vote.

1. What was the effect of the new voting law?

The elevator was an important invention. Since people could use an elevator to reach high levels easily, taller buildings were constructed.

2. What was one effect, or result, of the invention of the elevator?

Years ago, polio was a much more common disease than it is today. In 1953, Dr. Jonas Salk developed a new new special vaccine, or medicine. It is used to prevent polio. Today, fewer people get polio.

3. What is the cause of fewer polio cases today?

The Pilgrims did not have religious freedom in England. In 1620, they sailed on the *Mayflower* to America. They hoped to enjoy religious freedom in a new homeland.

4. What caused the Pilgrims to go to America?

In 1803, France controlled the Mississippi River. Farmers in the United States needed to use the river to send their goods to ships docked in New Orleans. When France refused to let the farmers use the river, the United States bought the entire area from France. The Louisiana Purchase, as it was called, allowed the farmers to use the Mississippi to transport goods.

5. What was a result of the Louisiana Purchase?

In 1608, Hans Lipperskey lined up two lenses, one behind the other, and saw that objects looked larger. He had invented the telescope. The telescope could be used to see distant objects in the sky.

6. What was one result of the invention of the telescope?

EXPLORATIONS

Each selection in "Explorations" describes something special about a journey to the West. Each essay, story, letter, or biography tells something different about pioneer travel. A journey to the West was often difficult and sometimes dangerous. Yet, many people were determined to reach their goals—and they succeeded.

Thinking About "Explorations"

1. Why were the covered wagons called "prairie schooners"?
2. How are Alfred Jacob Miller's paintings like a diary of his trip?
3. One characteristic of the tall tale is exaggeration. What are some examples of exaggeration in "Babe at the Circus"?
4. How were both the Reed family and the family in "A Pioneer Family" affected by the weather?
5. Grandma Brown told Rachael that American Indians were the first Americans. How do you think the pioneer movement changed the lives of the American Indians in the West?
6. How would you compare a trip you might take today to a pioneer's journey?
7. Imagine that you are traveling with a wagon train. Write a letter to your cousin describing one morning of your trip.

Glossary

This glossary will help you to pronounce and to understand the meanings of some of the unusual or difficult words in this book.

The pronunciation of each word is printed beside the word in this way: **o·pen** (ō′pən). The letters, signs, and key words in the list below will help you read the pronunciation respelling. When an entry word has more than one syllable, a dark accent mark (′) is placed after the syllable that has the heaviest stress. In some words, a light accent mark (′) is placed after the syllable that receives a less heavy stress.

The pronunciation key, syllable breaks, accent mark placements, and phonetic respellings in this glossary are adapted from the Macmillan *School Dictionary* (1981) and the Macmillan *Dictionary* (1981). Other dictionaries may use other pronunciation symbols.

Pronunciation Key

a	bad	**hw**	white	**ô**	off	**th**	that	**ə** *stands for*
ā	cake	**i**	it	**oo**	wood	**u**	cup	a *as in* ago
ä	father	**ī**	ice	**o͞o**	food	**ur**	turn	e *as in* taken
b	bat	**j**	joke	**oi**	oil	**yo͞o**	music	i *as in* pencil
ch	chin	**k**	kit	**ou**	out	**v**	very	o *as in* lemon
d	dog	**l**	lid	**p**	pail	**w**	wet	u *as in* helpful
e	pet	**m**	man	**r**	ride	**y**	yes	
ē	me	**n**	not	**s**	sit	**z**	zoo	
f	five	**ng**	sing	**sh**	ship	**zh**	treasure	
g	game	**o**	hot	**t**	tall			
h	hit	**ō**	open	**th**	thin			

A

a · ca · cia (ə kā′ ˙shə) *n.*   a tree with fernlike leaves and clusters of white, yellow, or orange flowers, found in warm regions throughout the world.

ac · cu · rate (ak′yər it) *adj.*   **1.** making few or no errors or mistakes; exact. **2.** without errors or mistakes; correct.

ac · quaint · ed (ə kwān′tid) *adj.*   familiar.

ad · mi · ra · tion (ad′ mə rā′ shən) *n.*   a feeling of high regard or esteem.

a · do · be (ə dō′bē) *n.*   a brick that has been dried in the sun, used as building material.

ad · ver · tise (ad′vər tīz′) *v.*   **ad · ver · tised, ad · ver · tis · ing.**   to make known to the public.

ag · i · ta · tion (aj′ ə tā′shən) *n.*   motion or movement.

a · ground (ə ground′) *adj.*   stranded, as in shallow water. –*adv.*   on or onto a reef or shoal.

aide (ād) *n.*   a helper or assistant.

ail · ment (āl′mənt) *n.*   an illness; sickness.

a · lert (ə lurt′) *adj.*   keenly watchful.

al · i · bi (al′ə bī′) *n.*   a claim or proof that one was somewhere else when a crime or other act was going on.

al · ien (āl′yən, ā′lē ən) *n.*   a person who is not a citizen of the country in which he or she is living.

am · ber (am′bər) *n.*   a hard yellowish-orange or yellowish-brown material used for jewelry and carvings.

an · ces · tor (an′ses′tər) *n.*   something from which another thing is developed or descended.

an · te · lope (ant′əl ōp′) *n. pl.,* **an · te · lopes.** any of various cud-chewing animals that are closely related to goats. Antelopes have unbranched horns and cloven hoofs. These animals are native to Africa and southern Asia.

antelope

anx · ious (angk′shəs) *adj.*   nervous, worried, or fearful about what may happen.

ap · pren · tice (ə pren′tis) *n.*   a person who works for a skilled worker in order to learn a trade or art.

ap · proach (ə prōch′) *v.*   to come near or close to.

ap · prox · i · mate (ə prok′sə mit) *adj.* nearly correct or exact.

a · quar · i · um (ə kwer′ē əm) *n.*   **1.** a tank, bowl, or other container in which fish, water animals, and plants are kept. **2.** a building that holds collections of fish, water animals, and water plants.

a · ris · to · crat (ə ris′ tə krat′) *n.*   a noble; person of high rank.

Ar · is · tot · le (ar′is tot′əl)   a Greek philosopher and scientist.

a · rouse (ə rouz′) *v.*   to stir up or excite.

ar · row · root (ar′ō rōōt′, ar′ō root′) *n.*   **1.** a tropical American plant with large leaves, white flowers, and starchy roots. **2.** a starch made from the roots of this plant.

ar · roy · o (ə roi′ō) *n.*   a dry bed of a stream; gully.

as · pire (əs pīr) *v.* **as · pired,
as · pir · ing.** to seek ambitiously to attain something; aim.

As · so · ci · at · ed Press (ə sō'shē āt'əd pres) a United States news agency that gathers and distributes news stories and pictures throughout the world.

as · sume (ə sōōm') *v.* **as · sumed,
as · sum · ing.** to take for granted as true; suppose as a fact.

a · stride (ə strīd') *adj.* with one leg on each side of.

as · tron · o · mer (əs tron'ə mər) *n.* a student of or an expert in astronomy.

as · tron · o · my (əs tron'ə mē) *n.* the science that deals with the planets, stars, and other heavenly bodies, including the study of their size, position, motion, and physical characteristics.

at · mos · phere (at'məs fēr') *n.* the air in a particular place.

au · di · to · ri · um (ô'də tôr'ē əm) *n.* a large room, often in a school, church, or other building, where people can gather.

Au · rum (ôr'əm)

au · to · mat · ic (ô'tə mat'ik) *adj.* **1.** acting, moving, or operating by itself. **2.** done without a person's control.

ax · is (ak'sis) *n. pl.,* **ax · es** (ak'sēz'). a real or imaginary line around which an object or body, such as the earth, rotates or seems to rotate.

B

bale (bāl) *n.* a large bundle of bulky goods compressed, tightly tied, or otherwise prepared for shipping or storage.

Bal · let Russe de Mon · te Car · lo (ba lā' rōōs'də mon'tē kär'lō) a ballet company of Russian dancers that was founded in the city of Monte Carlo, in the principality of Monaco.

Bal · ti · more (bôl'tə môr') the largest city in Maryland, located on the Chesapeake Bay.

ba · o · bab (bā' ō bab') *n.* a tree with a thick trunk and thick, spreading branches, found in tropical Africa.

Ba · ro · no · va, I · ri · na (bär'ə nō'və, ē rē'nə) a Russian ballet dancer.

Bar · thol · di, Fred · er · ic Au · guste (bär tôl'dē, frā dā rēk' ō goost') French sculptor who designed the Statue of Liberty.

bas · soon (bə sōōn') *n.* a wind instrument with a low range. A bassoon is made of a long doubled wooden tube and a curved metal mouthpiece which contains a double reed.

bat · ting av · er · age (bat'ing av'ər ij, bat'ing av'rij) a number expressing the average effectiveness of a baseball player's batting, figured by dividing the number of safe hits by the number of times at bat.

---

a b**a**d, ā c**a**ke, ä f**a**ther; e p**e**t, ē m**e**; i **i**t, ī **i**ce; o h**o**t, ō **o**pen, ô **o**ff; oo w**oo**d, ōō f**oo**d; oi **oi**l, ou **ou**t; th **th**in, th **th**at; u c**u**p, ur t**u**rn, yōō m**u**sic; zh trea**s**ure; ə **a**go, tak**e**n, penci**l**, lem**o**n, helpfu**l**

bawl (bôl) *v.*   **1.** to weep or sob loudly. **2.** to bellow, shout, or yell.

Bee · tho · ven, Lud · wig van (bā′tō′vən, lōōd′wig van)   a German composer.

be · wil · der (bi wil′dər) *v.*   to confuse or puzzle completely.

Big Dip · per (big′ dip′ər)   a group of seven stars in the constellation Ursa Major, forming the outline of a dipper.

bit · ter (bit′ər) *adj.*   **1.** having a sharp or biting taste. **2.** unpleasant to the mind; hard to bear.

black · smith · ing (blak′smith′ing) *n.*   the activities of a person who works with iron by heating it in a forge and hammering it into shape on an anvil.

blun · der (blun′dər) *v.*   to make a careless, stupid mistake; act blindly.

blurt (blurt) *v.*   to say suddenly or without thinking.

Blythe (blīth)

boar (bôr) *n.*   a wild hog that has a coarse, gray-brown coat and a pair of short tusks.

bog · gy (bog ē) *adj.*   marshy, wet, and spongy like a swamp.

bo · ler · o (bō lār′ō, bə lār′ō) *n.* *Spanish.*   **1.** a dance. **2.** a short, open jacket ending at or above the waistline.

bo · nus (bō′nəs) *n.*   something extra.

boul · der (bōl′dər) *n.*   a large, rounded rock, especially one lying on the surface of the ground.

bowed-down (boud′doun′) *adj.*   bent forward.

bra · ces (brā′səz) *n. pl.*   metal wires used to make teeth straight.

braille (brāl) *n.*   a system of writing and printing for the blind, in which the letters are formed in patterns of raised dots which may be recognized and read by touching.

bra · zen (brā′zən) *adj.*   **1.** of brass. **2.** like brass in color or other qualities.

bribe (brīb) *n.*   something offered or serving to influence or persuade. –*v.*   to give or offer a bribe to.

brin · dle (brin′dəl) *adj.*   gray or brownish-yellow colored, with irregular dark streaks or spots.

brisk (brisk) *adj.*   keen and bracing.

brit · tle (brit′əl) *adj.*   having hardness and rigidity; breaking readily.

bro · cade (brō kād′) *n.*   a heavy fabric woven with raised designs.

bron · co (brong′kō) *n.*   a small, untamed or partly tamed horse of the western United States.

bronco

Bu · ceph · a · lus (byōō sef′ə ləs)

Bud · dhist priest (bood′ist, bōō′dist prēst′)   a person who performs the religious ceremonies for a religion originating in India.

buf · fa · lo robe (buf′əl ō rōb′)   the hide of a North American bison, used as a blanket.

bulk (bulk) *n.*   size.

ca · ble (kā′bəl) *n.*   a bundle of wires that has a covering around it for protection. It is used to carry an electric current.

call · ing card (kô′ling kärd′) a small card with one's name on it, used for social or business purposes.

can · di · date (kan′də dāt′) *n.* a person who seeks, or is put forward by others for, an office or honor.

can · teen (kan tēn′) *n.* a small metal or plastic container for carrying water or other liquids.

Cap · i · tol Ro · tun · da (kap′it əl rōtun′də) the round room located under the dome of the building in which the U.S. Congress meets, in Washington, D.C.

cap · tion (kap′shən) *n.* a title or written description for a picture.

car · ri · er pig · eon (kar′ē ər pij′ən) a homing pigeon.

Cas · cades (kas kādz′) the Cascade Range; mountains in the northwestern United States and southwestern Canada.

cat · a · log (kat′əl ôg′, kat′əl og′) *n.* a publication that lists items, books, names, or subjects, and often describes each item.

Cat · a · lon (kat′ə lon)

cat · e · go · ry (kat′ə gôr′ē) *n.* a group or class of things.

cel · lo (chel′ō) *n.* an instrument of the violin family, between the viola and double bass in size and pitch.

cello

ce · re · al (sēr′ē əl) *n.* a food that is made from grain. Oatmeal is a cereal.

chal · lenge (chal′inj) *v.* **chal · lenged, chal · leng · ing.** to dare to fight or compete.

chem · i · cal (kem′i kəl) *n.* a substance made by or used in chemistry.

Chey · enne (shī en′, shī′an) *n. pl.,* **Chey · enne, Chey · ennes.** a member of a tribe of North American Indians formerly living on the Great Plains, now living mainly in Montana and Oklahoma.

chil · e (chil′ē) *n.* the pod of the pepper plant, used to make a hot spice.

chimes (chīmz) *n. pl.* a set of large bells, tuned to a musical scale, that produce tones when swung or struck.

Cho · pin, Fre · de · ric (shō′pan , shô pan′, fred′ər ik) Polish pianist and composer in France.

chor · e · og · raph · er (kô′rē og′rə fər) *n.* a person who designs or arranges the movements of a dance, especially a ballet.

chor · e · og · raph · y (kô′rē og′rə fē) *n.* the arrangement of the movements of a dance, especially a ballet.

cho · rus (kôr′əs) *n. pl.,* **cho · rus · es. 1.** a group of singers. **2.** music sung by a large group. **3.** something said by many people at one time.

cin · na · mon (sin′ə mən) *n.* a spice made from the dried or ground bark of a tropical Asian tree.

cir · cu · lar (sur′kyə lər) *adj.* **1.** having the form of a circle; round. **2.** moving in or forming a circle.

clas · si · cal (klas′ i kəl) *adj.* **1.** of or pertaining to the culture of ancient Greece and Rome. **2.** of the musical style that prevailed in Europe in the late part of the 18th century. **3.** of concert music or all music other than popular or folk music.

Cla · vi · us (klā′vē əs)   the name of a particular crater on the moon.

Cle · mens, Sam · u · el Lang · horne (klem′ənz, sam′yoo əl lang′hôrn′)

clothes · line (klōz′līn′, klōthz′līn′)   a rope or wire on which clothes are hung for drying or airing.

clot · ted (klot′təd) *adj.*   thickened into a lumpy mass.

co · bra (kō′brə) *n.*   a large, poisonous snake found in Africa and Asia. When a cobra becomes excited it spreads the skin about its neck so that it looks like a hood.

cock (kok) *v.*   to turn upward or tilt to one side.

cobra

col · lie (kol′ē) *n.*   a large, long-haired dog that has a long, narrow head. Collies were originally raised to herd sheep.

co · los · sus (kə los′əs) *n.* **1.** any statue of gigantic size. **2.** anything colossal or gigantic.

collie

Co · los · sus of Rhodes (kə los′əs ov rōdz′)   the legendary bronze statue of Apollo on the island of Rhodes.

com · bi · na · tion (kom′ bə nā′ shən) *n.*   something that is formed by combining; mixture; union.

com · et (kom′it) *n.*   a bright heavenly body made up of ice, frozen gases, and dust particles, and having a long, visible tail that points away from the sun.

com · mand car (kə mand′ kär′)   the car driven by the officer in charge of a unit.

com · mand per · for · mance (kə mand′ pər for′məns)   a performance of a play, a dance, or other entertainment put on for royalty, by command or request.

com · mer · cial (kə mur′shəl) *n.*   an advertising message on radio or television.

com · mit · tee (kə mit′ē) *n.*   a group of persons appointed or elected to perform certain duties.

com · mo · tion (kə mō′shən) *n.*   a noisy confusion; disorder.

com · pan · ion · ship (kəm pan′yən ship′) *n.*   friendship or fellowship.

com · pete (kəm pēt′) *v.* **com · pet · ed, com · pet · ing.**   to strive against another or others, as in a contest.

com · plain (kəm plān′) *v.*   to talk about one's problems, pains, or ills.

con · cen · trate (kon′sən trāt′) *v.* **con · cen · trat · ed, con · cen · trat · ing.**   to keep or direct all of one's attention, thoughts, or efforts.

con · cer · to (kən cher′tō) *n.*   a piece of music for one or more musical instuments accompanied by an orchestra.

Con · es · to · ga (kon′is tō′ gə) *n.*   a covered wagon with an arched canvas top and broad wheels. These wagons were used to cross the American prairies.

con · ges · tion (kən jest′shən) *n.* **1.** an overcrowded or overburdened condition. **2.** a condition in which too much blood collects in an organ or tissue of the body.

Con · gres · sion · al Re · cord
(kən gresh′ən əl rek′ərd)   an account in writing of the proceedings of the United States Congress.

con · scious (kon′shəs) *adj.*   **1.** knowing or realizing; aware. **2.** able to see and feel things. **3.** done on purpose.

con · stel · la · tion (kon′stə lā′shən) *n.*   a group of stars forming a pattern that suggests an object, animal, or mythological character.

co · or · di · nat · ed (kō ôr′ də nāt′ id) *adj.*   working well together.

cork · screw (kôrk′skrōō′) *n.*   a pointed metal spiral set in a handle or any other tool used for removing corks from bottles. –*adj.*   shaped like a corkscrew; spiral.

cor · ri · dor (kor′ə dər) *n.*   a long hallway or passageway.

coun · ter · mel · o · dy (koun′ter mel′ə dē) *n. pl.,* **coun · ter · mel · o · dies.** a secondary melody played or sung at the same time and in harmony with a main melody.

cov · er · age (kuv′ər ij) *n.*   the reporting and publishing or broadcasting of news.

cra · ter (krā′tər) *n.*   any hole in the ground resembling a bowl-shaped hollow, such as one made by a meteorite.

crit · i · cism (krit′ə siz′əm) *n.*   disapproval; faultfinding.

crude (krōōd) *adj.*   done or made without skill; rough.

cul · ture (kul′chər) *n.*   **1.** the way of life of a group of people at a particular time, including their customs, beliefs, and arts. **2.** a knowledge of intellectual and artistic accomplishments and what is considered to be fine in manners and taste.

curb · stone (kurb′stōn′) *n.*   stone or concrete edging of a sidewalk or pavement.

cur · rant (kur′ənt) *n.*   a small sour berry of any of several shrubs, used especially for making jelly, syrup, and wine.

cym · bal (sim′bəl) *n.*   a metal musical instrument that is shaped like a plate. One cymbal is hit against another to make a ringing sound.

D

dan · dy (dan′dē) *adj.*   excellent, very good.

date · line (dāt′līn′) *n.*   a line in a piece of printed material that gives its date and place of origin.

death-de · fy · ing (deth′ di fī′ing) *adj.* challenging death.

de · cep · tive (di sep′ tiv) *adj.*   misleading; meant to trick.

Dem · o · crat · ic (dem′ə krat′ik) *adj.*   of or belonging to the Democratic Party, one of the two major political parties in the United States.

Den · ver (den′vər)   the capital and largest city of Colorado.

---

a bad, ā cake, ä father; e pet, ē me; i it, ī ice; o hot, ō open, ô off; oo wood, ōō food; oi oil, ou out; th thin, <u>th</u> that; u cup, ur turn, yōō music; zh treasure; ə ago, taken, pencil, lemon, helpful

de · pres · sion (di presh'ən) *n.* **1.** sadness; lowness of spirits. **2.** a period marked by a severe reduction of business activity, a rise in unemployment, and falling wages and prices.

de · vice (di vīs') *n.* something made or invented for a particular purpose.

die · sel en · gine (dē'zəl en'jin) an engine that burns fuel oil. The oil is set on fire by heat produced by the compression of air in the engine.

di · et (dī'ət) *v.* to eat and drink a special selection of food and drink for reasons of health or for losing or gaining weight.

di · et · er (dī'ət ər) *n.* a person who diets.

dis · heart · en (dis härt'ən) *v.* to cause to lose hope or courage; discourage.

disk (disk) *n.* a flat, thin, circular object, such as a coin, plate, or phonograph record.

dis · o · be · di · ence (dis'ə bē' dē əns) *n.* failure to obey an order or rule.

dis · solve (di zolv') *v.* **dis · solved, dis · solv · ing** **1.** to mix and make or become liquid. **2.** to break up.

dis · tin · guished (dis ting'gwisht) *adj.* famous for an important achievement or excellent qualities.

dis · traught (di strôt') *adj.* distracted; bewildered; deeply agitated.

doc · ile (dos'əl) *adj.* easily managed, trained, or taught.

doge (dōj) *n.* the chief government officer in the former republics of Genoa and Venice.

dome (dōm) *n.* a round roof, resembling a half of a sphere.

dome

do · mes · ti · cate (də mes'tə kāt') *v.* **do · mes · ti · cat · ed, do · mes · ti · cat · ing.** to tame or develop for use by people.

do · mes · ti · ca · tion (də mes'tə kā'shən) the act of taming or adapting something for people's use.

Don Mar · cel · i · no de Sau · tu · o · la (don' mär sä lē'nō dä sou' tōō ō' la)

dra · mat · ic (drə mat'ik) *adj.* **1.** of or having to do with plays or acting. **2.** as exciting and interesting as a play.

dram · a · tize (dram'ə tīz') *v.* **dram · a · tized, dram · a · tiz · ing.** **1.** to write or perform something as a play. **2.** to make something seem very exciting.

dra · per · y (drā' pər ē) *n. pl.,* **dra · per · ies.** **1.** coverings, hangings, clothing of fabric. **2.** long curtains, usually of heavy fabric.

drear · y (drēr'ē) *adj.* **1.** sad, gloomy, depressing. **2.** dull or uninteresting.

dredge (drej) *v.* **dredged, dredg · ing.** to clear out, deepen, or enlarge with a machine equipped for scooping up or removing mud, sand, and other substances from the bottom of a body of water.

drought (drout) *n.* a long period of time when there is very little rain or no rain at all.

dug · out (dug'out') *n.* a long shelter in which baseball players sit when they are not playing.

dwell · er (dwel'ər) *n.* one who lives in a particular place.

E

ea · sel (ē zəl) *n.* an upright frame or tripod, used especially to hold an artist's canvas.

ed · it (ed′it) *v.* to correct and check something so that it is ready to be printed.

e · di · tion (i dish′ən) *n.* one of a day's several printings of a newspaper.

easel

ed · i · tor (ed′ə tər) *n.* a person who edits.

ed · i · to · ri · al (ed′ə tôr′ē əl) *n.* an article in a newspaper that expresses the opinions of the writer.

ed · u · ca · tion (ej′oo kā′shən) *n.* the process or act of teaching or training.

ef · fi · cient (i fish′ənt) *adj.* able to get the results wanted without wasting time and effort.

El · i · za (i lī′zə)

em · blem (em′bləm) *n.* an object or figure that stands for something.

em · broi · dered (em broi′dərd) *adj.* decorated with needlework designs.

e · merge (i murj′) *v.* **e · merged, e · merg · ing.** to come into view, come out, or come up.

em · i · grant (em′ə grənt) *n.* a person who leaves one place or country to live in another.

e · mo · tion (i mō′shən) *n.* a strong feeling. Love, hate, happiness, sorrow, and fear are emotions.

en · clo · sure (en klō′ zhər) *n.* something that encloses, such as a fence or wall.

en · cour · age · ment (en kur′ij mənt) *n.* something that encourages or gives hope or confidence to.

en · thu · si · asm (en thoo′zē az′əm) *n.* a strong feeling of excitement and interest about something.

e · rect (i rekt′) *v.* **1.** to build. **2.** to put or raise into an upright position.

er · ror (er′ər) *n.* something that is wrong; mistake.

Eu · rope (yoor′əp) the continent between Asia and the Atlantic Ocean.

e · vil · ly (ē′və lē) *adv.* in a wicked or harmful manner.

ex · haust (eg zôst′) *v.* to make very tired or weak.

ex · haus · tion (eg zôs′chən) *n.* the act of exhausting or being exhausted; weakness; tiredness.

ex · ile (eg′zīl, ek′sīl) *n.* a person who is sent away from his home or country.

ex · per · i · ment (eks per′ə mənt) *n.* a test that is used to discover or prove something.

ex · per · i · men · tal (eks per′ə ment′əl) *adj.* having to do with experiments.

ex · per · i · men · ter (eks per′ə ment′ər) *n.* one who experiments.

---

a bad, ā cake, ä father; e pet, ē me; i it, ī ice; o hot, ō open, ô off; oo wood, oo food; oi oil, ou out; th thin, th that; u cup, ur turn, yoo music; zh treasure; ə ago, taken, pencil, lemon, helpful

ex · pla · na · tion (eks′plə nā′shən) *n.* the act or process of making clear or understanding.

ex · plo · sion (eks plō′zhən) *n.* **1.** the act of bursting or expanding suddenly and noisily. **2.** a sudden outburst.

ex · treme · ly (eks trēm′lē) *adv.* severely; to a great extent.

F

Fed · er · al Trade Com · mis · sion (fed′ər əl trād′ kə mish′ən) FTC; the government agency that protects consumers from misleading advertising.

Fe · lix (fē′liks)

fic · tion (fik′shən) *n.* a written work that tells a story about characters and events that are not real.

fi · es · ta (fē es′tə) *n.* **1.** a religious festival, especially a saint's day as celebrated in Spain or Latin America. **2.** any festive celebration; holiday.

fil · i · gree (fil′ə grē′) *adj.* made of delicate ornamental work of intertwined gold or silver wire.

fi · na · le (fi na′lē) *n.* the last part of something; conclusion.

fire ex · tin · guish · er (fīr′eks ting′gwi shər) a device that contains chemicals that can be sprayed on a fire to put it out.

Fitz · pat · rick, Thom · as (fitz pat′rik′, tom′əs)

Flor · ence (flôr′əns, flor′əns) a city in central Italy.

fire extinguisher

floun · der (floun′dər) *v.* to struggle or move in a stumbling manner; to struggle in an embarrassed, awkward way.

fo · cus (fō′kəs) *v.* **1.** to bring into focus so as to make a clear image. **2.** to fix or direct.

ford (fôrd) *n.* a shallow place where a river, stream, or other body of water may be crossed — *v.* to cross a body of water at a shallow place.

Ford Foun · da · tion (fôrd′ foun dā′shən) an organization that gives money to support worthwhile projects.

fore · head (fôr′id, fôr′hed′) *n.* the part of the face above the eyes.

for · eign (fôr′ən, for′ən) *adj.* of or from another country; not native.

fore · tell (fôr tel′) *v.* **fore · told, fore · tell · ing.** to tell ahead of time.

fore · told (fôr tōld′) *v.* see foretell.

for · mu · la (fôr′myə lə) *n.* **1.** a set method of doing something. **2.** a set order of letters, symbols, or numbers that is used to express a rule or principle.

for · ty-nin · er (fôr′tē nī′nər) *n.* a person who went to California seeking gold in the gold rush of 1849.

frag · ment (frag′mənt) *n.* a part broken off; a small piece.

fra · grance (frā′grəns) *n.* a sweet or pleasing smell.

free · way frē′wā′) *n.* a highway with more than two lanes and no toll charges.

freight · er (frā′tər) *n.* **1.** a ship used mainly for transporting cargo. **2.** a person who receives and transports cargo.

full · sail (fool′sāl′) *adj.* with all sails set.

fu · ner · al (fyoo′nər əl) *n.* the ceremony for a dead person prior to burial or cremation.

fur · nish (fur′nish) *v.* **1.** to equip with furniture, fixtures, or appliances. **2.** to supply whatever is wanted; to provide.

fu · tile (fyo͞ot′əl) *adj.* useless or hopeless.

G

gal · ax · y (gal′ək sē) *n.* any of the vast groupings of stars, dust, and gases scattered throughout the universe.

Gal · i · le · i, Gal · i · le · o (gal′ə lā′ē, gal′ə lē′ō) Italian astronomer, physicist, and mathematician.

game (gām) *n.* **1.** a form of playing or amusement. **2.** wild animals, birds, or fish hunted or caught for sport or food.

gang · plank (gang′plangk′) *n.* a moveable bridge between a ship and a dock, used for boarding or leaving a ship.

gen · er · al pub · lic (jen′ər əl pub′ lik) everyone; people in general.

gen · er · a · tion (jen′ə rā′shən) *n.* **1.** a group of individuals born at about the same time. **2.** one step or degree in the line of natural descent, as of people, animals, or plants. Grandfather, father, and son make up three generations.

ging · ham (ging′əm) *n.* a strong cotton fabric. It usually has a pattern of checks, stripes, or plaid.

good-na · tured (good′ nā′ chərd) *adj.* having or showing a pleasant, cheerful disposition or mood.

gore (gôr) *v.* **gored, gor · ing.** to pierce with a horn or tusk.

gram (gram) *n.* a unit of weight in the metric system. One gram is equal to .035 ounces.

grasp (grasp) *v.* **1.** to take hold of firmly with the hand. **2.** to see the meaning of; understand.

grate (grāt) *v.* **grat · ed, grat · ing.** **1.** to shred by rubbing against a rough surface. **2.** to rub together in a way that produces a harsh scraping sound.

grav · i · ta · tion · al pull (grav′ə tā′shən əl pool′) the pull of gravity.

grav · i · ty (grav′ə tē) *n.* the force that pulls things toward the center of the earth. Gravity causes objects to fall when they are dropped and pulls them back to earth when they are thrown upward.

great-tusked (grāt′tuskt′) *adj.* having a long pointed tooth, or a pair of long pointed teeth that stick out.

green · horn (grēn′hôrn′) *n.* an inexperienced person; a person without training. Originally this word referred to a young animal with horns that were not fully grown.

grey · hound (grā′hound′) *n.* a slender dog with a smooth coat and a long nose. Greyhounds can run very fast.

grieve (grēv) *v.* **grieved, griev · ing.** **1.** to feel great sadness or pain; mourn. **2.** to make someone feel sorrow, sadness, or pain.

---

a bad, ā cake, ä father; e pet, ē me; i it, ī ice; o hot, ō open, ô off; oo wood, o͞o food; oi oil, ou out; th thin, th that; u cup, ur turn, yo͞o music; zh treasure; ə ago, taken, pencil, lemon, helpful

grip man (grip'man') *n.* the person who tightens and releases the grip on the cable that operates a cable car.

grub box (grub'boks') a container to hold food.

guitar (gi tär') *n.* a musical instrument having a long neck, six or more strings, and a body shaped somewhat like a violin. It is played by plucking or strumming the strings.

guitar

gul·ly (gul'ē) *n. pl.,* **gul·lies.** a ditch or channel cut in the earth by running water.

H

hab·it (hab'it) *n.* an action that is done so often that it is done without thinking about it.

ha·ci·en·da (hä'sē en'də) *n.* in Spanish-speaking countries, a large estate; large ranch; plantation.

hail (hāl) *v.* **1.** to shout in greeting or welcome. **2.** to shout to or after; attract the attention of by calling.

half-pint (haf'pīnt') *adj.* half of a unit of liquid measure. Half a pint equals one-fourth of a quart. — *n.* a small person.

hand·i·capped (han'dē kapt') *adj.* disabled; being at a disadvantage.

Han·ni·bal (han'ə bəl) a city in Missouri.

har·ass (har'əs, hə ras') *v.* to bother or annoy; to torment.

har·bor (här'bər) *n.* a sheltered place along a coast where ships and boats can anchor.

har·mo·ny (här'mə nē) *n. pl.,* **har·mo·nies.** **1.** a combination of musical notes that sound together, forming chords. **2.** any sweet or pleasant sound.

har·ness (här'nis) *n.* any combination of straps and bands resembling the gear by which a draft animal is attached to the load it is pulling.

hay fe·ver (hā'fē'vər) an allergy caused by breathing in the pollen in the air.

haze (hāz) *n.* mist, smoke, or dust in the air.

head·line (hed'līn') *n.* one or more lines printed at the top of an article, as in a newspaper, that tells what the article is about.

head·strong (hed'strông') *adj.* willful; determined to have one's own way.

head·wind (hed'wind) *n.* a wind blowing from the direction in which something, such as a ship, is headed.

heart·i·ly (här'tə lē) *adv.* in a friendly, sincere way.

hick·o·ry bow (hik'ə rē bō) *n.* a slender curved piece of hard wood used to support the canvas cover of a Conestoga wagon.

hip·po·pot·a·mus (hip'ə pot'ə məs) *n.* a very large plant-eating animal, native to central and southern Africa, living in and near rivers and lakes, and having a

hippopotamus

massive, thick-skinned, hairless body, short legs, and the largest mouth of any land animal.

hoist (hoist) *v.* to lift or pull up, especially by means of pulleys or a crane.

home · ly (hōm′lē) *adj.* **1.** having plain features; not good-looking. **2.** of a familiar or everyday nature; simple.

home · sick · ness (hōm′sik′nis) *n.* the state of being sad or sick because of being away from one's home or family.

hood (hood) *n.* **1.** a covering for the head and neck. **2.** something that looks like a hood or is used as a cover.

Ho · pi (hō′pē) *n.* a member of a tribe of Pueblo Indians living in northeastern Arizona and New Mexico.

ho · ri · zon (hə rī′zən) *n.* the line where the sky and the ground or sea seem to meet.

house · lights (hous′līts′) *n.* the lights in a theater that are used to illuminate the part of the theater where the audience sits.

hu · mor · ist (hyōō′mər ist) *n.* a professional writer or performer of humorous material; comedian.

hunch (hunch) *v.* to assume a bent, stooped, or crouched posture; draw up, raise, or bend. — *n.* a guess or feeling.

hurl (hurl) *v.* to throw hard and fast; fling.

I

Ic · a · rus (ik′ə rəs) a youth who escaped from Crete on wings made by his father, Daedalus. The wax holding the wings melted when he flew too near the sun, and he fell into the sea.

I · da · ho (ī′də hō) a state in the western United States.

i · den · ti · cal (ī den′ti kəl) *adj.* **1.** the very same. **2.** exactly alike.

ig · nore (ig nôr′) *v.* **ig · nored, ig · nor · ing.** to pay no attention to.

il · le · gal (i lē′gəl) *adj.* not legal; unlawful; against the law.

il · lus · tra · tion (il′əs trā′shən) *n.* **1.** something used to make clear or explain. **2.** a picture or diagram.

i · mag · i · na · tion (i maj′ə nā′shən) *n.* the ability or power to create or form new images or ideas.

im · i · tate (im′ə tāt′) *v.* **im · i · ta · ted, im · i · ta · ting.** **1.** to try to act or behave like another person does; copy. **2.** to look like; resemble.

im · mi · grant (im′ə grənt) *n.* a person who comes to live in a country in which he or she was not born.

im · mi · gra · tion (im′ə grā′shən) *n.* the act of entering a country or region in which one was not born in order to make a permanent home there.

im · pris · on (im priz′ən) *v.* to put or keep in prison; lock up.

im · pro · vise (im′prə vīz) *v.* **im · pro · vised, im · pro · vis · ing.** to make up and perform on the spur of the moment.

in · cre · du · li · ty (in′ krə dōō′ lə tē, in′krə dyōō′lə tē) *n.* refusal to believe; doubt.

in · di · cate (in′di kāt′) *v.* **in · di · cat · ed, in · di · cat · ing.** to show or to point out.

---

a bad, ā cake, ä father; e pet, ē me; i it, ī ice; o hot, ō open, ô off; oo wood, ōō food; oi oil, ou out; th thin, th that; u cup, ur turn, yōō music; zh treasure; ə ago, taken, pencil, lemon, helpful

in · dig · na · tion (in′dig nā′shən) *n.* anger caused by something unfair or cruel.

in · her · it (in her′it) *v.* **1.** to get the property or money of a person who has died. **2.** to get from one's parent or parents.

in · jec · tion (in jek′shən) *n.* the forcing of a liquid through the skin into a muscle, vein, or the like.

in · jure (in′jər) *v.* **in · jured, in · jur · ing.** to do or cause damage to; to hurt.

in · stru · ment (in′strə mənt) *n.* **1.** a tool, especially for fine work. **2.** a device for producing musical sounds, such as a guitar or violin.

in · sult (in sult′) *v.* to speak to or treat in a rude, disrespectful, or scornful way.

in · tense (in tens′) *adj.* **1.** very great or strong. **2.** having or showing strong or true feelings.

in · ten · tion (in ten′shən) *n.* plan or purpose.

in · ter · fere (in′tər fēr′) *v.* to interrupt; to become involved in the business of others without being asked.

in · ter · na · tion · al (in′ tər nash′ə nəl) *adj.* having to do with or made up of two or more countries.

in · tro · duc · tion (in′trə duk′shən) *n.* the act of introducing one person to another.

in · ves · ti · gate (in ves′ tə gāt′) *v.* **in · ves · ti · gat · ed, in · ves · ti · gat · ing.** to look into carefully in order to find facts and get information.

i · vo · ry (ī′və rē, īv′rē) *n. pl.* **i · vo · ries.** a smooth, hard, white substance that forms the tusks of elephants, walruses, and certain other animals.

J

jack rab · bit (jak′ rab′it) a hare that has a thin body and very long ears. Jack rabbits use their strong back legs for leaping, and they are one of the fastest of all animals.

jack rabbit

Jack · son, An · drew (jak′sən, an′drōō) the seventh president of the United States, from 1829-1837.

jag · ged (jag′id) *adj.* having sharp points that stick out.

Jap · a · nese (jap′ə nēz′) *n. pl.,* **Jap · a · nese** a person who was born or is living in Japan.

jazz (jaz) *n.* music of a style originated in America late in the nineteenth century.

jour · nal (jur′nəl) *n.* a record, diary, or account, especially one written every day. Journals include descriptions of events, experiences, or thoughts.

jump · line (jump′ līn′) *n.* a note in a newspaper telling a reader where an article is continued.

K

Kan · sas (kan′zəs) a state in the west central United States.

Kat · chin · a (kə chē′nə)

Ke · mi (ke′mē)

Ken · ya (ken′yə, kēn′yə) *n.* a country in eastern Africa.

Kil · i · man · ja · ro, Mt. (kil′ə mən jär′ō) the highest mountain in Africa.

kiln (kil, kiln) *n.* a furnace or oven for baking, drying, or burning pottery or bricks.

ki · lom · e · ter (ki lom′ə tər, kil′ə mē′tər) *n.* a unit of length in the metric system. A kilometer is equal to 1,000 meters, or about .62 of a mile.

kin · dle (kind′əl) *v.* **kin · dled, kind · ling. 1.** to set or catch on fire. **2.** to stir up or excite.

kin · ship (kin′ship′) *n.* a family relationship.

Ko · re · a (kô rē′ə) a country in eastern Asia, divided into North Korea and South Korea in 1948.

ko · to (kō′′tō) *n.* a Japanese stringed instrument.

L

La · fay · ette Square (lä′fē et′ skwer′)

land · ing mod · ule (land′ing moj′ool, mod′yool) a self-contained unit or part of a spacecraft used for landing.

land rov · er (land′rō′vər) a vehicle used for traveling on the ground.

land · scape (land′skāp′) *n.* **1.** a stretch or expanse of scenery that can be viewed from one place. **2.** a painting, photograph, or other picture showing such a stretch of scenery.

land · slide (land′slīd′) *n.* the sliding or falling down of soil and rock.

la · ser (lā′zər) *n.* a device that produces an extremely powerful beam of light consisting of light waves that are of the same wavelength and are in phase.

Laz · a · rus, Em · ma (laz′ə rəs, em′ə) a United States poet.

Le · an · dra (lē an′drə)

leg · gings (leg′ingz) *n. pl.* cloth or leather coverings for the legs that usually reach to the ankles.

lend (lend) *v.* **lent, lend · ing. 1.** to let someone have or use something for a while. **2.** to give someone money to use for a certain period of time at a set rate of interest.

lens (lenz) *n. pl.,* **lens · es.** a piece of glass or other clear material that is curved to make light rays move apart or come together. Lenses are used in eyeglasses, telescopes, and microscopes.

li · cense (lī′səns) *n.* a card, paper, or other object showing that a person has legal permission to do or show something.

life form (līf′fôrm′) *n.* the outward appearance of a living thing.

Lin · coln, A · bra · ham (ling′kən, ā′brə ham′) the sixteenth president of the United States, from 1861 to 1865.

lin · guist (ling′gwist) *n.* a student of or an expert in the scientific study of language.

li · on's paw ta · ble (lī′ənz pô′ tā′bəl) a table with legs that end in carved lion's feet.

lit · er (lē′tər) *n.* a basic unit of measurement in the metric system. A liter is equal to about 1.05 quarts of liquid.

log (lôg, log) *n.* an official record of speed, progress, and important events, kept on a ship or aircraft.

log · i · cal (loj′i kəl) *adj.* following as a natural result; reasonably expected.

a bad, ā cake, ä father; e pet, ē me; i it, ī ice; o hot, ō open, ô off; oo wood, oo food; oi oil, ou out; th thin, th that; u cup, ur turn, yoo music; zh treasure; ə ago, taken, pencil, lemon, helpful

lo · go (lō′gō) *n.* a symbol, letter, or word written in a particular way used as a trademark.

long-ant · lered (long′ant′lərd) *adj.* having long branched horns, like deer, elk, moose, and other related animals.

Lum · mox (lum′iks)

M

Mac · e · don (mas′ə don′) an ancient country north of Greece, the center of the empire created by Alexander the Great.

Ma · drid (mə drid′) the capital and largest city of Spain, located in the center of the country.

mag · ic glass (maj′ik glas′) an early expression for telescope.

ma · jor (mā′jər) *adj.* bigger or more important.

mam · moth (mam′əth) *n.* a prehistoric elephant with long, upward-curving tusks and black shaggy hair. Mammoths are extinct.

man · ger (mān′jər) *n.* a large box in which food for horses and cattle is kept.

man · u · al (man′yoo əl) *adj.* relating to, done by, or involving the hands.

man · u · al-dex · ter · i · ty (man′yoo əl deks ter′ə tē) *adj.* relating to, skill in using the hands.

man · za · ni · ta (man′zə nē′tə) *n.* any of several shrubs belonging to the heath family found in the western United States.

Ma · ri · ko (mä rē′kō)

mar · ma · lade (mär′mə lād) *n.* a jam made by boiling the peel and flesh of fruit, usually citrus fruit, like oranges.
   marmalade cat. a red tabby cat.

mar · vel · ous (mär′və ləs) *adj.* causing wonder or astonishment.

mast (mast) *n.* an upright pole in a sailing boat or ship to support the sails.

mate (māt) *n.* **1.** a husband or wife. **2.** one of a pair. **3.** an officer on a merchant ship, ranking next below the captain. **4.** a close friend.

math · e · ma · ti · cian (math′ə mə tish′ən) *n.* a student of or an expert in mathematics.

max · i · mum (mak′sə məm) *n.* the greatest possible amount.

May · flow · er (mā′flou′ər) the ship on which the Pilgrims came to America in 1620.

meas · ure · ment (mezh′ ər mənt) *n.* **1.** the size, height, or amount of something. **2.** a system of measuring.

med · i · cine man (med′ə sin man′) a person who performs religious rituals for a tribe of American Indians.

Mei Gwen (mā′ gwen′)

men · tion (men′shən) *v.* to speak about or refer to briefly.

mer · chan · dise (mur′chən dīz′, mur′chən dīs) *n.* things that are bought and sold.

me · te · or (mē′tē ər) *n.* matter from space that enters the earth's atmosphere, where it is heated by friction until it burns with a bright light during its fall.

me · te · or cra · ter (mē′tē ər krā′tər) a bowl-shaped hollow in the ground that is made when a meteor lands.

me · ter (mē′tər) *n.* the basic unit of length in the metric system. A meter is equal to 39.37 inches, or slightly more than 3¼ feet.

met · ric (met′rik) *adj.* of or having to do with the metric system.

mi · cro · phone (mī′krə fōn′) *n.* a device that is used to transmit sound or to make it louder.

Mi · das (mī′ dəs) a king in Greek legend who was given the power of turning everything he touched to gold.

Mid · do (mid′ō)

mid · sec · tion (mid′sek′shən) *n.* the middle section or part of anything.

min · i-sled (min′ē sled′) *n.* a skateboard with runners instead of wheels, used for sliding down snowcovered slopes.

Min · ne · ap · o · lis (min′ē ap′ə lis) the largest city in Minnesota, located in the southeastern part of the state.

Min · ne · so · ta (min′ə sō′ta) a state in the north central United States.

mi · rac · u · lous (mi rak′yə ləs) *adj.* **1.** having the nature of a miracle. **2.** like a miracle; marvelous; wonderful.

Mis · sis · sip · pi Riv · er (mis′ə sip′ē riv′ər) the principal river in the United States that flows from northern Minnesota to the Gulf of Mexico.

Mis · sou · ri Riv · er (mi zoor′ē, mi zoor′ə riv′ər) the longest river in the United States. It flows from Montana into the Mississippi River.

Miy · a · gi, Mi · chi · o (mē yô′gē, mē′shē ō)

mo · bile (mō′bēl) *n.* a piece of sculpture having delicately balanced units suspended in midair by wire or twine so that the individual parts can move independently, as when stirred by a breeze.

moc · ca · sin (mok′ə sin) *n.* a shoe with a soft sole and no heel. Moccasins are usually made from one piece of leather and were originally worn by American Indians.

moccasin

mod · ule (moj′ool, mod′yool) *n.* a self-contained unit or part of a spacecraft.

mol · ten (mōl′tən) *adj.* melted by heat.

mo · men · tous (mō men′təs) *adj.* of great importance.

mor · tal (môr′təl) *adj.* fatal, causing death.

mo · tion (mō′shən) *v.* to direct with a movement or gesture.

mot · to (mot′ō) *n.* a short sentence or phrase that says what someone believes or what something stands for.

moun · tain · eer (moun′tə nēı′) *n.* a person who lives in a mountainous region.

muf · fle (muf′əl) *v.* **muf · fled, muf · fling.** to soften the sound that something makes.

N

Nai · ro · bi (nī rō′bē) the capital of Kenya.

---

a bad, ā cake, ä father; e pet, ē me; i it, ī ice; o hot, ō open, ô off; oo wood, ōō food; oi oil, ou out; th thin, th that; u cup, ur turn, yōō music; zh treasure; ə ago, taken, pencil, lemon, helpful

Nam · pey · o (nam pā′ō)

Nan · tuck · et (nan tuk′it)   an island off southeastern Massachusetts.

Mass.

Nantucket →

nar · row (nar′ō) *v.* to make smaller in width or extent; reduce or limit.

na · tive (nā′tiv) *adj.*   **1.** belonging to a particular place or country. **2.** natural, possessed from birth.

nat · u · ral · ist (nach′ər ə list) *n.*   a person who studies natural sciences, especially one who studies plants or animals.

nau · ti · cal (nô′ti kəl) *adj.*   of or relating to ships, sailors, or navigation.

near · sighted (nēr′sī′tid) *adj.*   able to see objects that are close by more clearly than those that are far away.

neg · lect (ni glekt′) *v.*   to fail to give proper attention or care to; to leave undone.

net · work (net′wurk′) *n.*   **1.** a system of lines or structures that cross. **2.** a group of radio or television stations that work together so that they can all broadcast the same program at the same time.

New Or · le · ans (nyo͞o ôr′lē ənz), no͞o ôr′lənz)   a city in southeastern Louisiana, on the Mississippi River.

Louisiana

New Orleans

news · cast (no͞oz′kast′, nyo͞oz′kast′) *n.*   a radio or television program on which news is presented.

Ni · jin · ska, Bron · i · sla · va (ni zhin′skə, bron′ə släv′ə) a Russian ballet teacher and choreographer.

Ni · jin · sky, Vas · law (ni zhin′ skē, väts läf′) a Russian ballet dancer and choreographer.

no · ble (nō′bəl) *n.*   a person of high birth, rank, or title.

non · fic · tion (non fik′shən) *n.*   prose literature that deals with real situations, persons, or events. Essays and biographies are examples of nonfiction.

non · ver · bal (non vur′bəl) *adj.*   not in words; not spoken.

North Star (north′stär′)   another term for Polaris.

No · va Sco · tia (nō′və skō′shə)   a province of Canada, in the southeastern part of the country.

nub (nub) *n.*   a knob or lump.

nu · tri · tion (no͞o trish′ən, nyo͞o trish′ən) *n.*   food; nourishment.

O

oboe (ō′bō) *n.*   a woodwind instrument having a double reed and a high, penetrating tone.

ob · ser · va · tion (ob′zər vā′shən) *n.* **1.** the act or power of noticing. **2.** the fact of being seen; notice. **3.** something said; comment; remark.

oboe

ob · serv · a · to · ry (əb zur′və tôr′ ē) *n.* a place or building furnished with telescopes and other equipment for observing, studying, and collecting information on the moon, planets, or stars.

ob · vi · ous (ob′vē əs) *adj.* easily seen or understood.

old-fash · ioned (ōld′fash′ənd) *adj.* **1.** keeping to old ways, ideas, or customs. **2.** of former times; out-of-date.

o · pin · ion (ə pin′yən) *n.* a belief that is based on what a person thinks rather than on what is proved or known to be true.

op · ti · cian (op tish′ən) *n.* one who fills prescriptions for and specializes in fitting and adjusting eyeglasses and contact lenses.

op · tom · e · trist (op tom′ə trist) *n.* a specialist in the examination of the eyes for vision and the fitting of glasses.

or · bit (ôr′ bit) *n.* **1.** the path of a heavenly body as it revolves in a closed curve about another body. **2.** one complete trip of a spacecraft or artificial satellite along such a path.

or · ches · tra (ôr′kis trə) *n.* a group of musicians playing together on various instruments, usually including strings, woodwinds, brasses, and percussion instruments.

or · di · nar · y (ôrd′ən er′ē) *adj.* **1.** commonly used; habitual or regular. **2.** average; not distinguished from any other.

Or · e · gon (ôr′ə gon′, ôr′ə gən, or′ə gon′, or′ə gən) a state in the northwestern United States, on the Pacific Ocean.

O · res · tes (ô res′tēz)

or · na · ment (ôr′nə ment) *n.* a small decorative object.

or · tho · don · tist (ôr′thə don′tist) *n.* a dentist specializing in correcting and preventing irregularities of the teeth.

O · sage (ō sāj′, ō′sāj) *n.* **1.** the name of a tribe of Sioux Indians. **2.** a member of this tribe.

Os · sip (os′ip)

out · fit (out′fit′) *n.* a set of different articles for doing something. **2.** a set of clothing.

out · ing (ou′ting) *n.* a short pleasant trip; excursion.

out · raged (out′rājd′) *adj.* greatly angered.

o · ver · land (ō′vər land′) *adv.* **1.** by land. **2.** over or across the land.

P

pack (pak) *n.* **1.** a collection of things, wrapped or tied together, especially for carrying on the back. **2.** a group of animals living or hunting together.

Pain · ted Des · ert (pān′təd dez′ərt) a brilliantly colored desert in northeastern Arizona.

---

a bad, ā cake, ä father; e pet, ē me; i it, ī ice; o hot, ō open, ô off; oo wood, o͞o food; oi oil, ou out; th thin, th that; u cup, ur turn, yo͞o music; zh treasure; ə ago, taken, pencil, lemon, helpful

par · a · chute (par'ə shōōt') *n.* a device resembling an umbrella, used for slowing the speed of a body falling through the air.

parch · ment (pärch'mənt) *n.* **1.** the skin of sheep, goats, or other animals, prepared as a writing material. **2.** any of several types of paper made to resemble this material.

Par · is (par'is) the capital and largest city of France.

par · tic · u · lar (pər tik' yə lər) *adj.* **1.** taken by itself; apart from others. **2.** having to do with some one person or thing. **3.** unusual in some way. **4.** very careful about details; hard to please.

pas · ture (pas'chər) *n.* a field of land used for grazing cattle, sheep, or other animals.

pat · tern (pat'ərn) *v.* to make according to a pattern or example.

Pav · lo · va, An · na (päv lō'və, än'nä) a Russian ballet dancer.

ped · es · tri · an (pə des'trē ən) *adj.* of or for people traveling on foot.

pel · i · can (pel'i kən) *n.* a web-footed water bird having a large pouch beneath the bill that is used for storing fish.

per · fumed (pər fyōōmd') *adj.* pleasantly scented; having a pleasing odor.

per · mis · sion (pər mish'ən) *n.* a consent from someone in authority.

pet · ti · coat (pet'ē kōt') *n.* an underskirt.

phase (fāz) *n.* a stage of development of a person or thing.

Phil · o · ni · cus (fi lō'ni kəs)

phrase (frāz) *n.* **1.** a group of words expressing a single thought. **2.** a short expression.

phys · i · cist (fiz'ə sist) *n.* a person who knows a great deal about the science that deals with matter and energy and the laws governing them.

pi · geon (pij'ən) *n.* a bird that has a plump body, a small head, and thick, soft feathers. Pigeons live in the wild but are also found in nearly every city of the world.

pi · lot (pī'lət) *n.* **1.** a person who operates the controls of an aircraft or spacecraft. **2.** a person who steers a ship. **3.** any person who guides or leads.

pint (pīnt) *n.* a unit of measurement. It is equal to half a quart.

plan · ta · tion (plan tā'shən) *n.* a large estate or farm where one crop is grown.

play · ground (plā'ground') *n.* an area, often with equipment such as swings and teeter-totters, where children can play.

pla · za (plaz'ə, plä' zə) *n.* a public square or open space in a city or town.

plough (plou) *n.* a farm tool for turning over or breaking up the soil for planting.

pluck (pluk) *v.* **1.** to pull off; pick. **2.** to pull off hair or feathers from. **3.** to give a pull; tug.

plunge (plunj) *v.* **plunged, plung · ing. 1.** to put in forcefully. **2.** to dive or fall suddenly.

pneu · mo · nia (nōō mōn′yə, nyōō mōn′yə) *n.* any of several diseases that cause an inflammation of the lungs, usually caused by a bacterial or viral infection.

Po · lar · is (pō lar′is) a star located in the northern sky above the North Pole. It is the outermost star in the handle of the Little Dipper; North Star.

pomp (pomp) *n.* stately or brilliant display; splendor; magnificence.

por · poise (pôr′pəs) *n.* an animal that is warm-blooded and lives in the ocean. A porpoise has a round head with a short, blunt beak. Porpoises are very intelligent animals.

porpoise

port · fo · li · o (pôrt fō′lē ō) *n.* a portable case for carrying or holding loose papers, large drawings, or other materials; briefcase.

por · tion (pôr′shən) *n.* a limited amount or part of something.

port · o · phone (pôrt′ō fōn′) *n.* a portable telephone.

por · trait (pôr′trit, pôr′trāt) *n.* a painting, photograph, or other representation of a person.

post (pōst) *v.* to deposit in a mailbox or at a post office.

po · tion (pō′shən) *n.* a drink, especially one believed to have medicinal, magic, or poisonous powers.

pouch (pouch) *n. pl.*, **pouch · es.** a bag or sack made of a flexible material.

pout (pout) *v.* **1.** to thrust out the lips, as in displeasure or sullenness. **2.** to be sullen; sulk.

pow · der horn (pou′dər hôrn′) the horn of a cow or other animal, used for carrying gunpowder.

prac · ti · cal (prak′ti kəl) *adj.* **1.** having to do with real life; coming from experience. **2.** sensible; down to earth.

powder horn

prai · rie schoon · er (prär′ē skōō′nər) a covered wagon used by pioneers in crossing the prairies westward to the Pacific coast.

prairie schooner

pre · cau · tion (pri kô′shən) *n.* something done beforehand to prevent harm or danger.

pre · cise (pri sīs′) *adj.* exact, accurate, or definite.

pre · ci · sion (pri sizh′ən) *n.* accuracy; exactness.

pre · his · tor · ic (prē′ his tôr′ ik, prē′his tor′ik) *adj.* belonging to or relating to the period before recorded history.

---

a **b**ad, ā **c**ake, ä **f**ather; e **p**et, ē **m**e; i **i**t, ī **i**ce; o **h**ot, ō **o**pen, ô **o**ff; oo w**oo**d, ōō f**oo**d; oi **oi**l, ou **ou**t; th **th**in, th **th**at; u **c**up, ur **t**urn, yōō **m**usic; zh trea**s**ure; ə **a**go, tak**e**n, penc**i**l, lem**o**n, helpf**u**l

pres · en · ta · tion (prez′ən tā′shən, prē′zən tā′shən) *n.*   the act of presenting something.

press a · gent (pres′ ā′gənt)   a person who manages publicity or public relations for a person or organization.

pressed ham (prest′ham′)   a processed lunch meat made of ham and other things.

pre · ven · tion (pri ven′shən) *n.*   the preventing of something; keeping something from happening.

pro · ba · tion (prō bā′shən) *n.*   a testing or trial of the ability, qualifications, or suitability of a person, as a new employee, usually for a specified period of time.

pro · duc · tion (prə duk′shən) *n.*   **1.** the act of producing. **2.** the total amount of something that has been made. **3.** something that is produced, especially a play or motion picture.

pro · file (prō′fīl) *n.*   a side view, especially of a face or head.

prof · it (prof′it) *n.*   **1.** the amount of money left after all the costs of running a business or making or selling something have been paid. **2.** anything that is gained by doing something.

proj · ect (proj′ekt′) *n.*   a plan or activity to be done.

Pro · kof · iev, Ser · gei Ser · ge · ye · vich (prə kôf′yef, ser gā′ ser gā′yə vich)   a Russian composer.

proof (pr$\overline{oo}$f) *n.*   evidence that establishes a fact or shows something to be true.

prop · er · ty (prop′ər tē) *n. pl.*, **prop · er · ties. 1.** a possession. **2.** a piece of real estate; land. **3.** any movable article, except scenery and costumes, used on the set of theatrical production; prop.

pros · pec · tor (pros′pek tər) *n.*   a person who explores for gold or other minerals.

psy · chol · o · gist (sī kol′ə jist) *n.*   a person who knows a great deal about the mind and the way people behave.

pub · lish · er (pub′li shər) *n.*   a person or company whose business is the producing and offering of printed material for sale to the public.

Pu · litz · er Prize (pool′it sər priz′)   one of a group of annual prizes in journalism, literature, music, and other fields, established by Joseph Pulitzer.

pu · ny (py$\overline{oo}$′nē) *adj.*   small, weak, or unimportant.

Q

quart (kwôrt) *n.*   a unit of measure. It is equal to two pints.

ques · tion · naire (kwes′chə nār′) *n.*   a list of questions that is given to people to answer. The answers are analyzed for usable information.

quick · sand (kwik′sand′) *n.*   very deep, loose, wet sand that can swallow up or surround a heavy object that moves upon it.

R

range (rānj) *v.* **ranged, rang · ing.**   to move or wander over an area.

ran · som (ran′səm) *n.*   **1.** the release of a captive for a price. **2.** the price paid or demanded before a captive is set free. — *v.* to get a captive set free by paying a price.

ra · vine (rə vēn′) *n.*   a deep, narrow valley.

re · ac · tion (rē ak′shən) *n.*   an action in response to something that has happened or has been done.

re · al · is · tic (rē′ə lis′tik) *adj.*   having to do with what is real or practical.

re · al · i · ty (rē al′ə tē) *n. pl.,* **re · al · i · ties.** an actual or true thing, fact, or event.

re · a · lize (rē′ə līz′) *v.* **re · a · lized, re · a · liz · ing.** to understand completely.

Ream, Vinne (rēm, vin′ē)

re · as · sure (rē′ ə shoor′) *v.* **re · as · sured, re · as · sur · ing.** to restore confidence or courage in.

re · cit · al (ri sīt′əl) *n.*   a performance or concert of music or dance, often given by a single performer or devoted to the works of a single composer.

re-en · try (rē en′trē) *n.*   **1.** the act or instance of entering again. **2.** the return of a missile or spacecraft to the earth's atmosphere.

re · flect (ri flekt′) *v.*   to turn or throw back.

re · gret · ful (ri gret′fəl) *adj.*   feeling or expressing regret.

re · hearse (ri hurs′) *v.* **re · hearsed, re · hears · ing.** to practice or train in order to prepare for a performance.

rein (rān) *n.*   either of two long, narrow, leather straps attached to a bit at either side of a horse's mouth that are used to control the movement of the horse.

rein

re · lay (rē′lā′) *n.*   a fresh set or team of men or animals prepared to relieve another.

rep · re · sent · a · tive (rep′ri zen′ tə tiv) *n.* a person who is chosen to speak or act for others. The members of the Congress are our elected representatives in the federal government.

re · pub · lic (ri pub′lik) *n.*   a form of government in which the final authority of the state rests with voting citizens and is exercised by elected officials, rather than by a monarch.

Re · pub · li · can (ri pub′li kən)   of or belonging to the Republican Party, one of the two main political parties in the United States.

re · quest (ri kwest′) *n.*   something that has been asked for or requested.

re · spect · ful (ri spekt′fəl) *adj.*   with regard or consideration for someone or something; full of respect; courteous.

---

a bad, ā cake, ä father; e pet, ē me; i it, ī ice; o hot, ō open, ô off; oo wood, o͞o food; oi oil, ou out; th thin, th that; u cup, ur turn, yo͞o music; zh treasure; ə ago, taken, pencil, lemon, helpful

re · spond (ri spond') *v.*   **1.** to give an answer. **2.** to act in return; react.

re · sume (ri zōōm') *v.*   **re · sumed, re · sum · ing.**   to continue again after stopping.

re · tire (ri tīr') *v.* **re · tired, re · tir · ing.**   to take oneself away from a business, job, or office.

re · treat (ri trēt') *v.*   to withdraw, as from battle; to draw back.

re · view (ri vyōō') *n.*   a critical summary or discussion.

re · volve (ri volv') *v.*   **re · volved, re · volv · ing. 1.** to move in a circle around a central point or object. **2.** to depend on.

rhi · noc · er · os (rī nos'ər əs) *n.*   a large, thick-skinned animal of Africa and Asia, having one or two horns on the snout.

Rhodes (rōdz)   an island in the eastern Mediterranean Sea, southwest of Turkey.

ri · dic · u · lous (ri dik'yə ləs) *adj.*   very silly or foolish.

rig · id (rij'id) *adj.*   not yielding, not bending, stiff.

rill (ril) *n.*   a large crack on the moon's surface.

ri · val (rī'vəl) *n.*   a competitor.

riv · et (riv'it) *n.*   a metal bolt used to fasten metal or leather in a firm, usually permanent way.

rivet

Rock · y Moun · tains (rok'ē moun'tənz)
a mountain range that extends for more than 3000 miles through the United States. They extend from central New Mexico to northern Alaska.

ro · de · o (rō'dē ō', rō dā'ō) *n.*   **1.** a show in which people compete in various events, such as horseback riding, calf roping, and steer wrestling, often for cash prizes. **2.** a roundup of cattle.

Rol · lins, James (rol' ənz, jāmz)

Rome (rōm)   the capital of Italy, located on the Tiber River.

Ros · si · ni, Gio · ac · chi · no An · to · nio
(rō sē'nē, jo'ä kē'nō än tō'nyō) an Italian composer of operas.

ro · tate (rō'tāt) *v.*   to turn around on an axis.

rou · tine (rōō tēn') *n.*   a fixed way of doing something.

roy · al · ty (roi'əl tē) *n.*   a royal person or persons. Kings, queens, princes and princesses are royalty.

ru · mor (rōō'mər) *n.*   a report or statement passed from person to person as truth without any evidence to support it; unverified story.

run · a · way (run'ə wā') *n.*   a person or thing that runs away, such as a fugitive or a horse that has gone out of control.

rut (rut) *n.*   a groove or track made in the ground by a wheel or by many wheels.

S

sa · cred (sā'krid) *adj.*   **1.** of or relating to religion. **2.** deserving respect or reverence.

sa · fa · ri (sə fär'ē) *n.*   a hunting expedition, especially in Africa.

San · chez, Se · ñor (sän'chez, se nyōōr')

sand · bar (sand'bär') *n.*   a ridge of sand built up by the action of waves and currents.

sa · van · na (sə van′ə) *n.* a broad, grassy plain with widely scattered trees and shrubs.

scale (skāl) *n.* **1.** the proportion that a plan, map, or model has to what it represents. **2.** a series of tones that go up or down in pitch according to fixed intervals.

sched · ule (skej′o͞ol, skej′o͞o əl, skej′əl) *n.* **1.** a list of the times when certain events are to take place. **2.** a plan or group of things to do at a particular time.

sci · ence fic · tion (sī′əns fik′shən) stories that draw imaginatively on scientific knowledge and speculation in plot, setting, and theme.

score (skôr, skōr) *n.* **1.** a record of points made in a game or contest. **2.** a grade or rating on a test or examination. **3.** written or printed music.

script (skript) *n.* the written text of a play, movie, or television or radio show.

script writ · er (skript′rī′tər) a person who writes scripts for movies, radio, or television.

scroll (skrōl) *n.* a roll of parchment, paper, silk, or other material, especially one with writing on it, often wound around a rod or a pair of rods so as to be able to be easily stored.

scroll

scuff (skuf) *v.* to scratch the surface of by scraping or by wear.

sculp · ture (skulp′chər) *n.* a three-dimensional statue that is carved, chiseled, or modeled.

seamed (sēmd) *adj.* marked by ridges or furrows, like the joined edges of two pieces of cloth sewn together.

sen · a · tor (sen′ə tər) *n.* a member of a senate.

sen · sor (sen′sər) *n.* a device that senses sound, light, or the like.

ser · geant (sär′jənt) *n.* a police officer ranking above a patrol officer and below a captain or a lieutenant.

shab · by (shab′ē) *adj.* worn-out and faded.

Shang · hai (shang′hī) a city in China.

shin (shin) *v.* **shinnied, shin · ny · ing.** to climb by using the hands or arms and the feet or legs in grasping or pulling.

Sho · sho · ni (shə shō′nē, shō shō′nē) *n.* a member of the tribe of North American Indians living in Idaho, Montana, Nevada, Oregon, Wyoming, and Utah.

shrine (shrīn) *n.* **1.** a case or other container that holds sacred objects. **2.** a place set aside for worship.

Si · be · ri · a (sī bēr′ē ə) a region of the Soviet Union that extends from the Ural Mountains to the Pacific Ocean.

Si · er · ra Ne · va · da (sē er′ə nə vad′ə, sē er′ə nə vä′də) a mountain range in eastern California.

---

a bad, ā cake, ä father; e pet, ē me; i it, ī ice; o hot, ō open, ô off; oo wood, o͞o food; oi oil, ou out; th thin, th that; u cup, ur turn, yo͞o music; zh treasure; ə ago, taken, pencil, lemon, helpful

Sioux (sōō) *n. pl.,* **Sioux** (sōō, sōōz) a member of a group of North American Indian tribes that speak a Siouan language.

sire (sīr) *n.* **1.** a male parent. **2.** a form of address once used in speaking to a king or noble.

sketch (skech) *n.* a rough, preliminary drawing or painting.

ski · board (skē′bôrd′) *n.* a low, flat board having small runners attached to the bottom instead of wheels as with skateboards.

skiboard

sky · light (skī′līt′) *n.* a window in a roof or ceiling.

slav · er · y (slā′ vər ē) *n.* **1.** the institution or practice of owning slaves. **2.** the condition of being a slave.

slug · gish (slug′ish) *adj.* without vigor; slow moving.

Smith · so · ni · an In · sti · tu · tion (smith sō′nē ən in′stə tōō′shən) an institution in Washington, D.C., founded with funds left by James Smithson, for the increase and spread of knowledge.

smoth · er · ing (smu<u>th</u>′ər ing) *adj.* depriving of air; suffocating.

smudge (smuj) *n.* a mark or a stain made by smearing; a blurred mark.

snick · er (snik′ər) *v.* to laugh slyly, usually expressing scorn or disrespect.

snug · gle (snug′ əl) *v.* **snug · gled, snug · gling.** to lie close to or hold closely for warmth or protection, or to show love.

so · ber (sō′bər) *adj.* very serious and solemn.

soil · bound (soil′bound′) *adj.* firmly set in or attached to the soil.

som · brer · o (som brer′ō) *n.* a hat with a broad brim, worn especially in Mexico and the southwestern United States.

sombrero

sound ef · fect (sound′i fekt′) any sound, other than music or speech, that is artificially reproduced to create an effect in a dramatic presentation.

spec · u · la · tive · ly (spek′yə lə′tiv lē) *adv.* in a serious or thoughtful way.

splotch (sploch) *n. pl.,* **splotch · es.** a large irregular spot, stain, or blot.

sprawl (sprôl) *v.* **1.** to lie or sit with the body stretched out in an awkward or careless manner. **2.** to spread out in a way that is not regular or organized.

spurt (spurt) *n.* a sudden, brief spell, as of activity or effort.

sput · ter (sput′ər) *n.* a popping or spitting noise.

spy · glass (spī′glas′) *n.* a small telescope.

squash (skwosh) *n.* the round or oblong fruit of any of a group of plants related to the gourd, cooked and eaten as a vegetable.

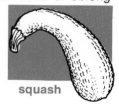

squash

squat (skwot) *v.*
squat · ted, squat · ting.
to crouch or sit with the knees bent and
drawn close to or under the body.

squeal (skwēl) *v.* to make a loud, shrill cry
or sound.

squint (skwint) *v.* to partly close the eyes.

staid (stād) *adj.* sober; sedate; settled
and steady.

star · gaze (stär′gāz′) *v.* **star · gazed,**
star · gaz · ing. to gaze at or study the
stars.

star · ling (stär′ling) *n.* a bird with a plump
body, pointed wings, and a short tail.
Starlings are found in most parts of the
world.

sta · tion · ar · y (stā′shə ner′ē) *adj.* having a fixed place; not moving.

stat · ue (stach′ōō) *n.* a representation,
often life-size or larger, of a human or
animal figure, carved, cast, or modeled in
stone, bronze, clay, or some other material.

stern · ly (sturn′lē) *adv.* in a strict, harsh,
or severe manner, especially one show-
ing displeasure.

stir (stur) *v.* **stirred, stir · ring. 1.** to mix
by a continuous circular movement. **2.** to
excite deep feelings or emotions.

stir · rup (stur′əp, stir′əp) *n.* one of a pair
of metal, wooden, or leather loops or
rings, flattened at the bottom and suspended from a saddle, used to support a
rider's foot in mounting and riding.

sto · ried (stôr′ēd) *adj.* famous in story
and history.

stout · ly (stout′lē) *adv.* in a brave,
courageous manner.

stow · a · way (stō′ə wā′) *n.* a person
who hides on a ship or airplane, especially in order to obtain free passage.

Strad · i · var · i, An · to · nio (strad′ə
vär′ē, än tō′nyō) an Italian violin maker.

stroll (strōl) *v.* to walk in a slow, relaxed
way.

stu · di · o (stōō′dē ō′, styōō′dē ō′) *n.* a
place where an artist works.

sub · ject (sub′jikt) *n.* a person or thing
that is under the control of another.

suf · fer (suf′ər) *v.* **1.** to have pain or sorrow. **2.** to be harmed or damaged.

sul · len (sul′ən) *adj.* withdrawn or
gloomy because of bad humor or anger;
sulky.

sum · ma · rize (sum′ə rīz′) *v.*
sum · ma · rized, sum · ma · riz · ing.
to make or give a brief account of.

su · pe · ri · or (sə pēr′ē ər) *adj.* **1.** higher
or greater. **2.** proud; haughty.

su · per · no · va (sōō′pər nō′və) *n.* a star
that suddenly becomes extremely bright
and then fades to its original brightness.

su · per · vise (sōō′pər vīz′) *v.*
su · per · vized, su · per · vis · ing. to
watch over or direct.

---

a **b**ad, ā **c**ake, ä **f**ather; e **p**et, ē **m**e; i **i**t, ī **i**ce; o **h**ot, ō **o**pen, ô **o**ff; oo w**oo**d,
ōō f**oo**d; oi **oi**l, ou **ou**t; th **th**in, <u>th</u> **th**at; u **c**up, ur **t**urn, yōō m**u**sic; zh trea**s**ure;
ə **a**go, tak**e**n, penci**l**, lem**o**n, helpf**u**l

su · per · vi · sor (sōō′pər vī′zər) *n.*   a person who watches over or directs.

surge (surj) *v.* **surged, surg · ing.** to move with a violent, heaving motion.

sur · vey (sur′vā) *n.*   a detailed study.

sus · pi · cious · ly (sə spish′əs lē) *adv.* in a manner arousing or likely to arouse suspicion.

swarm (swôrm) *v.*   to come together or move in a large mass or group.

sym · pho · ny (sim′ fə nē) *n.*   **1.** a long musical composition written for an orchestra. **2.** a large orchestra.

symp · tom (simp′təm) *n.*   a sign of a disease or other disorder.

T

tact · ful (takt′fəl) *adj.*   having or showing the ability to do or say the right thing when dealing with people or difficult situations.

taf · fet · a (taf′i tə) *n.*   a shiny, somewhat stiff fabric, usually woven out of silk or rayon.

tal · ent (tal′ənt) *n.*   **1.** a special natural ability. **2.** a person having special ability. **3.** an ancient unit of weight and money.

tal · ent · ed (tal′ən tid) *adj.*   having a natural or acquired ability, especially of superior quality; gifted.

tal · low (tal′ō) *n.*   the fat from cattle and sheep, used chiefly for making soap, candles, and margarine.

tam · bou · rine (tam′bə rēn′) *n.*   a small drum that has metal disks attached loosely around the rim. A person plays a tambourine by shaking it or hitting it with the knuckles.

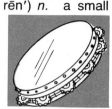
tambourine

team · ster (tēm′stər) *n.*   **1.** a person whose work is driving a truck. **2.** a person whose work is driving a team of horses or other animals.

tel · e · graph (tel′ə graf′) *n.*   the system or equipment used for sending messages over a long distance. The message is sent in code over wires by electricity.

tel · e · scope (tel′ə skōp′) *n.*   an instrument for making distant objects, such as heavenly bodies, appear nearer and larger. The eyepiece contains a magnifying lens or lenses.

tel · e · view · er (tel′ə vyōō ər) *n.*   a receiver used for television viewing.

tem · pest (tem′pist) *n.*   a violent and extensive wind, especially one accompanied by rain, hail, or snow.

ten · or sax · o · phone (ten′ər sak′sə fōn′) a wind instrument with a high range.

ten · ta · cle (ten′tə kəl) *n.*   a long, slender flexible growth coming from the head or mouth of certain animals.

ter · rain (tə rān′, te rān′) *n.*   a region of land, especially with regard to its natural features.

tes · ti · fy (tes′tə fī′) *v.*   **tes · ti · fied, tes · ti · fy · ing.** to give evidence or proof.

tes · ti · mo · ny (tes′tə mō′nē) *n.*   **1.** a statement made under oath by a witness in a court of law. **2.** proof of evidence.

theme (thēm) *n.*   **1.** the main subject or idea of something. **2.** the main tune from a piece of music.

there · upon (<u>th</u>ār′ə pôn′, <u>th</u>ār′ə pon′) *adv.*   immediately after that; at once.

Thes · sa · ly (thes′ə lē)   the region in northern Greece bordering the Aegean Sea.

Thessaly

thud (thud) *n.*   a dull heavy sound.

time · piece (tīm′pēs′) *n.*   any device that records, measures, or keeps time, especially a watch or clock.

tor · ment (tôr ment′) *v.*   to cause physical or mental pain or suffering.

tor · til · la (tôr tē′yə) *n.*   a flat, unleavened corn cake baked on an iron plate or flat stone, used as the equivalent of bread in Mexico and some parts of the southwestern United States.

tost (tôst, tost) *v.*   a poetic form of *tossed*.

tow · el (tou′əl) *n.*   a piece of material, especially used for drying or wiping.

trade · mark (trād′märk′) *n.*   a picture, word, or mark that a manufacturer uses to show that it made a product.

trad · ing post (trād′ing pōst′)   a store or station set up by a trader or trading company in a sparsely settled region.

trag · e · dy (traj′ə dē) *n.*   **1.** a story in which life is treated in a serious way and which usually has a sad ending. **2.** a sad or dreadful event.

train · ee (trā nē′) *n.*   a person who is undergoing training, especially in a job or in the military service.

tram · ple (tram′pəl) *v.* **tram · pled, tram · pling.** to step heavily on something so as to injure, crush, or destroy it.

tran · quil (trang′kwəl) *adj.*   calm, peaceful, free from disturbance.

trans · for · ma · tion (trans′fər mā′shən) *n.*   a change in form, appearance, nature, or character.

tran · sis · tor (tran zis′tər) *n.*   **1.** a very small electronic device that is used instead of vacuum tubes to control and to increase the strength of the electric current in television sets, computers, and other electronic equipment. **2.** a radio equipped with transistors.

Traz (traz)

treach · er · ous (trech′ər əs) *adj.*   **1.** disloyal or traitorous. **2.** dangerous.

tri · al (trī′əl) *n.*   **1.** an examination of a case in court; **2.** a difficult test.

tri · umph (trī′ umf) *n.*   **1.** success. **2.** exultation derived from victory.

---

a **b**ad, ā **c**ake, ä **f**ather; e **p**et, ē **m**e; i **i**t, ī **i**ce; o **h**ot, ō **o**pen, ô **o**ff; oo **w**oo**d**, o͞o **f**oo**d**; oi **oi**l, ou **ou**t; th **th**in, <u>th</u> **th**at; u **c**up, ur **t**urn, yo͞o **m**usic; zh **t**rea**s**ure; ə **a**go, tak**e**n, penc**i**l, lem**o**n, helpf**u**l

tri · um · phant (trī um′ fənt) *adj.* successful or victorious.

trum · pet (trum′pit) *n.* a brass musical instrument made up of a cylindrical metal tube coiled into a long loop and flaring out at the end. The tones of a trumpet are varied by the pressure of a player's lips and by the use of three valves.

trumpet

trun · dle (trund′ əl) *v.* **trun · dled, trun · dling.** to cause to roll along by pushing; to move in a rolling fashion.

Tsa · vo Na · tion · al Park (säv′ō) a national park in southern Kenya.

tu · ber · cu · lo · sis (too bur′kyə lō′sis, tyoo bur′kyə lō′sis) *n.* a disease caused by bacteria which may affect any organ of the body, especially the lungs or joints.

tur · bu · lent (tur′byə lənt) *adj.* not calm or smooth; agitated.

U

UFO an abbreviation for *unidentified flying object.*

un · con · fined (un kən fīnd′) *adj.* without limits.

un · der · ground (un′dər ground′) *adv.* below the earth's surface.

un · der · ground rail · road (un′dər ground rāl′rōd) an arrangement by people who opposed slavery for helping runaway slaves to places of safety.

un · earth (un urth′) *v.* to dig out of the earth; to discover.

un · for · tu · nate (un fôr′chə nit) *adj.* not lucky.

u · ni · form (yoo′nə fôrm′) *adj.* always the same; unvarying. — *n.* the special or official clothes worn by the members of a group.

u · ni · son (yoo′nə sən, yoo′nə zən) *n.* complete agreement; corresponding exactly.

u · ni · verse (yoo′nə vurs′) *n.* all that exists, including the earth, the heavens, and all of space; entire physical world.

un · veil · ing (un vāl′ing) *n.* the act of revealing or uncovering something.

un · wa · ver · ing · ly (un wā′vər ing lē) *adv.* in a steady, firm way.

up · right (up′rīt′) *adj.* in a vertical position.

ut · ter (ut′ər) *v.* to give voice to; express out loud.

ut · ter · ly (ut′ər lē) *adv.* completely or perfectly.

V

vague (vāg) *adj.* not clear or definite.

vain (vān) *adj.* not successful.

val · u · a · ble (val′yoo ə bəl, val′yə bəl) *adj.* having great value.

van · ish (van′ish) *v.* to disappear, especially suddenly.

var · nish (vär′nish) *v.* to coat with a liquid preparation usually made up of resins dissolved in alcohol or mixed with an oil, such as linseed oil.

vast (vast) *adj.* very great in size or amount.

vault (vôlt) *v.* to jump over; to spring over.

ve · hi · cle (vē′ə kəl) *n.* a device designed or used for transporting people or goods.

Ven · ice (ven′is) a port city in northern Italy, built on 118 small islands in the Adriatic Sea.

vi · a · duct (vī′ə dukt′) *n.* a bridge that carries a road or railroad over a highway or valley.

vi · bra · tion (vī brā′shən) *n.* rapid movement back and forth or up and down.

vic · tim (vik′təm) *n.* **1.** a person who is injured, killed, or ruined. **2.** a person who is cheated or tricked.

vid · e · o · tape (vid′ē ō tāp′) *n.* an electromagnetic tape on which the video and audio portions of a television program or motion picture are recorded.

vig · or (vig′ər) *n.* healthy strength.

vi · ol · a (vē ō′lə) *n.* a stringed instrument of the violin family, slightly larger and lower in pitch than the violin.

vol · ume (vol′yŌŌm) *n.* the number of issues of a newspaper printed to date.

vol · un · teer (vol′ən tēr′) *n.* a person who offers to help without pay.

vote (vōt) *n.* the formal expression of a wish or choice.

W

wag · on box (wag′ən boks′) the rectangular part of a wagon that holds whatever is to be carried.

wail (wāl) *v.* to make a long mournful cry, especially as an expression of grief or pain.

waist (wāst) *n.* the part of the human body between the ribs and the hips.

ware · house (wār′hous′) *n.* a building where merchandise is stored.

wash (wôsh, wosh) *n.* **1.** the act of washing. **2.** a flow of water. **3.** a thin coat of ink or paint.

well-gnawed (wel nôd′) *adj.* chewed up; showing signs of repeated bites.

whale-oil (hwāl′oil′) *adj.* of, related to, or using oil from the fatty part of whales.

whal · ing com · mu · ni · ty (hwā′ling kə myŌŌ′nə tē) a town whose chief business is hunting and killing whales for their oil, flesh, and bones.

wharf (hwôrf) *n.* a structure that is built along a shore, used as a landing place for boats and ships; dock.

wharf

whit · tle (hwit′əl) *v.* **whit · tled, whit · tling.** to cut shavings or small bits or pieces from.

a bad, ā cake, ä father; e pet, ē me; i it, ī ice; o hot, ō open, ô off; oo wood, ŌŌ food; oi oil, ou out; th thin, th that; u cup, ur turn, yŌŌ music; zh treasure; ə ago, taken, pencil, lemon, helpful

wick · er (wik'ər) *n.* slender, flexible twigs woven together, used in making baskets, furniture, and the like. — *adj.* made of, or covered with such woven twigs.

wil · de · beest (wil'də bēst') *n.* any of several swift antelopes of Africa having a head like that of an ox, short horns that curve sharply upward, and a long tail; also, a gnu.

wing (wing) *n.* in the theater, the part of the stage that is not seen by the audience.

win · ter · ize (win'tə rīz') *v.* **win · ter · ized, win · ter · iz · ing.** to prepare something for cold weather.

wit · ness (wit'nis) *n.* a person who has seen or heard something.

worth · while (wurth'hwīl') *adj.* good enough or important enough to spend time, effort, or money on.

wound · ed (woond'əd) *adj.* injured; hurt.

wretch · ed (rech'id) *adj.* deeply distressed or unhappy; miserable; unfortunate.

wrist (rist) *n.* the joint between the hand and the arm.

Yer · ba Bue · na (yär'bə bwā'nə) an island in San Francisco Bay between Oakland and San Francisco.

yoke (yōk) *n.* **1.** a collar-like frame for joining two work animals. **2.** a pair of work animals, especially oxen, joined together by a yoke.

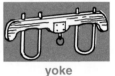

yoke

young · ster (yung'stər) *n.* a young person.

Z

zone (zōn) *n.* an area, a region or a section distinguished from surrounding areas or sections by some quality, condition, or use.

zo · ol · o · gy (zō ol'ə jē) *n.* the study of all forms of animal life.

Y

yal · ler (yal'ər) *adj. non-standard English.* yellow.

yearn (yurn) *v.* to be filled with longing or desire.

Yed · do Ski-Kre · do (yed'ō skē krē'dō)